The Iranian Revolutionary Guard Corps

Studies in Contemporary Warfare

The state of war in the modern world is in flux. Both the methods of warfighting and the actors involved in the process are changing. Landmark events in modern global affairs represent important turning points in the direction of contemporary war: the end of the Cold War forced a shift in the state relations that drive conflict; the 9/11 attacks spurred a focus on terrorists as the predominant strategic concern of the West; and the evolution of cyber technology has spurred a rapid development in the means of war-waging.

This series seeks to attract internationally-excellent scholarship that concentrates on one of three key elements:

- Evaluations of specific contemporary wars (including: the War in Afghanistan; the War in Iraq; the Gulf War; the Kosovo intervention; the Crimea crisis; the Libya intervention)
- Evaluations of types of contemporary war (including: Drone Warfare; Hybrid Warfare; Cyber Warfare; Proxy Warfare)
- Themes and issues running through contemporary wars (including: Intelligence; Torture; DDR; Special Forces; Targeted Killing; Gender & Violence; Private Military Contractors; Airpower)

Series Editor:

Andrew Mumford is Professor of War Studies at the University of Nottingham, UK.

The Iranian Revolutionary Guard Corps

Defining Iran's Military Doctrine

Alma Keshavarz

BLOOMSBURY ACADEMIC
LONDON • NEW YORK • OXFORD • NEW DELHI • SYDNEY

BLOOMSBURY ACADEMIC
Bloomsbury Publishing Plc
50 Bedford Square, London, WC1B 3DP, UK
1385 Broadway, New York, NY 10018, USA
29 Earlsfort Terrace, Dublin 2, Ireland

BLOOMSBURY, BLOOMSBURY ACADEMIC and the Diana logo are
trademarks of Bloomsbury Publishing Plc

First published in Great Britain 2023

Copyright © Alma Keshavarz, 2023

Alma Keshavarz, 2023 has asserted her right under the Copyright,
Designs and Patents Act, 1988, to be identified as Author of this work.

For legal purposes the Acknowledgments on pp. xii–xiii constitute
an extension of this copyright page.

Series design by Adriana Brioso
Cover image © Morteza Nikoubazl/ZUMA Wire/Alamy Stock Photo

All rights reserved. No part of this publication may be reproduced or
transmitted in any form or by any means, electronic or mechanical,
including photocopying, recording, or any information storage or retrieval
system, without prior permission in writing from the publishers.

Bloomsbury Publishing Plc does not have any control over, or responsibility for, any
third-party websites referred to or in this book. All internet addresses given in
this book were correct at the time of going to press. The author and publisher regret
any inconvenience caused if addresses have changed or sites have ceased to exist,
but can accept no responsibility for any such changes.

A catalogue record for this book is available from the British Library.

Library of Congress Cataloging-in-Publication Data
Names: Keshavarz, Alma, author.
Title: The Iranian Revolutionary Guard Corps : defining Iran's
military doctrine / Alma Keshavarz.
Description: London ; New York : Bloomsbury Academic, 2023. |
Series: Studies in contemporary warfare | Includes bibliographical references and index.
Identifiers: LCCN 2023001429 (print) | LCCN 2023001430 (ebook) | ISBN 9781350255654
(paperback) | ISBN 9781350255661 (hardback) | ISBN 9781350255678 (epub) |
ISBN 9781350255685 (pdf) | ISBN 9781350255692
Subjects: LCSH: Iran. Sipāh-i Pāsdārān-i Inqilāb-i Islāmī. | Iran.
Sipāh-i Pāsdārān-i Inqilāb-i Islāmī. Nīrū-yi Quds. | Iran–Military policy.
Classification: LCC UA853.I7 K42 2023 (print) | LCC UA853.I7 (ebook) |
DDC 355/.033555–dc23/eng/20230605
LC record available at https://lccn.loc.gov/2023001429
LC ebook record available at https://lccn.loc.gov/2023001430

ISBN:	HB:	978-1-3502-5566-1
	PB:	978-1-3502-5565-4
	ePDF:	978-1-3502-5568-5
	eBook:	978-1-3502-5567-8

Series: Studies in Contemporary Warfare

Typeset by Integra Software Services Pvt. Ltd.
Printed and bound in Great Britain

To find out more about our authors and books visit www.bloomsbury.com
and sign up for our newsletters.

To my parents

Contents

Preface	x
Acknowledgments	xii
List of Abbreviations	xiv

1	US Foreign Policy and Hybrid Warfare	1
	Applying the concept	3
	US foreign policy toward Iran	6
	Scope of hybrid warfare	13
	Chapters and book plan	16
2	Questions Remain Unanswered	19
	Hybrid warfare	20
	Iran and the IRGC	28
	Proxy wars are different	33
	Integrating the IRGC into broader Middle East scholarship	34
3	The Offspring of the Islamic Republic of Iran	37
	Structure and ideology	37
	Quds Force (QF)	42
	State sponsorship	44
	Understanding history	47
4	Laying the Foundation	49
	The purge	51
	Ineptitudes in battle	52
	Growth	53
	From conventional to asymmetric warfare	54
	The Tanker War	57
	Lessons learned	58

5	A Civil–Military Revolution in Post-War Expansion	61
	Integrating Iran's civil–military relations within the study of hybrid warfare	62
	Akbar Hashemi Rafsanjani	65
	Seyyed Mohammad Khatami	68
	Has Iran's civil–military transformation impacted its strategic calculus?	69
6	The IRGC Economy	73
	Iran's economy reimagined	74
	Khatam al-Anbia	76
	Iran's nuclear program and sanctions as US policy	77
	"Introspection has never been Mahmoud Ahmadinejad's strong suit"	79
7	The Iranian Way of War	83
	Does Iran have its own hybrid war strategy?	86
	The US invasion and Iran's emerging shadow network	90
	Badr (بدر)	93
	Asa'ib Ahl al-Haq (عصائب اهل الحق)	94
	Kata'ib Hizballah (KH) (كتائب حزب الله)	94
	Kata'ib Sayyid al-Shuhada (KSS) (كتائب سيد الشهداء)	95
	Harakat Hizballah al-Nujaba (HaN) (حركة حزب الله النجبا)	96
	Popular Mobilization Forces (الحشد الشعبي)	96
	Lebanon and Syria	97
	Yemen (انصار الله)	100
	Iran's strategic investments and US policy	101
8	Rouhani and the Shadow Government	107
	"The diplomatic Sheikh"	108
	The IRGC under Rouhani	110
	An intelligence unit divides leadership	112
	The Joint Comprehensive Plan of Action (JCPOA)	113
	US withdrawal from the JCPOA	115
	The "resistance economy" and FTO designation	116
	There is no status with Iran	118

9	An Iranian Cyber Command?	121
	Stuxnet	122
	Capabilities and networks	123
	Hybridity in practice	125
	Cyber as a tool for hybrid wars	127
10	A Modern Foreign Policy in the Age of Hybrid Warfare	131
	The unintended consequences of maximum pressure and the influence of the militant networks	133
	Policy concepts and strategic thought	137
	The future of foreign policy	140
Notes		143
Bibliography		179
Index		198

Preface

The idea for this book stemmed from my research experience in a range of topics related to the Middle East. I realized that in my search for answers I was asking more questions. Hybrid warfare is not a new phenomenon, as I explain in this book; however, it has become more relevant as a concept over the last two decades. State and non-state actors have found meaningful ways to engage in hybrid warfare against the United States and the West. Adversaries who do not have the same level of conventional superiority have identified hybrid wars as a way to impose costs and extend the length of conflict to burdensome levels.

Iran's Islamic Revolutionary Guard Corps (IRGC) is a prime example of a hybrid actor that blends various modes of conflict to achieve its strategic ends. Aside from regional hegemony, Tehran seeks to remove US influence from the Middle East. Iran's military doctrine is designed in a way that allows them to identify their adversaries' vulnerabilities for exploitation. Washington's foreign policy toward Iran has followed a systemic method of trial and error. Unlike the goals of the Cold War or even the Global War on Terror, for instance, it is hard to conclusively define an overarching policy toward Iran. It ranges anywhere from preventing Tehran from reaching nuclear capability to curbing malign influence, but US foreign policy toward Iran has been dictated by dynamics since the 1979 Islamic Revolution and has largely been reactionary.

As such, the study of hybrid warfare as applied to specific actors, such as Iran, should be included in policy debates. We continue to face challenges when addressing the issue of Iran and the IRGC. The signing and implementation of the Joint Comprehensive Plan of Action (JCPOA) was a critical juncture in Middle East policy, as was the subsequent withdrawal of the US. Tehran's actions and reactions during both periods provided greater insight into the IRGC's mindset and overall thought process when faced with obstacles. These are opportunities for further exploration and study to better understand an adversary that does not adhere to traditional norms of warfare.

This book seeks to address this gap in the literature and help shed light on how hybrid warfare can be useful to foreign policymaking. The IRGC was born out of necessity and grew to possess unsurmountable power over time. And it cannot be reversed. The objective of a book such as this is to assess the role of the IRGC from a different perspective. This book is an assessment of how the IRGC has rooted itself into Iran's foreign policy, which extends beyond its original intent. The IRGC's military doctrine is its foreign policy. While hybrid warfare is not a new concept in practice or theory, there is merit behind the growing interest in this area of research and the inclusion of this topic in the framing of policy and strategy.

Acknowledgments

I did not have answers for every question when developing this concept and sought guidance from experts and practitioners to fill knowledge gaps. I am grateful for all the assistance and support I received during the development and drafting of this book. I would like to particularly thank those who were willing to be interviewed—in some cases multiple times, with follow-up questions and discussions. Past and current US government officials graciously offered their time despite their busy schedules. I would like to first express my gratitude to former Secretary of Defense Jim Mattis, for his invaluable insights and for answering my questions with exceptional detail, and Ambassador James Jeffrey, who engaged in the most thought-provoking discussions with me, which helped me shape this book. I built this book around these conversations, and it is all the better for it.

Several officials of the Department of Defense and Department of State, who shall have to remain anonymous because of their current standing in the government, provided meaningful assessments, and I am appreciative of their time. I would also like to thank—alphabetically—Elliott Abrams, Ali Alfoneh, John Arquilla, Russell Berman, Michael Connell, David Crist, Michael Eisenstadt, Thomas Mahnken, Peter Mansoor, Samantha Ravich, Henry Rome, Daveed Gartenstein-Ross, Barbara Slavin, John Yaros, and unnamed others who offered their insights and opinions through phone calls, emails, and impromptu coffee meetings. A range of diverse thinkers helped me better understand the subtle nuances from a different perspective and to do my best to capture multiple viewpoints.

I would also like to extend my gratitude to my research assistants from my time at the Institute for Politics and Strategy at Carnegie Mellon University. Having also been my students at some point, they were always eager and enthusiastic to support me in my research. This book would not have been realized without the constant encouragement from my family, friends, and mentors. My deepest gratitude to Kiron Skinner, whose support makes anything possible. I have learned so much from her, and I would not be where I am today without her. I would also like to thank Robert Bunker and Robert Kaufman, whose years of guidance continue to shape my outlook. And Michael Warner continues to be the voice of reason, constantly reminding me of what I can do. I am forever grateful for the endless support and encouragement.

I would also like to recognize my closest confidants who have listened to me ramble about Middle East policy for many years. From drafts to late night calls, thank you for taking the time to listen to me and provide honest feedback. Lastly, to my parents and brother—my family—whose infinite care and optimism make things possible.

Chapters 2 and 3 were adapted from a previous work of the author: Keshavarz, Alma. "Hybrid Warfare: The Islamic State, Russia, and Iran's Islamic Revolutionary Guard Corps (IRGC) Threats, Challenges, and US Policy Response." Claremont Graduate University Proquest Dissertation Publishing, 2018.

Abbreviations

4GW	Fourth Generation Warfare
5GW	Fifth Generation Warfare
6GW	Sixth Generation Warfare
A2/AD	Anti-Access Aerial Denial
AAH	Asa'ib Ahl al-Haq
AEI	American Enterprise Institute
AFGS	Armed Forces General Staff
AP	Additional Protocol
APT	Advanced Persistent Threat
AQ	al-Qaeda
ATGM	Anti-Tank Guided Missile
BoG	Board of Governors
CDA	Congressionally Directed Action
CENTCOM	US Central Command
CIA	Central Intelligence Agency
CIS	Commonwealth of Independent States
CISADA	Comprehensive Iran Sanctions, Accountability, and Divestment Act
CRS	Congressional Research Service
CSIS	Center for Strategic and International Studies
CVE	Common Vulnerability and Exploit

DDoS	Distributed Denial of Service
DIA	Defense Intelligence Agency
DoD	Department of Defense
DoS	Department of State
DoT	Department of the Treasury
DPRK	Democratic Republic of North Korea
E3	France, Germany, United Kingdom
EFP	Explosively formed penetrator
EO	Executive Order
EU	European Union
FDD	Foundation for the Defense of Democracies
FTO	Foreign Terrorist Organization
GAO	Government Accountability Office
GCC	Gulf Cooperation Council
HaN	Harakat Hizballah al-Nujaba
IAEA	International Atomic Energy Association
IDF	Israeli Defense Forces
IED	Improvised Explosive Device
IG	Inspector General
IISS	International Institute for Strategic Studies
IRGC	Islamic Revolutionary Guard Corps
IRGCN	Islamic Revolutionary Guard Corps Navy
ISA	Iran Sanctions Act
ISCI	Islamic Supreme Council of Iraq

ISIL	Islamic State in the Levant and Syria
IT	Information Technology
JCPOA	Joint Comprehensive Plan of Action
JFQ	*Joint Force Quarterly*
JPL	Jet Propulsion Lab
JPoA	Joint Plan of Action
KH	Kata'ib Hizballah
KSS	Kata'ib Sayyid al-Shuhada
LAN	Local Area Network
LIC	Low-Intensity Conflict
MANPADS	Man-Portable Air Defense Systems
MeK	Mujahedin-al Khalq
MODAFL	Ministry of Defense and Armed Forces Logistics
MOIS	Ministry of Intelligence and Security
NPS	Naval Postgraduate School
NPT	Non-Proliferation Treaty
NSC	National Security Council
OCO	Offensive Cyber Operations
OFAC	Office of Foreign Assets Control
OIR	Operation Inherent Resolve
OSD	Office of the Secretary of Defense
P5+1	China, France, Germany, Russia, United Kingdom, United States
PFLP-GC	Popular Front for the Liberation of Palestine
PMF	Popular Mobilization Forces

QF	Quds Force
RFE/RL	Radio Free Europe/Radio Liberty
SAR	Synthetic Aperture Radars
SCADA	Supervisory Control and Data Acquisition
SCIRI	Supreme Council for the Islamic Revolution in Iraq
SIGINT	Signals Intelligence
SLO	Supreme Leader's Office
SMG	Shia Militia Groups
SNSC	[Iran] Supreme National Security Council
SOC	Special Operations Command
SOFA	Status of Forces Agreement
SPGD	South Pars Gas Development
TTP	Tactics, Techniques, and Procedures
UAE	United Arab Emirates
UAV	Unmanned Aerial Vehicle
UK	United Kingdom
UN	United Nations
UNGA	United Nations General Assembly
UNSC	United Nations Security Council
UNSCR	United Nations Security Council Resolution
US	United States
USG	United States Government
WMD	Weapons of Mass Destruction

1

US Foreign Policy and Hybrid Warfare

Hybrid wars have changed the dynamics of strategic planning and foreign policy. Political scientists have extensively researched and developed models and databases to both blueprint and explain wars. Sometimes, wars are fought over miscalculations and misunderstandings. Other times, though, wars are a product of political differences: they make take the form of civil wars domestically, or they may cross the borders of states that vie for influence or regional hegemony. Prussian theorist Carl von Clausewitz wrote, "If war is part of policy, policy will determine its character."[1] Foreign policy is the driving force behind the desired outcomes that are played out in theater, and according to Clausewitz, "as policy becomes more ambitious and vigorous, so will war, and this may reach the point where war attains its absolute form."[2] Hybrid warfare is connected to this notion and has been for at least the last two decades, if not longer. It is not a new phenomenon; there are a number of historical cases that exemplify this concept. United States (US) foreign policy has, over time, helped shape the subtle nuances of regional dynamics, most notably in the Middle East. This book aims to show that there is a connection between foreign policymaking and hybrid warfare in modern times.

The most contemporary case study is Iran. The 1979 Islamic Revolution in Iran changed the landscape of the Middle East and forced the United States to reconsider its approach toward foreign policy in the region. Indeed, Iran's foreign policy since the 1979 Islamic Revolution has grown increasingly ambitious. Though its intensity has varied across regimes, it has certainly shown its resilience and survivability, particularly since the time of former Iranian President Mahmoud Ahmadinejad to the present. As a result, Iran's policies have determined the nation's character. However, Washington has not adapted strategically to implement policies toward Iran that further US interests. Since the 1979 Revolution, US policy toward Iran has been reactionary without much progress toward either curbing Iran's malign influence or finding a path to diplomatic off-ramps.

Herein lies the need for laying the groundwork for incorporating hybrid warfare into broader strategic thought and foreign policy. As noted before, hybrid warfare is certainly not a new concept, and it does not need a rigid definition. The basic tenet of hybrid warfare is maneuverability in strategy and operations. It is a kind of situational awareness on the part of an adversary to adjust tactically when the strategy is not working to plan. Over time, our adversaries have observed operational vulnerabilities and ways to circumvent policies, which is arguably the most fundamental component of hybrid warfare. The greatest danger that the United States faces from a policy perspective is an adversary who knows to adjust when we are not expecting it. The idea behind a book such as this is to reassert that the United States must understand all the potential tactics, techniques, and procedures (TTP) of an adversary and reconsider where the adversary fits on the warfare spectrum to devise and implement all-encompassing strategies. Increasingly, adversaries such as Russia, China, Iran, and even non-state actors have tailored their performances to their strategic advantage while targeting the vulnerabilities of the United States and the West.

While this book focuses on Iran, the overarching premise is hybrid warfare. How has hybrid warfare enabled Iran's foreign policymaking and how has that in turn influenced US foreign policy toward Iran? Iran has gradually transitioned into hybrid warfare and defined its military doctrine around it. Without engaging in various modes of conflict, Iran would not have had the same level of successful sustainability in the face of economic pressures, increased international isolation, and military encroachments. Over the last four decades, Iran's foreign policy has been driven by its defensive strategy. The Iran–Iraq War turned into a hybrid war for Iran, and it used the lessons it learned from the war to design the course of its hybrid trajectory, which led to the rise of the Islamic Revolutionary Guard Corps (IRGC) and the formation of a shadow government.

Hybrid warfare has become policy-speak for many within government and academic circles. The concept has been defined in several different ways, but the foundational understanding of the theory must be applied to strategy and foreign policy processes. Strategy should be as much an evolving phenomenon as warfare is. The synergy of multiple modes of conflict characterizes hybrid warfare. Any US strategy for hybrid wars requires a whole-of-government approach that considers all modalities, and most importantly, it should be incorporated into policymaking. US policy toward the renewal of influence in the Middle East, Indo-Pacific, and Europe has had mixed reviews. While blending various modes of conflict is not new, it has conceptually become more prevalent in foreign policy circles.

Hybrid warfare ultimately applies to an overmatched adversary.[3] It is important to repeatedly stress that this concept is not new; however, its use against the United States has given cause to revive a broader discussion on the nature of wars and strategic thought. As a senior official at the Department of Defense explained, "Hybrid warfare came out of the necessity to compete and fight with the US, no matter who the adversary was."[4] Adversarial ambitions came to fruition when they broadly questioned what they could do to thwart, deter, or antagonize the United States in a meaningful way. The contours of hybrid warfare changed over time as our adversaries identified exploitable vulnerabilities. Groups such as al-Qaeda (AQ), the Islamic State in the Levant and Syria (ISIL), Lebanese Hizballah, and other terrorist organizations are not hybrid actors, but they developed an asymmetric platform that contributes to the overall discussion. Terrorist organizations exposed weaknesses that state adversaries such as Russia, China, and Iran studied. As a result, if the state actors can reasonably measure how the United States may respond, they will be able to adjust their approach accordingly. Developing the concept of hybrid warfare within the context of these types of state adversaries allows us to better prepare for the unexpected. The outcome will in turn help us produce more robust strategies and foreign policy frameworks. From a policy perspective, the goal should be to prevent threats without being reactionary. However, with Iran, the United States has unfortunately fallen more in the reactionary column than not.

Applying the concept

Extant scholarship on hybrid warfare is mostly related to Russia, especially because of the ongoing war in Ukraine at the time of writing this book. The concept is also sometimes applied to Iran but with caveats as Iran is closely associated with the concept of proxy warfare, which will be discussed later. This book will specifically apply hybrid warfare to Iran's Islamic Revolutionary Guard Corps (IRGC) (in Farsi, *sepāh-e pāsdārān-e enqelāb-e eslāmi*, سپاه پاسداران انقلاب اسلامی). Since its inception, the IRGC has altered its predetermined identity and reached beyond its original scope by intimately linking itself to Iran's foreign policy objectives. The IRGC is an agent of pursuing foreign policy and has gradually sidelined foreign policymaking bodies in Iran. Hybrid warfare is not simply a means to an end; it incorporates far more expansive strategic ends. The IRGC's hybridity has changed its form over time, beginning with the Iran–Iraq War. While there is an abundance of literature analyzing the Iran–Iraq War, the main takeaway is that it was the source of Iranian hybrid warfare. During this time, the IRGC was not suited for conventional battle in terms of capabilities, human capital, and training. They needed to adjust and thereby returned to guerilla and irregular styles of fighting that ultimately garnered some success. Though Iran lost the war, it was the lessons it learned from the war that served as a point of departure for the growth of IRGC into a multifaceted body with foreign policy ambitions.

This book most closely aligns with the version of hybrid warfare developed by former US Secretary of Defense James Mattis, and the conceptual framework outlined in an edited volume by historians Peter R. Mansoor and Williamson Murray. In 2005, the then General Mattis co-authored an article that articulated the concept of hybrid wars. Mattis noted that "our conventional superiority creates a compelling logic for states and non-state actors to move out of the traditional mode of war and seek some niche capability or some unexpected combination of technologies and tactics to gain an advantage."[5] A combination of assorted TTPs can thus be termed hybrid warfare. Several examples of hybrid warfare can be identified in history, including the Greek Civil War after the Second World War, internal conflicts in Djibouti and Somalia, and communist conflicts in Indonesia. Moreover, the United States spent many years fighting what we today term as irregular wars with Native Americans.[6]

As Mansoor wrote in the introduction to *Hybrid Warfare: Fighting Complex Opponents from the Ancient World to the Present*, "the lines of warfare in the twenty-first century are becoming increasingly blurred. America's security challenges include state-on-state wars, counterinsurgency conflicts, terrorism, and combinations thereof."[7] The authors of the edited volume define hybrid warfare as a "conflict involving a combination of conventional military forces and irregulars (guerrillas, insurgents, and terrorists), which could include both state and nonstate actors, aimed at achieving a common political purpose."[8] Agreeably, hybrid wars do not "change the nature of war; it merely changes the way forces engage in its conduct ... [and] is a useful construct to analyze conflicts involving regular and irregular forces engaged in both symmetric and asymmetric combat."[9] Like Mattis, the volume engages in a historical survey of hybrid wars to illustrate that the concept in practice is not new. The contributers to the volume trace the concept as far back as the Peloponnesian War before moving to more modern conflicts such as the French and Indian War in North America from 1735 to 1763 and the Second Sino-Japanese War with Mao Zedong.

Hybrid actors have historically shown that they can prolong conflict, and as terrorist organizations and insurgencies have proven, it costs the United States more in terms of blood and treasure to counter such threats than it does the adversary to employ their tactics. Hybrid actors also have the advantage of time,[10] and Iran is a prime example of this. As Thomas G. Mahnken, president and chief executive officer of the Center for Strategic and Budgetary Assessments, explained when asked for his thoughts on hybrid warfare, "From the Iranian perspective, it is about conflict or confrontational warfare, and it is using all the means that they have at their disposal as effectively as they can to confront us and achieve political objectives. It is about trying to take any and all resources and use them most effectively to achieve ends."[11] Since the political aims of hybrid actors vary, it is difficult to fight an adversary who ignores the traditional laws of warfare. Iran has continually confronted the United States with fewer resources and inferior weaponry but has nonetheless inflicted considerable damage.

In Iran, the IRGC's defense strategy has evolved since losing the Iran–Iraq War. The 1979 Islamic Revolution set a religious standard for what Iran wanted in terms of its stature in the region. Ayatollah Ruhollah Khomeini, Iran's inaugural supreme leader, stood on what he stated as "neither East, nor West, but the Islamic Republic." He intimated that the newly branded Islamic Republic was to spread the ideas of the revolution across the Middle East. Iranian foreign policymaking has come a long way since 1979. Indeed, religion was the single most significant factor when this new form of government took shape, but each regime brought different challenges and presented new fault lines. As the IRGC grew in strength, authority, and capability, the religious fervor waned in favor of IRGC predilections. However, it is not as though foreign and domestic policies are no longer rooted in safeguarding the revolution; Iranian Iranian leadership continues to guard its foundational revolutionary ideas. Many among the IRGC ranks, most notably the late Quds Force (QF) commander General Qasem Soleimani, have steadfastly guarded the original revolutionary intent. But religion is no longer the force behind the policymaking decisions; it is merely a tool to achieve regional goals.

Iran's experiences since 1979, including the Iran–Iraq War, the Arab Spring, and the Joint Plan of Action (JPoA) culminating in the Joint Comprehensive Plan of Action (JCPOA), have both directly and indirectly shaped the future of the Iranian regime and its foreign policy outcomes. What started as religious fervor has transformed into the sustainability of a style of warfare—hybrid warfare. For the IRGC specifically, religion now takes a backseat to its ambitions for greater political autonomy, which includes the realm of both defense and foreign policy.

US foreign policy toward Iran

The interplay of US foreign policy and Iranian strategy helped to design the IRGC's shadow government. For more than four decades, US foreign policy toward Iran has fluctuated from lack of coordination to miscalculation. It is difficult to pinpoint an overarching policy toward Iran that adequately captures the grand strategy. James Jeffery, former US ambassador to Iraq and Turkey and special envoy to the Global Coalition to Defeat ISIS, noted that there is a formula for understanding the relationship between Iraq and US foreign policy. Ambassador Jeffrey called it "F^3 + P:" Francis Fukuyama, Thomas Friedman,[12] Milton Friedman, plus Colin Powell.[13] Without going into the details of each "variable," the central point that Ambassador Jeffrey conveys here is how the thought-provoking concepts formulated by these intellectuals helped shape US strategy toward Iraq. These concepts are evident not just in their writings but also in their personal experiences, especially in the case of Colin Powell, the late former secretary of state. The takeaway of this author is that while there has been some formulaic understanding of the influences that shaped US strategy toward Iraq since 2003, there has been no such understanding, or historical trajectory, toward Iran.

This is partly due to the lack of foundational understanding of Iran since 1979 and the resultant changes to the overall political climate of the region. As one author notes, "The Islamic Republic of Iran has a strategic culture that is a confluence of and contestation between history, ideology, religion and modernity."[14] And there are other variables to study as well, including culture—both before the revolution and after—and language. All of these must be considered to fully understand Iran's perspectives and global, strategic outlook.

The 1979 Islamic Revolution changed the Middle East, and the international community is still struggling to fully capture the dynamics in Iran; this is largely because of misinterpretation. President Jimmy Carter shifted his stance on Iran almost overnight. From celebrating with the shah of Iran, Reza Pahlavi, in Tehran and unequivocally voicing US support, Carter changed his tune and turned into an advocate for change, which brought Khomeini out of exile. The rest is history. But from a policy perspective, upon the sudden change, US policy analysts were left deliberating religious overtures to understand how an Ayatollah would rule a nation and how this was going to alter the overall character of the Middle East. More importantly, how was this going to affect US foreign policy? What followed was complete chaos, with a series of aftershocks from the revolution, and a lack of understanding failed to facilitate any progress. Most notable were the events of November 4, 1979, when Iranians, mostly youth, stormed the US Embassy in Tehran and took American diplomats hostage for 444 days. The Carter administration had no substantive response nor any fruitful ideas to free the American hostages. Much of the failure was due to the lack of experience and understanding of the new regional dynamics. There was no preparation for this rapid change in the region, and the United States no longer had a staunch ally in Tehran—it was now an enemy.

Nonetheless, the Carter administration worked tirelessly to bring the American hostages home, and a deal was reached five minutes after Carter passed the presidency to Ronald Reagan.[15] What followed shortly thereafter was another hostage crisis that would be tied to what became known as the Iran-Contra Affair during the Reagan administration. While the deeper interagency, bureaucratic nuances of Iran-Contra are about the rise of the National Security Council (NSC) and the rift between the Department of State (DoS) and Department of Defense (DoD), the processes and outcome of Iran-Contra are variables in the broader study of US policy toward Iran. President Reagan tied his anti-Sandinista policy to the latter Iran hostage crisis, which was fully under the purview of the NSC staff to avoid stringent congressional oversight. During this time, it was suspected that Iranians had ties to both the 1983 Beirut Bombings in Lebanon and the hostages taken by Lebanese Hizballah. The Reagan administration supported the Nicaraguan Contras' fight against the Sandinistas while providing arms to Iran in an unsuccessful effort to coerce Iran to convince Hizballah to release the Western hostages. Reagan's National Security Advisor Robert "Bud" McFarlane and McFarlane's NSC staffer Lieutenant Colonel Oliver North employed an "arms-for-hostages" deal with Iran during the Iran–Iraq War, and a portion of these funds was transferred to the Nicaraguan Contras.[16] The broader design of the strategy was that it would not only free the Western hostages but also open a diplomatic channel with Iran.[17] Operational authority that is traditionally left to the Departments of State and Defense—and specifically to the Central Intelligence Agency (CIA) in this case—was instead with the NSC, which led to an unfavorable outcome.

The Reagan administration's Iran policy was pieced together on a whim by a group of NSC insiders, and the Iranian regime took full advantage of this disorderly strategy. On December 1, 1986, President Reagan established a presidential commission in response to the Iran-Contra Affair, which came to be known as the Tower Commission. Reagan tasked Texas Senator John Tower, former Secretary of State Edmund Muskie, and former National Security Advisor Brent Scowcroft to evaluate Iran-Contra and assess the role of the NSC more broadly, given how it was the NSC that was primarily running an operation typically left to the Departments of State and Defense. According to the Commission's report, the United States initiated the arms deal with Iran in exchange for the release of the kidnapped Americans held hostage in Lebanon. Interestingly, Israel was also supplying Iran with US weapons, and in turn, the United States was resupplying Israel.[18] The Commission explained that while "large sums changed hands," other large sums were "unaccounted for, and may have been diverted to guerilla groups in various countries, including the resistance in Nicaragua, or to middlemen."[19] It was a case study on how not to implement policy, but it was the best idea that could have been devised under the circumstances. Washington analysts were still reeling under the sudden change in the Middle East while trying to put out other fires.

The United States imposed economic sanctions against Iran in November 1979 and officially broke diplomatic ties in 1980 with additional sanctions. The fallout from the Iran-Contra Affair was still looming even after Reagan left office. President George H.W. Bush was more focused on Iraq than Iran, but the Bush administration was still working toward releasing the hostages from Lebanon. Bush's emphasis in his inaugural address in 1989 that "goodwill begets goodwill" was a signal to the Iranian regime that Washington and Tehran could still work toward a goal.[20] With the help of a United Nations (UN) career officer Giandomenico Picco, Bush secured the release of all Western hostages from Lebanon. But there was no tradeoff by the United States, which angered Tehran. US policy toward Iran during Bush's term was minimal as the priority was the Gulf War, which was sparked by Saddam Hussein's invasion of Kuwait in 1990.[21]

When President Bill Clinton took office, he surveyed Middle East politics before tackling either Iran or Iraq. Clinton's inner circle, however, seized the opportunity to shape the US Middle East policy. At the time, the NSC's director for Near Eastern and South Asian Affairs Martin Indyk and special envoy for the Middle East Dennis Ross devised a strategy to forge stronger Arab ties as part of a peace process that would also serve as a buffer for Israel. Clinton's core Middle East team focused on the US–Israel relationship and believed that the Islamic Republic was inflexible. The Clinton administration began implementing a series of additional sanctions against Iran to curb its behavior.[22] What occurred in response was Tehran courting Hamas, which was the beginning of Iran's influence beyond Lebanon. As the IRGC and its elite paramilitary, the Quds Force (QF), expanded, Hamas became a test case outside of Iran and Iraq.

While US and international sanctions persisted, the IRGC and QF slowly spread throughout the region, learning from failures and ramping efforts to gain greater influence. However, following the attacks of September 11, 2001, Tehran facilitated the movement of US troops during the invasion of

Afghanistan. It came as a surprise to Tehran when President George W. Bush included Iran as part of the "Axis of Evil" in his State of the Union Address on January 29, 2002. The administration shifted its focus to Saddam Hussein in 2003, and while the war raged on, the IRGC and QF exploited the situation. The United States did not factor Iran into its calculations.[23] For several years during the Iraq War, the Iranian regime feared that the United States would develop a similar campaign for Iran. Eventually, Tehran no longer felt threatened that it would be next but used the Iraq War as an opening to forge alliances and covertly foster political influence. Ultimately, given the circumstances, as of this writing, it succeeded.

The Iraq War was ongoing when President Barack Obama took office in 2008, but the United States took a different approach toward Iran. Obama implemented a flurry of sanctions against Iran, specifically targeting Tehran's nuclear program, weapons procurement, and even the QF. These targeted sanctions really hit Iran economically. As a result, Washington and Tehran began talks toward a deal, hoping to open a diplomatic pathway. The JPoA, the precursor to the JCPOA, resulted from what is known as "critical dialogue" between the E3 (France, Germany, the United Kingdom) and Iran from 2003 to 2005 over Iran's nuclear program.[24] The deal required Iran to stop uranium enrichment, sign the Additional Protocol (AP)[25] of the Non-Proliferation Treaty (NPT), and grant the International Atomic Energy Association (IAEA) access for routine inspections. However, the IAEA in August 2005 urged Iran to

> re-establish full suspension of all enrichment related activities including the production of feed material, including through tests or production at the Uranium Conversion Facility, on the same voluntary, non-legally binding basis as requested in previous Board resolutions, and to permit the Director General to re-instate the seals that have been removed at that facility.[26]

The IAEA also highlighted the Board of Governors' (BoG) concerns that stemmed from the August 1, 2005, notification to the IAEA, which stated that

> Iran had decided to resume the uranium conversion activities at the Uranium Conversion Facility in Esfahan, at the Director General's report that on 8 August Iran started to feed uranium ore concentrate into the first part of the process line at this facility and at the Director General's report

that on 10 August Iran removed the seals on the process lines and the UF4 at this facility.[27]

After more than a year of back and forth between Iran, European foreign ministries, and the IAEA, the United Nations Security Council (UNSC) began the implementation of international sanctions for Iran's noncompliance. United Nations Security Council Resolution (UNSCR) 1737 was unanimously adopted on December 23, 2006. This blocked the import or export of sensitive nuclear components and equipment and placed a freeze on financial assets belonging to persons or entities supporting Iran's proliferation of sensitive nuclear activities or the development of nuclear-weapon delivery systems. The resolution was adopted under Article 41 of the Charter's Chapter VII:

> Iran should, without further delay, suspend the following proliferation sensitive nuclear activities: all enrichment-related and reprocessing activities, including research and development; and work on all heavy-water related projects, including the construction of a research reactor moderated by heavy water."[28]

The Security Council required a report within sixty days from the director general of the IAEA on whether Iran had returned to compliance. On March 24, 2007, UNSCR 1747 was unanimously passed, which "widened the scope" of UNSCR 1737 "by banning the country's arms exports and freezing the assets and restricting the travel of additional individuals engaged in the country's proliferation-sensitive nuclear activities."[29] On March 3, 2008, UNSCR 1803 imposed additional sanctions against Iran, calling on member states to "inspect cargo entering or leaving Iran reasonably suspected of transporting goods prohibited as part of any one of the three Council resolutions on this issue," and subsequently inform the Security Council.[30]

Nuclear talks took years, and finally, on November 11, 2013, in Tehran, the IAEA and Iran agreed on a "Joint Statement on a Framework for Cooperation," which set the basis for future nuclear talks:

> In this regard, it was agreed that Iran and the IAEA will cooperate further with respect to verification activities to be undertaken by the IAEA to resolve all present and past issues. It is foreseen that Iran's cooperation will include providing the IAEA with timely information about its nuclear facilities and

in regard to the implementation of transparency measures. Activities will proceed in a step-by-step manner.[31]

An interim deal that would be implemented over the next six months was signed on November 24, 2013, between Iran and the P5+1 (China, France, Germany, the Russian Federation, the United Kingdom, the United States) in Geneva, Switzerland.[32] Over the course of six months, Iran agreed to halt uranium enrichment, reduce its stockpile, and cease construction of new facilities; it also agreed to more intrusive inspections by the IAEA. The United States and EU agreed to not impose new sanctions and loosened the grip on Iran's oil sales and petrochemical exports.

The IAEA continued to issue reports confirming Iran's commitments and obligations by the deal's standards.[33] Talks persisted, and verification measures routinely showed that Iran was not in violation of any measures. On July 14, 2015,[34] all parties officially signed the JCPOA. Iran agreed to limit its enrichment levels to 3.67 percent and reduce its stockpile of low-enriched uranium over fifteen years; enrichment facilities would continue to be monitored by the IAEA, no new facilities would be erected, and existing centrifuges would be reduced by two-thirds.[35] In exchange, sanctions would steadily be lifted. However, if Iran violated any aspect of the JCPOA, sanctions could be "snapped back" into place. Implementation Day of the JCPOA, January 16, 2016, brought additional relief for Iran. Most notably, Iran received $1.7 billion in cash payments for undelivered military equipment during the Shah period.[36]

However, the JCPOA was short-lived. President Donald J. Trump withdrew the United States from the deal on May 8, 2018, and enacted what his administration called a "maximum pressure campaign" against Iran to "curb Iran's malign behavior."[37] Whether the maximum pressure campaign was a success or failure depends on which side of the argument one is on. But as this author has previously written,[38] maximum pressure had unintended consequences then and now. Against the backdrop of JPoA and then JCPOA, the IRGC was working toward its own agenda of economic expansion and political authority. The JCPOA did indeed curb the IRGC's illicit activities, which are their predominant sources of funding. With legal finance channels opening in Iranian markets, the IRGC was certainly feeling the pinch. The maximum pressure campaign's unintended consequences included the resurgence of the IRGC's illicit activities and also an opportunity for the IRGC to better understand US sanctions policy. As a result, the IRGC became experts at sanctions evasion.

The maximum pressure campaign had its successes as well, and proponents will certainly argue that it was more successful than any prior sanctions campaigns against Iran. Despite this, there is still no clear thought or inquiry on US strategy toward Iran. Washington has either miscalculated or failed to factor Tehran into the equation when developing Middle East strategies since 1979. Beginning with Iran-Contra, for instance, as one author correctly notes,

> single actors cannot be held solely responsible for the course of events that unfolded. To assign blame for the whole episode to individual actors and not to the institutions they represented would be an inaccurate representation of the problems that caused the Iran-Contra Affair: the lack of cooperation between various government agencies cannot be overlooked as a major factor in the operation. An analysis of key Iran-Contra actors reveals this imperfect cooperation and other problems in the US national security interagency structure.[39]

Bureaucratic dynamics stunted US policy toward Iran. Too many conflicting views and a lack of cohesion have prevented a broader strategy toward Iran and by default, also influenced US policy toward the Middle East in general. Since the Iran-Contra Affair, US policy toward Iran has not decidedly executed a strategy with any off-ramps, and Iran gradually started to exert influence from Tehran to Lebanon, Syria, Iraq, Yemen, and elsewhere. Washington's overall disregard of the IRGC's growth over the last four decades has guided this hybrid war in which the outcome is yet to be realized.

Scope of hybrid warfare

Hybrid warfare is a blurry phenomenon; it is not a constant. Understanding the IRGC's political milieu and operational environment can assist with shaping our own foreign policy approach toward Iran. The Iranian regime, through the IRGC, has proven that it is far better at pairing modalities than the United States. We can expect Iran and the IRGC to continually adapt to their political and strategic environments, as they have successfully demonstrated so far. The IRGC's approach to hybrid warfare is this systemic understanding of their strengths and weaknesses. But they also have a situational awareness of US policy. It would be ignorant of us to believe that Iranian leaders do not understand how our processes and system of governance work. After all, scholars, academics, and practitioners alike are committed to particular fields of study, and so too are Iranian leaders. They understand our branches of government to a degree, but most important to their policies, Iranian leadership—which includes the IRGC—has a solid comprehension of sanctions. Otherwise, they would not have been as successful in sanctions circumvention over the last four decades. They have even written on what they define as their version of hybrid warfare as applied to their defense and security, which will be discussed in the following chapters.

But where does the US government (USG) stand on hybrid warfare? It has largely been absent in policy, but do the branches of our armed forces incorporate the concept of hybrid warfare in their teachings and training doctrines? The United States Air Force, Army, Marine Corps, Special Operations Command (SOC), and Navy have their own conceptions of hybrid warfare. The Air Force defines hybrid warfare as characterized by "increased tempo, complexity, diversity, and wider orchestration across national borders; adversaries can communicate more easily, obtain funding and more sophisticated weaponry."[40] Special Operations Command does not view hybrid warfare any different from "current doctrinal forms of warfare across conflict spectrum."[41] To the Navy, hybrid warfare is "synonymous with full spectrum and encompasses both conventional and unconventional warfare," while the Marine Corps does not view it as a new form of warfare but uses the concept to describe potential threats by state and non-state actors.[42] Interestingly, a 2010 report from the Government Accountability Office (GAO) noted that the DoD officials agreed that "hybrid warfare encompasses all elements of warfare across the spectrum. Therefore, to define hybrid warfare risks omitting key and unforeseen elements."[43] These characterizations are merited. There is no absolute need to define hybrid warfare, but it is worth acknowledging the phenomenon on the conflict spectrum so that we may better understand our adversaries. The IRGC is indicative of why we should integrate hybrid warfare into the process of designing strategic doctrines and outlining policy goals.

Clausewitz believed that a precept of strategy is that "war is merely the continuation of policy by other means."[44] Strategies should prepare for emerging hybrid threats. Not that we should reject traditional paradigms; rather, we should expand on them, which will help policymakers have a clearer understanding of already complex situations. While conflict changes over time, the traditional paradigms from which we can learn are constant. For example, we can attribute the rising interest in hybrid warfare over the last fifteen years to the tactics employed by Lebanese Hizballah during the Israel–Hizballah War in 2006.[45] Hizballah showed successful defense against the Israeli Defense Forces (IDF) between July 12 and August 14, 2006, a total of thirty-three days.[46] Hizballah had an unexpected advantage over the IDF as they received continued support from the Iranian regime in the form of financial aid and weapons procurement.[47] Hizballah used tactical combinations with innovations of modern technology, such as the use of anti-tank guided missile (ATGM) systems, unmanned aerial vehicle (UAV) systems, and signals intelligence (SIGINT). They possess thousands of short- and intermediate-range rockets and missiles, thanks to Iranian state sponsorship. Iranian QF soldiers, in their role as advisors, offered tactical support. Equally important to Hizballah's capabilities was the IDF's apparent weaknesses. Though Hizballah is not a hybrid actor, Iran is to be credited for their success as their state sponsor. Israel was not prepared for a UAV-capable Hizballah, nor did they assess the group as organized enough to maneuver with adaptability.

Relatedly, the IRGC exists across the non-state to state spectrum by engaging in hybrid warfare. Following the end of the Iran–Iraq war, the IRGC transitioned from an institution originally meant to be vanguards of the revolution within Iran's borders to an elite military hydra with economic, political, and foreign influence. This has directly impacted US foreign policy toward Iran, impeding Washington's ability to develop a strategy toward a sound solution by fostering wide differences in opinion and subjecting it to groupthink. From a policy perspective, the focus should be more on alliances than on deterrence. Both concepts should work in tandem rather than independently. As former Secretary Mattis explained, the United States should "identify and focus on vital interests. Whatever builds alliances and allies is most important because that is what will temper adversaries. We must build up allies because we can't deter adversaries or win wars alone."[48]

Chapters and book plan

Following this introduction, Chapter 2 is a survey of literature on hybrid warfare, Iran, and IRGC. It is certainly not comprehensive but is limited to the most widely cited and most valuable contributions to both fields. The overview of the literature is intended as a reflection on the pertinent questions that must be answered and the issues that must be rectified. Chapter 3 is an introduction to the IRGC for readers who may be unfamiliar with their origins. It is intended to be informative but also poses as a structure for outlining the IRGC's trajectory, which will be charted in detail as the book progresses. Chapter 4 assesses how the Iran–Iraq War laid the groundwork for Iran's hybrid warfare strategy. Though Iran lost the war, the lessons learned were pivotal in gaining perspective on how to best exert strength by exploiting fault lines. Chapter 5 transitions into the post-war reconstruction era, focusing on former Iranian presidents Ali Akbar Hashemi Rafsanjani and Mohammad Khatami, both of whom promoted the IRGC's strength through rebuilding efforts but simultaneously wanted to restrain their limits to prevent heightened authority in politics and the economy. Civil–military tensions flared during both regimes, and despite their best efforts, there were unintended consequences, and the IRGC's gains were never rolled back; in fact, they grew exponentially. Chapter 6 follows chronologically, beginning with the election of former President Mahmoud Ahmadinejad and tracing how his presidency ushered in an era of economic superiority for the IRGC. The IRGC was further pulled into political affairs, including foreign policy. Ahmadinejad redefined the IRGC's status, particularly in Iraq. Chapter 7 focuses specifically on Iran's Shia militia groups (SMG) across the Middle East and how they are critical to Iran's broader hybrid strategy. These groups are crucial to Iran's political engagement in Syria, Iraq, Lebanon, and Yemen and its narrative of minimizing US footprint in the region. Chapter 8 examines former President Hasan Rouhani's regime, with special emphasis on the JCPOA and the maximum pressure campaign of the United States. As part of the IRGC's hybridity, circumventing sanctions has been a logistical tool. Iran has weathered sanctions for the better part of four decades, but it is the IRGC's long game to fund their activities, and sanctions circumvention has become a form of art. Chapter 9 introduces the latest element in hybrid warfare—cyber. An exploration of Iranian cyber capabilities would be valuable to the overarching study of hybrid wars as it is an understudied area in this field. Chapter 10, the concluding chapter, provides policy implications. It is not a summation but an analysis from a policy perspective.

This book is part of an ongoing research project on hybrid wars. It is being written during a time when the IRGC is exhibiting exceeding growth and capability. Since 2015, the international community has witnessed a nuclear deal with Iran—the JCPOA—the United States' withdrawal from the deal in 2018, and a new US administration under President Joe Biden that is set on returning to the deal. As of this writing, we have not reached the basis for a new deal or a return to the original JCPOA. Dozens of interviews with current and former government officials in various capacities, think tank experts, and academics have been conducted to gain greater insight on not just the IRGC but also defense strategies and US policy. These discussions, as well as past professional experiences, have helped shape the framework for this theoretical account.

In the present climate, state adversaries are engaged in hybrid wars that are continually challenging US interests. We have a responsibility to identify these threats, then develop and implement strategies to combat them. To achieve this, the United States must identify an end goal and decide how to achieve it instead of using available tools to fit a vague end. The United States should be better prepared for action by strengthening its alliances in all corners of the world, and that includes in the Middle East. While the strategic focus has shifted toward the Indo-Pacific, it does not mean that interests in the Middle East are on hold. Identifying threats early on puts the United States at a greater strategic advantage to prevent attacks and the rise of extremist movements. Understanding the operational environment is crucial, as personnel will have the skills to recognize unusual changes.[49] The United States should maintain capabilities and develop strategies that can combat actors that blend various modes of conflict. Hybrid warfare in its rawest form involves prolonging conflict and mounting costs for the opposing side. Most times, it is a political struggle and not a military one, Iraq being a case in point.

The future operational environment will be more complex than the current. Terrorism never really becomes extinct but festers until a group grows larger and its leadership devises a strategy to challenge Western influence and authority.[50] Aggressive states like Russia will continue to encroach near peer states to gain more regional influence, which further challenges US authority.[51] Both state and non-state actors have already employed destabilization efforts and will continue in this age of rapid information.[52] Indeed, hybrid wars are not replacing traditional wars; however, the United States should not expect to fight hybrid wars with traditional tools. The international community should be prepared to fight hybrid wars as hybrid actors are proving to be more challenging and complex. This necessitates a deeper understanding of regional atmospherics, people, and policies as well as the resources to act quickly and with little planning time. It also means that we should incorporate this concept into our policy debates and strategic doctrines.[53]

Whether it is a shift over time or an interplay of circumstances, there will always be a trigger that will cause decision-makers to take a closer look at an actor. Typical models of strategy have become too rigid. We can improve security by strengthening partnerships and establishing new ones. The United States should be committed to assisting nations that face hybrid challenges, especially regions US influence is being contested. This requires a whole-of-government approach and a strategy that would help guide action against the hybrid threats that are seeking to displace US influence.[54]

2

Questions Remain Unanswered

This chapter presents a review of existing literature by engaging in a survey of the spectrum of scholarship on hybrid warfare and Iran. It is important to address the various contributions made to both fields before applying the concept to the case study. Literature on hybrid warfare continues to change, for instance. There are a variety of definitions and conceptualizations as applied to either case studies or stand-alone overviews of the theory. However, scholarship on Iran is boundless, and this book will not cover all of it. While this book's focus is on Iran's IRGC, it falls under the thematic umbrella of hybrid warfare. There is no clear-cut definition of hybrid warfare; rather, it is conceptualized as a technique embraced by one of the most challenging adversaries of the United States over the course of its development.

A number of scholars have written on the IRGC, but they constitute only the minority when considering literature on Iran as a whole. Any scholarship on the IRGC is timely and relevant. However, across the literature on hybrid warfare—though mostly within the literature on the IRGC—questions that relate to US foreign policymaking remain unanswered. The United States has largely avoided including the IRGC into broader strategies toward Iran save for sanctions policies related to terrorism and, of course, the JCPOA. Scholarship in this field can be categorized into two based on their focus on either the IRGC's capabilities or Iranian politics. But there needs to be a baseline that combines the two perspectives to demonstrate the true breadth of the IRGC, particularly in the realm of Iran's foreign policymaking. Considering hybrid warfare, this cumulative approach can assist with better policy decisions that broaden the scope of regional dynamics.

Hybrid warfare

While the literature exploring hybrid warfare varies, there is one constant, and that is that hybrid warfare is a blending of various modes of conflict. This section will outline the most significant pieces of scholarship within the hybrid warfare subfield. It is not comprehensive by any means but offers a thematic overview of the conceptual trajectory.

To begin with, "New Modes of Conflict," an early piece on low-intensity conflict (LIC) by terrorism expert Brian Michael Jenkins, prepared for the Defense Nuclear Agency in 1983, discusses conventional and guerrilla warfare and international terrorism. Jenkins opined that these three components will "coexist in future warfare, with both government and subnational entities employing them individually, interchangeably, sequentially, or simultaneously."[1] Jenkins, writing in 1983, was ahead of his time and rightly predicted the plight of the international community as it faces terrorists and insurgents today:

> Warfare in the future ... will be less coherent ... The distinction between war and peace will dissolve ... Hostilities will be endless, and nominal peace will be filled with continuing confrontations and crises. Armed conflict will not be confined by national frontiers. Local belligerents will mobilize foreign patrons. Wars will spill floods of refugees on other countries, many of whom will carry their quarrels with them and many of who will also be targets for factions in their native countries. Terrorists will attack foreign targets both at home and abroad.[2]

Jenkins goes on to detail all three modes of conflict, but none is more interesting than his discussion on international terrorism. Jenkins explains that "present-day terrorism is a derivative of twentieth-century theories of guerrilla warfare, for which Mao Zedong deserves the most credit."[3] As Jenkins—and later, others—notes, Mao developed the concept of a "people's war," combining political power with military strategy, which defined the concept of guerrilla warfare. Mao recognized that political strength in Chinese peasants could supplant the resources and technological capabilities of a conventional military. Terrorism was and continues to be "that proposition pursued to its most violent extreme."[4]

Israeli military historian Martin van Creveld revitalized LIC and conceptualized the modern era of studying warfare with his 1991 book, *The Transformation of War*. According to van Creveld, the world is no longer enthralled by the Clausewitzian conventional state-on-state conflict because warfare is not about a rational political conflicts between states. Rather, the very nature of warfare has transformed into ideological conflicts, which has set a new standard of warfare. Non-state actors will soon dictate the battle space: "We are entering an era, not of peaceful economic competition between trading blocks, but of warfare between ethnic and religious groups."[5] van Creveld departs from Clausewitz in arguing that politics does not play a part in this type of warfare because politics is an object of states and not non-state actors. Highlighting the rise of Islamic Jihad at the time of his writing, van Creveld noted that the Clausewitzian norm could not apply to such actors, predicting instead that future warfare will be led by terrorists, insurgents, and guerrillas driven by ideology, who will make use of the advanced technology and weaponry that were typically employed by state actors.

Relatedly, cybersecurity experts John Arquilla and David Ronfeldt coined *netwar* in their 1996 RAND research, "The Advent of Netwar." Netwar is a subfield of LIC and "refers to conflicts in which a combatant is organized along networked lines or employs networks for operational control and other communications."[6] Arquilla and Ronfeldt posited that netwar actors are layered by organization, doctrine, technology, and socially, and engage in "conflicts short of war involving actors who may or may not be military."[7] The term "netwar" is what the authors, at the time of their writing, believed was an emerging genre of conflict at the societal level, in which the actors use "network forms of organization, doctrine, strategy, and communication." These actors comprise "dispersed, often small groups who agree to communicate, coordinate, and act in an internetted manner, often without a precise central leadership or headquarters."[8] Netwar actors use information technology (IT) and cyberspace either to disrupt or to destroy their adversaries. The authors argued the likelihood of hybrids, highlighting the possibility of cases with an element of state sponsorship and those wherein non-state actors may sponsor states. Arquilla and Ronfeldt's netwar concept[9] anticipated the current climate and how non-state actors have used technology; non-state actors use cyberspace and media platforms to recruit, propagandize, and disrupt or destroy, or even both.

However, the first case study on hybrid warfare—though indirectly—was presented by Col. William J. Nemeth while at the Naval Postgraduate School (NPS) in 2002. In his widely cited master's thesis, "The Future War and Chechnya: A Case for Hybrid Warfare," Nemeth writes that devolving societies are turning into hybrid societies. He identifies societies that are "returning to more traditional forms of organization," adding that they are "either a multitude of warring clans contained within the previous state boundaries, or a mostly homogenous socio-political unit that is fighting against a perceived oppressor."[10] Nemeth used Chechnya as a case study to prove this hypothesis. According to Nemeth, these societies are hybrids because they are a blend of the modern and traditional and have "organized hybrid military forces, and it is these forces that will challenge military and diplomatic planners in the future."[11] Nemeth discovered that when Chechens sense their culture, society, and territory to be threatened, they respond as a unified force, making their defeat all the more challenging. While they are used to fighting in the style of guerrilla warfare, Chechens also have conventional groups with an unconventional flair. Chechens showed that they could also transition back and forth, when necessary, which was characteristically unique.[12] The Chechen case study shows that devolution yields the "legacies of modernity": religion, political ideologies, technology, and modern social norms.[13] This blend composed a weak central government and equally unstable society. But according to Nemeth, "this new warfare paradigm foresees warfare becoming increasingly focused between states and non-states."[14]

Against this backdrop, the 2005 National Defense Strategy (NDS) was the first to recognize that "uncertainty is the defining characteristic of today's strategic environment,"[15] though it did not explicitly use the term "hybrid." Rather, the NDS acknowledged that the challenges the United States faced in modern times cannot be treated by adopting a case-by-case or reactionary approach. The United States must adapt. Since 2005, Frank G. Hoffman, Distinguished Research Fellow at the National Defense University, has published extensively on hybrid warfare, including his most widely cited essay, "Conflict in the 21st Century: The Rise of Hybrid Wars," written in 2007. Hoffman defines hybrid warfare as a mode of conflict in which the "adversary ... simultaneously and adaptively employs a fused mix of conventional weapons, irregular tactics, terrorism, and criminal behavior in the battlespace to obtain their political objectives."[16] He further adds that "hybrid wars can be conducted by both states and a variety of non-state actors."[17] According to Hoffman, hybrid warfare challenges the conventional military thought of the United States because the "blurring of modes of war, the blurring of who fights, and what technologies are brought to bear, produces a wide range of variety and complexity."[18]

Hoffman further developed his framework and argued that states and non-states alike will take advantage of whatever weaponry and technology they have at their disposal. For example, a terrorist organization like Lebanese Hizballah may learn modern military tactics such as calling in air strikes or using man-portable air defense systems (MANPADS). Hybrid modes of conflict pose a threat to Western interests and challenge the West's war-fighting strategies. As Hoffman notes, hybrid warfare will "continue to thwart the West's core interests and world order over the next generation."[19]

In a 2009 article, Hoffman states that "instead of separate challengers with fundamentally different approaches (conventional, irregular, or terrorist), we can expect to face competitors who will employ *all* forms of war and tactics, perhaps simultaneously."[20] Counterinsurgency expert David Kilcullen similarly agrees. In *Accidental Guerrilla*, published in 2009, Kilcullen notes that the term "hybrid warfare" best describes modern conflicts, with the blending of irregular modes, including civil wars, insurgency, and terrorism.[21] His works since have been among leading scholarship on counterterrorism issues.

Other scholars, such as Russell W. Glenn, assert that hybrids exist across physical and conceptual dimensions. In "Thoughts on 'Hybrid Conflict,'" published in 2009, Glenn purports that physical dimensions are a "struggle against an armed enemy" and conceptual dimensions are a "wider struggle for, control and support of the combat zone's indigenous population, the support of the home fronts of the intervening nations, and the support of the international community."[22] Glenn adapts his definition from Colonel John McCuen[23] and states that hybrid conflicts seek "to secure and stabilize the indigenous population," while "intervening forces must immediately rebuild or restore security, essential services, local government, self-defense forces and essential elements of the economy."[24]

In 2012, Christopher O. Bowers authored "Identifying Emerging Hybrid Adversaries," in which he argues that there is a need for a "methodological attempt to identify where, and in what capacity, these organizations will emerge over the coming decades."[25] Bowers explains that hybrid threats have three components: capability, maturity, and complex terrain. First, these threats must have some modern, conventional military capabilities to qualify as a hybrid. This includes having advanced weaponry or technology, knowledge of their use, and the capability to maintain subsistence.[26] Maturity is the next important factor, and it includes several components: (1) organization and cohesions; (2) depth of leadership; (3) responsiveness to internal leadership and foreign state sponsors; (4) population support; and (5) extent to which the group is goal-oriented with an effective strategy.[27] The third component is terrain, which has human and geographic elements. Complex terrain helps with tactical and organizational abilities but also "provides sanctuary by impeding a modern military's ability to conduct effective targeting."[28] Bowers also includes cyberspace within complex terrain. He explains that "a hybrid group's cyber capabilities may enable it to take advantage of the complex terrain of cyberspace in the same manner it leverages physical and human terrain."[29] Where are all three variables overlap is what Bowers calls the "sweet spot," in which adversaries fully develop into hybrid threats. Hybrid threats will use cyberspace, which includes social media, transnational crime networks, and high-tech tools such as UAVs, among other weaponry. According to Bowers, "this 'middle range' of capabilities—less than a modern state military, more than a guerrilla or insurgent force, with aspects of both—makes hybrid threat organizations problematic for advanced western militaries."[30] Bowers presents a method to identify potential threats that are developing into hybrids and devise ways for the United States to prepare for these threats in future conflicts.

Fourth Generation Warfare (4GW) scholarship is also closely related to hybrid warfare in that 4GW "uses all available networks—political, economic, social, and military—to convince the enemy's political decision makers that their strategic goals are unachievable or too costly for the perceived benefit."[31] William S. Lind and his co-authors were the first to present the concept of 4GW. In their 1989 article titled "The Changing Face of War: Into the Fourth Generation," the authors argue that 4GW "seems likely to be widely dispersed and largely undefined; the distinction between war and peace will be blurred to the vanishing point."[32] The first generation of warfare followed the medieval period. It was the era "of the smoothbore musket, the tactics of line and column."[33] The first generation extended up to the Napoleonic Wars, when it transitioned into the second generation, with warfare tactics that were "based on fire and movement."[34] With both a growing population and economy, second generation warfare was more about manpower and firepower. Third generation warfare was like its predecessor, though emphasized ideas over technology. Hitler's Germany is credited for third generation of warfare because of the new tactics they developed. Therefore, third generation warfare tactics "were the first truly nonlinear tactics,"[35] the transition into the period marked by "Blitzkrieg." Germans were operationally advantaged with new tactics that the Allies were unprepared to face, which included tanks and heavy machinery. The authors maintained that 4GW "may emerge from non-Western cultural traditions, such as Islamic or Asiatic traditions," since 4GW may potentially be based on ideas.[36]

T.X. Hammes, in his 2006 book, *The Sling and the Stone: On War in the 21st Century*, notes that 4GW attacks "the minds of enemy decision makers to destroy the enemy's political will."[37] As such, 4GW is an evolution from previous generations of warfare. Hammes explains 4GW has "evolved in conjunction with the political, economic, social, and technological changes that are modifying our world"[38] and "will target specific messages to policy-makers and those who can influence the policy makers."[39] Iraq and Afghanistan are contemporary examples, where insurgents utilize all forms of networking to distribute propaganda.[40]

However, 4GW comes with its own problems. In "The Transition to Fourth Epoch War," Robert J. Bunker explains that one of the main challenges is decoupling technology from ideas because "warfare is carried out by military systems—war fighting institutions that represent a unique set of mutually supporting structures, a synthesis of technology and ideas that enable a polity to conduct war."[41] Bunker is of the opinion that the generations of warfare identified by Lind and others are "incorrectly conceptualized, and the conclusions drawn regarding the emerging fourth generation are based on faulty premises."[42] The second issue is that Lind and others did not go far back enough historically. Last, "the theory is not firmly anchored to the material culture of Western civilization. Relationships to either modes of production or basic energy technology are not planned."[43] Rather, there are epochs separated by "differing energy foundations of civilization that exist for each one" and there is is an "energy sequence, or sequences, based initially on the experimental exploitation of, and then later the institutionalization of, an energy source by society"[44] within each epoch. The first epoch was Classical warfare that transitioned to Raider warfare during the Medieval period. Bunker follows that Feudal warfare changed to Dynastic warfare, which signaled a transition from Medieval to Modern times. As such, the present era has transitioned from a mechanical to a post-mechanical energy foundation, allowing "for the fielding of such advanced technology weaponry as lasers, rail guns, and robotic war-fighting units."[45] According to Bunker, "this transition has been greatly complicated by the simultaneous rise of growing external threats to our modern military system based on terrorist/low-intensity conflict."[46]

Similarly, hybrid warfare endorses an evolution in conflict and is not a new form of warfare, but a blend of existing modes. Some like Max G. Manwaring define Fifth Generation Warfare (5GW) as using information—or propaganda—and high technology that are aimed at civilian and military organizations.[47] He explains that "on one level, it involves the propaganda-oriented strategy derived from Maoist insurgency doctrine against a vulnerable government or set of targeted institutions,[48] while on the level of information and technology, "fifth-generation conflict includes but is not restricted to financial war, trade war, economic warfare, media war, cyber war, net war and bond-relationship targeting."[49] Hammes too believes in the possibility of 5GW, citing the anthrax and ricin attacks on Capitol Hill could have been the earliest strands of 5GW, though it is still uncertain. There have been signs that 5GW will signal a transition to biological and chemical warfare.[50] In 2007, George Friedman explained in "Beyond Fourth Generation Warfare" that the difference between 4GW and 5GW conflict "is that the lead time to deploy capabilities in Fifth Generation warfare is much longer than Fourth Generation warfare. Fourth Generation is a question of training and mindset, with a limited technological evolution required. Fifth Generation warfare requires an extended weapon development timeline."[51] Friedman recommended that the United States should increase spending on space-based systems, survivable fleets, and advanced infantry systems, to name a few.

In 2008, Donald J. Reed further developed the potential for 5GW in "Beyond the War on Terror: Into the Fifth Generation of War and Conflict." Reed believed that 5GW went beyond 4GW by "expanding the domain of conflict" into the physical (land, air, and sea), information (cyber), cognitive, and social (political) domains.[52] According to Reed, conventional warfare is the physical domain, which includes land, sea, air, and space, while cyberspace is the information domain. The cognitive domain is tactics and techniques, and lastly, the social domain is human intelligence where information sharing occurs. Additionally, Reed explains that there are four axes to 5GW: Axis (A)—new domains of conflict (Where will future wars be fought?); Axis (B)—changing nature of adversaries (Who will fight in future wars?); Axis (C)—changing nature of objectives (Why will future wars be fought?); and Axis (D)—changing nature of force (How will future wars be fought?).[53] These are at the core of Reed's argument on 5GW development. Examples include computer hackers, the anthrax and ricin incidents on Capitol Hill, the Madrid bombings, and al Qaeda:

> They can dissipate centers of gravity across the omnipresent battlefield so that they become virtually non-existent. Despite extensive countermeasures taken by nation-states the success of organized computer hackers continues unabated; the number of super-empowered individuals capable of carrying out attacks similar to the 2001 anthrax and 2003–2004 ricin attacks is virtually limitless; the Madrid bombers successfully brought about regime change in a sovereign Western European nation-state; and al Qaeda has demonstrated great resiliency and has achieved levels of capability equal to 2001 and earlier.[54]

These and others have shown how 5GW has changed warfare through the "successful application of multiple kinetic and non-kinetic sources of force."[55]

While these examples have hybrid warfare as their conceptual theme, there has since also been an abundance of literature interweaving hybrid warfare as applied to Russian aggression. This began most notably following the Russo-Georgian War in 2008, followed by the Russian annexation of Crimea in 2014, and again with Russia's full invasion of Ukraine in February 2022. Many authors have developed their own characterizations of hybrid warfare as applied to Russia, and their significance to the overall body of hybrid warfare scholarship is worth mentioning.

Relatedly, in 2018, an edited volume by Western and Russian authors examined hybrid and information warfare and how both have changed over time. Edited by Ofer Fridman, Vitaly Kabernik, and James D. Pearce, *Hybrid Conflicts and Information Warfare: New Labels, Old Politics* uses case studies to demonstrate the differences in perspectives. The volume incorporates social media as an added element in the rise of hybrid conflicts. Brin Najžer's *The Hybrid Age: International Security in the Era of Hybrid Warfare*, published in 2020, is an exceptional primer that provides an updated analysis of hybrid warfare. Najžer establishes a theoretical framework and guides the reader through case studies for a more inclusive understanding. Another edited volume published in 2021, *Hybrid Warfare: Security and Asymmetric Conflict in International Relations,* edited by Mikael Weissmann, Niklas Nilsson, Björn Palmertz, and Per Thunholm, is a collection of articles by US and European experts and practitioners who offer characterizations of hybrid warfare from their respective perspectives. Case studies include Russia, China, and Iran but also incorporate cyberwarfare. It is a relevant collection of essays that encapsulates the current climate of global affairs by avoiding a stringent definition of hybrid warfare while characterizing the nature of each case's environment.

Iran and the IRGC

There is an abundance of literature available on Iran, and certainly this review cannot include every piece of scholarship. However, this section will highlight the works that have not just influenced this book but have also endured a long shelf life.

A discussion of the IRGC begins with the earliest publications by Nikola B. Schahgaldian and Sepehr Zabih in 1987 and 1988, respectively. Both authors are concerned with Iran's creation of an elite military that was separate from its regular military (*artesh*). Schahgaldian and Zabih, respectively, argue that the creation of the IRGC by the supreme leader was a move toward establishing an "Islamic" army or an army that would maintain the principles of the Islamic

Revolution. Zabih focuses on the IRGC's loyalty to the supreme leader and the zeal of the Islamic Revolution. Schahgaldian explains that Iran's military was a political element and that it has matured since 1979. Anyone writing on the IRGC must acknowledge the contribution made by both Schahgaldian and Zabih as the earliest IRGC scholars in this field.

Focusing specifically on the Iran–Iraq War, Williamson Murray and Kevin M. Woods co-authored a vivid historical analysis in *The Iran-Iraq War: A Military and Strategic History*. The authors offer an expertly researched narrative on not just the rise of the IRGC but also the political dynamics that were playing out in the background as added context to the war. The selection of literature available on the Iran–Iraq War varies on the particular aspects that authors choose to cover at length. This author is especially grateful for the available scholarship that has detailed a range of deadly battles and political conflicts that are integral pieces of the larger puzzle. This was critical in framing this theoretical argument that the IRGC's hybridity began during the Iran–Iraq War and not afterward.

Renowned Iran expert and Congressional Research Service (CRS) scholar Kenneth Katzman has extensively covered Iran and the IRGC. His 1991 dissertation compares the IRGC to the Soviet Red Army, the People's Liberation Army in China, and the French Revolutionary Army. According to Katzman, these three armies became professionalized. The IRGC has become institutionalized because it has "not lost ideological zeal."[56] Katzman uses Samuel P. Huntington's measures of institutional development—adaptability vs. rigidity; vs. rigidity; complexity vs. simplicity; autonomy vs. subordination; and coherence vs. disunity—to assess the IRGC and demonstrate its adaptability and tenacity to overcome challenges, particularly during the Guards' infancy.[57] The regime developed smaller units, like the IRGC Navy (IRGCN), Air Force, and later the QF, for a more well-rounded of military force. As such, the IRGC became autonomous by protecting its own interests. Katzman expands on this theory in his 1993 book, *The Warriors of Islam: Iran's Revolutionary Guard*, and concludes that by protecting its interests the IRGC maintained the principles of the 1979 Revolution. Anthony H. Cordesman is a similar scholar who has covered Iran and the IRGC. In a 1994 report, he discusses Iran's military forces following the Iran–Iraq War, during which Iran was forced to rebuild its land forces. According to Cordesman, "Iran stepped up its arms imports in late 1989, and took advantage of the fact that Iraq's invasion of Kuwait gave Iran a new respectability that eased its ability to order arms and add oil revenues."[58] Cordesman accurately predicted that the IRGC Navy (IRGCN) would "play a critical role in Iranian military action in the Gulf region," as has been the case since 2016.[59] Both Katzman and Cordesman have written countless pieces covering Iran, which continue to influence Iran watchers.

On Iranian politics, there are several notable pieces of literature, including Barbara Slavin's *Bitter Friends, Bosom Enemies: Iran, the US, and the Twisted Path to Confrontation*, published in 2007. Slavin was the first woman to interview former Iranian president Mahmoud Ahmadinejad, among other high-ranking Iranian leaders, and she expertly chronicled her time in Iran with acute attention to detail. Slavin's book is not an overview of the Iranian governing system; it has levels of nuances that are unpacked purely through personal interviews with figureheads such as Mohsen Rezaei whose personalities are incorporated into the narrative.

Similarly, Saïd Amir Arjomand's 2009 book, *After Khomeini*, discusses the IRGC specifically during the Ahmadinejad years. Ahmadinejad's election was bolstered by the Basij first and hen the IRGC, in which they were generously rewarded for their support.[60] Arjomand extensively chronicles the IRGC's political and economic climb under Ahmadinejad's watch. A 2009 report prepared for the Office of the Secretary of Defense (OSD) has contributed significantly to the study of the IRGC. The authors of the report argued that the IRGC is more than just a military; by being a part of Iran's society, economy, and politics which now extends to foreign policy. Frederic Wehrey, the lead author of the report, claims that the "IRGC has primacy over Iranian unconventional warfare options, it maintains tight control over the development and deployment of Iran's ballistic missiles, and it wields an external terrorism capability through its elite Quds Force."[61] However, the IRGC's entry into Iran's economy followed the end of the Iran–Iraq War and strengthend under the late president Rafsanjani. The authors note that "the IRGC's industrial activities began not long after the Iran–Iraq war, when President Rafsanjani's government encouraged the IRGC to use economic activities to bolster its budget."[62] Military historian Steven R. Ward's *Immortal: A Military History of*

Iran and its Armed Forces, also published in 2009, is an important historical primer on Iran and its military. Beyond this, Ward made a lasting impact on the field of Iran studies in general and the IRGC's development in particular.

In 2012, Steven O'Hern addressed the topic of the IRGC in *Iran's Revolutionary Guard: The Threat that Grows while America Sleeps.* It is an exceptional outline of the IRGC's beginnings, key players, evolution, global activity, and the IRGC's operations in Iraq following the United States' invasion in 2003. Abraham D. Sofaer built on O'Hern's book in *Taking on Iran: Strength Diplomacy, and the Iranian Threat*, published in 2013. Sofaer's text is a discussion on the IRGC's weapons and the IRGCN, among other technical specifications.

This author will argue that there is no book more important to Iran studies than military historian David Crist's *The Twilight War: The Secret History of America's Thirty-Year Conflict with Iran* published in 2012. According to Crist, the relationship between the United States and Iran is a "war of the shadows, largely unknown, arguably the most important and least understood conflict in recent history. It is the twilight war."[63] This is still true as of this writing. Crist weaved in his experience and extensive knowledge of the region to masterfully outline the Islamic Republic's trajectory. The intricate details on early Iranian wave makers such as Mostafa Chamran and others involved in the IRGC's development such as Ali Shamkhani are foundational elements for research in this area. *The Twilight War* should continue to be a point of reference for any author writing on Iran as Crist presents several details in each chapter that could be developed further and updated to reflect the events that have unfolded since 2012.

The most recent publications on the IRGC offer a different perspective and seem to indicate a shift in how the topic is approached for research. What used to be strategic studies is now more academic, with more history and theory. This author believes that, beginning with Afshon Ostovar of the Naval Postgraduate School, the small community of IRGC and Iran scholars have taken a sociological approach towards the Guards' role in Iran. In his 2009 dissertation, "Guardians of the Islamic Revolution: Ideology, Politics, and the Development of Military Power in Iran (1979–2009)," Ostovar examines a post-revolutionary Iran through the Revolutionary Guards. Since previous literature on the IRGC was primarily meant for audiences such as defense analysts and policymakers, studies such as Ostovar's took an opportunity to define sociological nuances surrounding the Guards. Ostovar builds on his own work in his 2016 book *Vanguard of the Imam: Religion, Politics, and Iran's Revolutionary Guards* and traces the origins of the IRGC up through the present at the time of writing. He discusses the Guards within a historical and religious context, arguing that the IRGC was a tool for state-building, establishing and maintaining control, and state survival.

Similarly, Bayram Sinkaya's 2016 book, *Revolutionary Guards in Iranian Politics: Elites and Shifting Relations*, views the IRGC as the regime's protectors. He argues that the "guard's increasing political clout in current Iranian politics is derived from its involvement, interventions, and interferences in the political sphere, rather than its being a constitutionally mandated authority."[64] The book employs case study analysis as its methodology and considers the French Revolution (1789), the Bolshevik Revolution (1917), and the Chinese Revolution (1949) to examine whether there is a relationship between revolutionary armies and political leadership. Sinkaya offers more details on the rise of the IRGC, specifically through Iran's economy, the Houthi rebels, and other relevant conflicts involving Iranian sponsorship and the IRGC.

While "The US Army in the Iraq War," a 1,400-page two-part volume published by the United States Army War College is about the US Army in the Iraq War what the title suggests, it provides invaluable insight into Iranian influence in Iraq, particularly into the various militia groups. It is an analytical volume that details the way in which the United States approached Iraq from both a tactical and policy perspective. The authors involved in this project were in some way connected to the war on various occasions, and the expertise behind the volumes skillfully explain the nuances of the Iraqi government and the breadth of Iranian influence.

Relatedly, Nader Uskowi's *Temperature Rising: Iran's Revolutionary Guards and Wars in the Middle East*, published in 2019, is a concise narrative of the Guards' warfare origins and traces their involvement across Middle East conflicts. Uskowi focuses primarily on the QF and Qasem Soleimani's impact on Iraq and Syria. The book offers detailed accounts of key battles the IRGC and QF were involved in across Syria and Iraq. Though this predates the targeted killing of Soleimani, its relevancy is still integral to the study of the

IRGC and QF. Lastly, a 2020 textbook by Ofira Seliktar and Farhad Rezaei, *Iran, Revolution, and Proxy Wars* is a chronological exploration of Iran; beginning with the 1979 Islamic Revolution, the book traces the tenure of each Iranian president, building a narrative of the evolution of the Islamic Republic. It is a succinct analysis of how Iran has evolved over time and how the country's policies have shaped its standing in the Middle East. It is filled with plenty of details that have been overlooked by some preceding scholarly works on Iran.

Proxy wars are different

It is a common practice across scholarship to use "proxy war" and "hybrid warfare" synonymously or interchangeably. Some argue that Iran is engaged in a proxy war using various Shia militia groups (SMG), but this book will differentiate the term "proxy" from "partners" in the subsequent chapters. Proxy wars are different from hybrid wars. For instance, Tyrone L. Groh, associate professor of global security and intelligence at Embry-Riddle College, designated Iran as being engaged in a "proxy war," defined as

> directing the use of force by a politically motivated, local actor to indirectly influence political affairs in the target state. An indirect intervention demands that an intervening state's forces engage tangentially in the conflict as advisors or in a capacity that augments a proxy's ground forces (such as providing air power or intelligence) without participating directly in the fighting on the ground. Once the intervening state begins to use its own forces to engage in the fighting, the conflict becomes a direct intervention.[65]

The author offers case studies dating from 1945, including Iranian sponsorship of the Houthis in Yemen, what he calls America's proxy war in Laos, South Africa's proxy war in Angola, and India's proxy war in Sri Lanka.

Andrew Mumford defines proxy wars as

> the product of a relationship between a benefactor, who is a state or non-state actor external to the dynamic of an existing conflict, and the chosen proxies who are the conduit for the benefactor's weapons, training, and funding. In short, proxy wars are the logical replacement for states seeking

to further their own strategic goals yet at the same time avoid engaging in direct, costly and bloody warfare.[66]

Mumford continues that, "more often than not, many of the proxy wars of the Cold War (such as the US's indirect intervention in Afghanistan during the 1980s) and after (like the recent Iranian proxy involvement against the US military in Iraq) could not have happened without existing local tensions ready to be exploited."[67] This is true but is only part of the story. In hybrid conflicts, this is more directly linked to the foreign policy of the sponsoring state, which is often trying to achieve a certain foreign policy end through the conflict.

The IRGC has also been discussed in relation to "surrogate warfare." Andreas Krieg and Jean-Marc Rickli adopt a sociological approach to describing post-revolutionary Iran in *Surrogate Warfare: The Transformation of War in the Twenty-First Century*. Specifically, surrogate warfare is presented as a "sociopolitical phenomenon rather than just another mode of war."[68] The authors focus on the development and societal aspect that contributed to Iran's government formation, particularly through a lengthy discussion on the Constitution of Iran. Though, theoretically, the authors try to differentiate their concept from proxy wars, in practice, it is quite similar. It is the use of external forces to do one's bidding. Regardless of terminology, proxy—and surrogate—wars differ from hybrid wars operationally.

Integrating the IRGC into broader Middle East scholarship

This research aims to fill gaps and build on the extant literature in Middle East scholarship—those presented in this review and otherwise. Historical details are important in understanding the origins and overall nature of the IRGC. Previous authors have been explaining "why" the IRGC has grown but not much "how" to approach them strategically. The same conclusion has been reached repeatedly: the IRGC behaves as it does both domestically and internationally to preserve the ideals of the Islamic Revolution. With the various conflicts playing out in the Middle East, it is now impossible to ignore the wider impact that Iran and the IRGC have on the region. This influence should be captured in scholarship to better understand the role of this challenging adversary with whom, as Crist has previously argued, the United States has been engaged in a twilight war for the last four decades.

More importantly, the conceptual framework of hybrid wars as applied to the IRGC should navigate within foreign policy circles to develop targeted strategies that aim for regional goals within US interests. Thus far, Washington has developed a habit of recycling information while trying to reach different conclusions. This lack of adaptation has not moved the needle on policymaking. Strategic thinking requires a whole-of-government approach that necessitates adaptation and a clear understanding of not just the history of an adversary but its development over time.

The Offspring of the Islamic Republic of Iran

The 1979 Islamic Revolution in Iran ended the reign of Iran's monarch Reza Shah Pahlavi. When Ayatollah Ruhollah Khomeini returned to Tehran from exile, there were already competing factions in Iran, which were not sold on his vision. The solution was to create an organization that would install and maintain a domestic order adhering to the newly established principles of the Islamic Republic. As the Marxist group the Mujahedin-al Khalq (MeK) waged rebellions and ethnic divisions ran rampant across the country, the IRGC exerted greater authority and use of force. They were essentially the national law enforcement, and they arguably still are today, having vastly grown in strength and responsibility.[1]

However, the IRGC is not just a stand-alone military organization. There exists a hierarchical system with responsibilities. This chapter will not serve as a deep dive into the IRGC's creation, as there are a variety of available literature that cover its origins, but as an overview of its structure. Historical context rests against the backdrop of the hybrid war theory because it explains the IRGC's ascendency. This framework will serve as a roadmap to how the Guards propelled themselves to dominance and broke away from its domestic mold.

Structure and ideology

Shortly after Khomeini inaugurated the Islamic Republic of Iran in February 1979, he issued a decree to establish a military that would protect the ideals of the revolution. According to Michael Eisenstadt, Kahn Fellow and director of the Washington Institute's Military and Security Studies Program, "Iran was born at war with the international system because from their point of view it was a system that was under American hegemony and thus inherently hostile to their interests. Accordingly, we must look at Iranian actions in that light."[2] Domestic problems following the revolution were also problematic. Regime leaders believed a purge of the Shah's Imperial Army (the Artesh) was the first step. Mostafa Chamran,[3] a US-educated radical who was instrumental in training the Guards in guerrilla and irregular warfare and who later established the Amal Movement in Lebanon, was tasked to develop a strategy to approach this purge. Chamran stated of his task,

> We need to purge the armed forces and more importantly change the existing system which was constructed by the Satanic regime. Firstly, (1) we should change the philosophical outlook of a military created to defend Zionism and imperialism; (2) we should purge it and redirect its goal to the defense of the revolution and Iran's independence; (3) purge will be based on the criteria of belief in Iran's independence and territorial integrity, belief in the Islamic Revolution and its leader Khomeini, and obedience to and acceptance of the government's sovereignty. Secondly, we must consolidate control within the armed forces by full acceptance of governmental authority and obedience to higher ranks.[4]

Meanwhile, Iran's future president Ali Akbar Hashemi Rafsanjani chartered the guidelines for the creation of the IRGC. As the author of the IRGC's constitution, Rafsanjani was subsequently appointed to manage the new institution, though this task was short-lived. In early 1980, Khomeini selected Ali Khamenei, another future Iranian president and would-be successor as supreme leader, as the Guards' caretaker. According to Barbara Slavin, director of the Future of Iran Initiative and nonresident senior fellow at the Atlantic Council, "Khamenei has had a symbiotic relationship with the IRGC. He was a minor cleric and regime loyalist when he was elevated to supreme leader and had no real political base of his own."[5] This relationship of convenience later strengthened and spurred the IRGC's growth, while Khamenei grew dependent on his predecessor's creation. Khamenei promoted a wider role for the organization and later used them to wield power.

Khamenei publicly explained that "the duty of the Sepah [IRGC] was to defend the regime against internal and external enemies, and especially to protect Iran against the arrogant powers and all others who intended to overthrow the regime."[6] He called the IRGC the Islamic Republic's "offspring":

> I believe that if Sepah did not exist or was weak, defending ourselves against absolute threats to our existence would be impossible for us. You are familiar with my views regarding armed forces—as His Eminence Imam held this belief until the end of his life—that the Sepah and the military (Artesh) must not be dissolved into each other, but that the two have to remain separate. Artesh, like the Sepah, will remain. But I believe that the only force that is capable of defending the revolution and the Islamic Republic in a revolutionary manner is the Sepah.[7]

Principally, the IRGC was intended to maintain order domestically. This included clearing out any defectors and Shah loyalists.

According to Article 150 of the Islamic Republic's Constitution, the span of the IRGC's responsibility is governed by the state's ideological laws:

> The Islamic Revolutionary Guards Corps, organized in the early days of the triumph of the Revolution, is to be maintained so that it may continue in its role of guarding the Revolution and its achievements. The scope of the duties of this Corps, and its areas of responsibility, in relation to the duties and areas of responsibility of the other armed forces, are to be determined by law, with emphasis on brotherly cooperation and harmony among them.[8]

Initially, the regime left the Guards' duties and responsibilities vague. Institutionally, the IRGC interprets constitutional law as they see fit. While the intention was never for the Guards to be involved politically, this ambiguity paved the way for constitutional abuse.

The IRGC swore an oath to the principle of *velayat-e faqih* (the Guardianship of the Jurisprudent; ولایت فقیه in Farsi). This is a strict Islamic practice that not only pertains to how one lives but also to how one views political matters. According to the Islamic Republic's Constitution, both the Artesh and the IRGC are unified under Shia Islam:

> In the formation and equipping of the country's defense forces, due attention must be paid to faith and ideology as the basic criteria. Accordingly, the Army of the Islamic Republic of Iran and the Islamic Revolutionary Guards Corps are to be organized in conformity with this goal, and they will be responsible

not only for guarding and preserving the frontiers of the country but also for fulfilling the ideological mission of jihad in God's way; that is, extending the sovereignty of God's law throughout the world (this is in accordance with the Qur'anic verse "Prepare against them whatever force you are able to muster, and strings of horses, striking fear into the enemy of God and your enemy, and others besides them" [8:60]).[9]

The IRGC, however, is primarily responsible for safeguarding these principles and enforcing the law. But that does not mean that the IRGC's sole purpose is safeguarding the revolution as it was originally established. While some maintain this notion, it can be alternatively argued that the IRGC has gone far beyond its original role. The circumstances in Iran and the Middle East required for the Islamic Republic to shape its defense strategy to meet its needs, and that began with the development of the IRGC.

The Guards' initial duties were to protect the supreme leader, preserve the principles of the revolution, and prevent any internal plots seeking to overthrow the new governing bodies. In short, the IRGC was a domestic force designed to "maintain Iran's religious nature and spirit."[10] According to *The Analytical History of the Iran–Iraq War*, an Iranian text by Hossein Alaei, a former a high-ranking IRGC official and member of Iran's Defense Ministry, on April 24, 1979, the Revolutionary Council and Ayatollah Khomeini concluded that a military establishment separate from the Artesh was necessary.[11] Following the events of the revolution, the supreme leader and his inner circle publicly displayed their suspicions and distrust of the Artesh.[12] The IRGC's standing was elevated; while they had previously answered to the Revolutionary Council, which was part of the supreme leader's cabinet, they now answered directly to the supreme leader himself.

At the time of its establishment, the Revolutionary Council was tasked with a list of duties (*"Asas Nameh-ye Sepah"* or اساسنامه سپاه *in Farsi*):

- Protect the Islamic Revolution;
- Defend Iran against domestic and international attacks;
- Detain and imprison anyone who poses a threat to the Islamic Revolution;
- Confiscate arms from the public;
- Gather intelligence;
- Assist with implementing the principles of the Islamic Revolution;

- Act as local law enforcement;
- Assist Muslim groups or states that are "oppressed" (such as Muslims in Sudan or other parts of the world).[13]

This established the parameters for the IRGC's responsibilities but also showed that they would aid others who wanted an Islamic Revolution. Additionally, the IRGC was committed to supporting the Palestinians with their fight against Israel.[14] Most of those credited with creating the IRGC were also involved in taking over the US Embassy in Tehran.

Iranian texts and research are significant sources of insight into the mindset of the Guards and those associated with its origins according to a 2014 volume produced by the Holy Defense Research and Document Center, which is an IRGC affiliated institute, the IRGC was created for two primary reasons: defense and exporting the Islamic Revolution. Defense means that the IRGC is meant to protect Iran's borders. The text furthers that the supreme leader and the Revolutionary Council envisioned a malleable IRGC that could quickly adjust and take on the role of the army, diplomatic officers, financial associates, policy advisors, and even authorities on societal issues.[15] Khomeini envisioned in an IRGC that would defend all Muslims and aid sympathetic rulers. He also sought unity across all Muslim countries under "Jahan-e Islam" (the way of Islam in the Koran, جهانه اسلام in Farsi) and that defending other Muslim countries is a duty; by extension, this implied that non-Muslim countries need not get involved in Islamic matters.[16]

This kind of rhetoric was a catalyst for the Iran–Iraq War, which will be discussed in the following chapter. The war posed greater challenges for Iran, not just domestically but internationally. It was catastrophic, though a prime case study for the Guards. In 1988, the regime wanted to merge the two state militaries under one authority. As a result, the Armed Forces General Staff (AFGS) was born. The Artesh and the IRGC would be separate but housed under the AFGS for organizational purposes.[17] In the aftermath of the Iran–Iraq War in 1989, Iran created the Ministry of Defense and Armed Forces Logistics (MODAFL) as the overarching state defense authority. There are several entities that fall under its purview, such as the equivalent to US defense and war colleges, and research and development for defense, which includes Iran's missile program.[18] Ultimately, the AFGS and its bodies were incorporated under the MODAFL's domain.[19] At the top of the hierarchy sits the supreme leader as the commander-in-chief of the armed forces, which was constitutionally mandated in October 1979. The Supreme National Security Council (SNSC) includes the president, and the secretary of the SNSC acts as a national security advisor. Interestingly, the Ministry of Intelligence and Security (MOIS) does not fall under the armed forces category. It is the supreme leader who appoints the leadership of the armed forces, not the president.[20] All of this is to show that Iran is not compartmentalized and should not be treated as such. It is more linear than commonly perceived.

Though there is a hierarchy, that does not necessarily mean a chain of command is followed. The Artesh and the IRGC are distinct, but both include parallel branches of armed forces: ground forces, navy, air force. The Artesh is outside the scope of this book, and we will therefore focus on the IRGC's branches. Aside from the QF, which is the IRGC's elite paramilitary, the IRGCN is emblematic of Iran's strategic thinking. It has nothing to do with the IRGCNs capability and resources but how Iran plays to its strengths. Iran focuses on maritime activities to police international waters and threaten commerce. The IRGCN is "the main executor of Iran's asymmetric naval guerilla warfare strategy and has full operational jurisdiction over Iran's maritime forces in the Persian Gulf."[21] As will be discussed in the following chapters, the IRGCN was a part of several attacks against the United States and the Gulf countries. With a situational understanding of this strength, the IRGCN either improved existing vessels or developed small new boats designed for fast attacks, in addition to anti-ship missiles and mines. They have significantly contributed to Iran's overall anti-access aerial denial (A2/AD) capabilities.[22] Strength awareness is not limited to the IRGCN. The IRGC ground and aerospace forces are also capable in their own right, as particularly evidenced in Syria.[23]

Quds Force (QF)

The QF became an official unit in 1988. They serve as a clandestine service under the IRGC umbrella. It is unclear how many soldiers compose the QF, but estimates suggest that the number conservatively ranges anywhere between 10,000 and 15,000.[24] They are akin to the green berets of the United States, an elite unit that conducts clandestine operations and is primarily tasked with external operations. According to IRGC scholar Ali Alfoneh, the QF was intended to be a compilation of "the armies of Islamic countries and their combatant people who will both end the life of dependent regimes of the region and the criminal and shameful life of Israel."[25] Ahmad Vahidi was the first QF commander; Qasem Soleimani took over in 1998 and vastly altered the scope and authority of the QF. Even though the QF is under the IRGC's purview, Soleimani had a direct line to the supreme leader. Over the course of almost twenty-two years, Soleimani executed multi-pronged strategies across the Middle East, which included the creation of various militia groups that reap the rewards from Iranian state sponsorship. Soleimani was a true believer in the revolutionary principles and wanted to shape the region within this framework. Through a variety of operations across Iraq and Syria, he was well versed strategically and tactically. He also had a remarkable ability to resonate with non-Iranian populations that would be explicitly loyal to him and but not necessarily Iran. These qualities were what made him particularly dangerous.

The QF additionally supports groups such as Lebanese Hizballah, Hamas, and Palestinian Jihad, among others. As Soleimani's authority expanded, he took charge of special projects, such as creating militias in his image and defining their roles through the prism of Iran's defense strategy. He fostered relationships with local leaders and joined in community engagements predominately in Iraq. Young Iraqis were eager to join any group that was part of Soleimani's vision.

While QF is technically a separate branch of the IRGC, they act independently and especially did so while under Soleimani.[26] Their intended purpose was to operate across Iran's borders while the IRGC tended to domestic matters. Specifically, the QF fostered "relationships with people, often building on existing socio-economic ties with the well-established Shia diaspora."[27] They have a massive global presence and continually support ally militant groups through a variety of activities, including training, advising, and equipping. As an operationally independent entity, the QF have been called "soldiers of the Last Days, or "holy warriors who do the bidding of Iran's Shia clerics."[28] Over time, notably following the US invasion of Iraq, the international community studied and evaluated this faction within the IRGC and recognized not just how embedded they are within state systems but also the breadth of its capabilities. Through the QF, the IRGC penetrated foreign policy matters as both war and policy blurred the lines of civil–military relations.

State sponsorship

Since 1984, Iran has been designated as a state sponsor of terrorism.[29] Iran engages in international terrorism through Lebanese Hizballah and other militia groups. Along with its main partner, Hizballah, Iran has engaged in terrorist activities since the mid-1980s, especially with a series of suicide bombings that targeted US forces. In 1983, Iranian and Hizballah operatives were linked to the Marine barracks bombing in Beirut, Lebanon. But the September 1984 attack at the US Embassy annex in Beirut put Hizballah on the map. It was not until *Brewer v. Islamic Republic of Iran* in 2009 that a US district court found that Iran, through the MOIS and the IRGC, had provided "material support and resources,"[30] to Hizballah and that the executors of the bombing were Hizballah fighters. *Brewer* and *Welch v. Islamic Republic of Iran* both exposed the breadth of Iran's involvement, specifically uncovering satellite reconnaissance images of "an identical, life-size model of the Embassy Annex in the training camps in the Bekaa Valley."[31] Other early, high-profile attacks that involved Hizballah included the AMIA Jewish Community Center attack in Buenos Aires, Argentina, in 1994 and the Khobar Towers bombing in Saudi Arabia in 1996.[32]

Iran's state sponsorship had a starting point, though. Hizballah publicly acknowledged the then supreme leader Ayatollah Ruhollah Khomeini as their supreme leader in 1985.[33] As Mohsen Rafighdoost, one of the Guards' founders, indicated, "Hizballah are descendants of Iran's Revolution."[34] The QF is primarily responsible for providing support to Hizballah, "which Iran views as an essential partner for advancing its regional policy objectives."[35] Lebanon was engulfed in a civil war before the Islamic Revolution in Iran. Between 1975 and 1990, Lebanon faced domestic turmoil, leading thousands of Lebanese to immigrate to other parts of the world. After the 1979 Revolution in Iran, however, the new clerical regime seized the opportunity to strengthen the small guerrilla group in Lebanon. It was the first area in which Iran began expanding ties with a Shia population.

Since 1982, the IRGC has been vital to the foundation of Hizballah, and it continues to be so even today. The QF "provides financial, weapons, training, and logistical support to Lebanese Hizballah," and Hizballah in turn trains Iraqi insurgents in the region through the prism of Iranian interests.[36] Hizballah provides "training, tactics and technology to conduct kidnappings, small unit tactical operations and employ sophisticated improvised explosive devices (IEDs), incorporating lessons learned from operations in southern Lebanon."[37]

While SMG will be discussed later in more depth, it is worth mentioning them at this stage to better place the IRGC in context. For example, attacks in Iraq were overt since not only did the IRGC enlist the support of Hizballah following the US overthrow of Saddam Hussein in 2003, but IRGC soldiers also targeted US troops. Iran consistently supplied weapons and training to Shia militant groups. For instance, the C-4 explosives found on Shia militiamen were identified as Iranian made.[38] In 2009, reports revealed that US troops found a supply of weapons, which included 150 copper plates to be specifically used as explosively formed penetrators (EFP) and "sophisticated launching rails for rockets that are designed to increase range and accuracy."[39] It was no longer a secret that Iranian-backed SMG were using Iranian weapons to kill US troops.[40] Other weapons included "improvised explosive devices (IED); anti-aircraft weapons; mortars; 107 and 122 millimeter rockets; rocket-propelled grenades and launchers; explosives and small arms."[41] The IRGC, QF, and Hizballah have provided considerable aid to Shia militias, which includes teaching war-fighting tactics at specialized training camps.[42]

One of the militant groups was an extension of the Islamic Supreme Council of Iraq (ISCI), known as the Badr Corps (or the Badr Organization). The IRGC also had previous connections with Muqtada al Sadr's group, Jaysh al-Mahdi (the Mahdi Army), and the Da'wa party. Second to Lebanese Hizballah, the most powerful Shia group is Soleimani's creation, Kata'ib Hizballah (KH) in Iraq. Many of these groups became active beyond Iraq's borders to aid with Iran's defense of Bashar al-Assad in Syria in the aftermath of the Arab Spring in 2011. Iranian-backed Shia militiamen were flown into Syria from Abadan, Iraq, on daily flights by Iran's Mahan Airlines.[43] While Shia militias are present in Syria, Iran's paramilitary force, the Basij, has also had an increasing presence since at least 2015.[44]

Iran also provides monetary aid and weapons to Palestinian terrorist groups such as Hamas, the Palestinian Islamic Jihad, and Popular Front for the Liberation of Palestine (PFLP-GC). Though these groups are not Shia, Iran's association with them proves its willingness to provide aid to groups that will support Iran's strategic objectives. The IRGC extended into parts of the African continent beginning in the 1990s. Many Lebanese immigrated to West Africa during the civil war, and Hizballah fighters followed close behind to establish a subtle foothold. It took time before direct action was taken despite the IRGC continuing to sponsor terrorism internationally. In October 2007, the QF was sanctioned by the US Department of the Treasury (DoT) under Executive Order 13224 for providing material support to the Afghan Taliban and terrorist organizations like Hizballah and Hamas.[45] Identifying QF for its support of terrorism, the designation recognizes it as the "Iranian regime's primary instrument for providing lethal support to the Taliban," such as "frequent shipments of small arms and associated ammunition, rocket propelled grenades, mortar round, 107mm rockets, plastic explosives, and probably man-portable defense systems."[46] The designation also includes the QF support to Hizballah as well as the lethal support to "select groups of Iraqi Shia militants who target and kill Coalition and Iraqi forces and innocent Iraqi civilians."[47]

The IRGC, QF, and SMG took advantage of the situations in Iraq and Syria and established a base of operations that serves the Iranian regime's overarching national and regional interests. Overall, terrorism worked to Iran's advantage with logistical support and weapons to pro-Iranian groups and SMG in Lebanon, Iraq, Syria, Persian Gulf, Gaza-West Bank, Afghanistan, and Central Asia.[48] When the fragile Iraqi government was threatened by the Islamic State in 2014, Iran quickly supplied QF "advisors, intelligence drone surveillance, weapons shipments, and other assistance."[49] The range of experience they gained facilitated a shift in strategy, which was more emboldened and calculated.

Understanding history

The IRGC's hybrid trajectory can be traced from its origins. Iranian documents on the IRGC explicitly link its founding members and early leaders to Arab countries where they trained for guerilla warfare, which they imported to Iran. Some were in Iraq in the mid-1970s, while others trained in guerrilla tactics in Syria and Palestinian territory.[50] According to military historian Steven M. Ward, the IRGC's "first loyalty was to the clerics and not the new government."[51] At the onset, the IRGC was deeply rooted in Khomeini's Twelver Shia and the Islamic Revolution itself. Gradually, as this book will discuss, this ideological zeal tempered, and the strategic doctrine vested in hybrid warfare became the driving force. That is not to say, however, that there are no elements within the regime and across the IRGC that believe in the original intent of the revolution. But the background of the early founders and influencers suggests that they were a motley crew of outsiders that facilitated the revolution and pushed to establish a military vanguard. It is critical to understand that the Guards' original war-fighting tactics were imported and that they had to adapt accordingly.

As such, Iran's clerics used the IRGC as a tool not only to defend the country's borders and export the revolution but also to prevent any domestic unrest that would threaten regime stability. As Steven O'Hern wrote in 2012,

> The most dangerous aspect of the IRGC is its transformation from a tool of Iran's supreme leader and senior clerics into an independent power unto itself. The Revolutionary Guard has eclipsed the revolutionary leaders it was formed to protect. This transformation of the IRGC is aided and accelerated by three factors: its position as an economic power, its role in maintaining internal security with Iran, and its ever-growing status as a political power.[52]

The IRGC's transformation into its present form is the culmination of its experiences over the last four decades. Eisenstadt observed that

> from the very beginning of the revolution and then 1982, Iran was in Lebanon, and there were connections that even preceded the Revolution. Then, the Israeli invasion of Lebanon in 1982 created an opportunity. Iran's efforts to export the revolution in the early years via the IRGC were an

expansive kind of effort, followed by retrenchment after the Iran–Iraq war, but not in Lebanon though.[53]

Over the last four decades, the IRGC has grown to independently act on Iran's foreign policy, which is a far cry from simply defending domestic borders.

Nonetheless, Khomeini's vision for a national law enforcement grew into a conglomerate, which has been the greatest unintended consequence. As will be discussed in upcoming chapters, four Iranian presidents—one of whom later became the next supreme leader—tried to place checks on the IRGC, and all failed in the process. Both Khomeini and Khamenei, as supreme leaders, used the IRGC as tools to protect their individual control and authority, not realizing that the Guards' growth was irreversible. Having learned that senior leadership will utilize the Guards to pursue self-interests, the IRGC leadership has manipulated this relationship and essentially extorted the regime for authority. According to Alfoneh, the Guards have become "indifferent to the preferences of civilian leadership, and the IRGC uses disunity among the civilians to pursue its own corporate interests."[54] As a result, the IRGC is essentially a shadow government, impervious to civilian leadership, which at this point includes even the supreme leader.

4

Laying the Foundation

Surveying the Iran–Iraq War through the prism of hybrid warfare is one way to better understand the IRGC's expansive reach. Formed in the vision of a conventional military, the IRGC found its war-fighting space in irregular campaigns, which challenged the Iraqi military tactically and operationally. Christopher Bowers posits three variables to understand emerging hybrid adversaries—maturity, capability, and complex terrain—and notes that the overlap of these variables is "the point of maximum, tactical, operational, and strategic effectiveness for a hybrid threat."[1] A "fully developed" hybrid can transition between irregular and guerrilla war while blending conventional modes.[2] During the Iran–Iraq War, the IRGC was not yet a mature force, but the lessons they learned from the war helped them steadily reach that point.

Iran was not prepared institutionally to fight a conventional war with Iraq, but Khomeini was convinced that the Islamic Republic could defeat its enemy through will alone. Khomeini issued the decree for the IRGC's establishment to restore order in the country following the revolution that brought him to power, and this included purging opposition groups and shah loyalists. The IRGC's role was strengthened after the declaration of a national emergency on September 22, 1980.[3] The Iran–Iraq War was yet another defining moment in Middle East history. There is still a purpose to studying the war and how it changed the landscape of the region. The current political and military dynamics of the region are arguably a result. Iran used the outcome as a "lessons learned" to integrate the IRGC more broadly in defense and foreign affairs. The consequences of the war, whether intentional or unintended, are still felt by regional states, even as of this writing.[4] To this effect, this chapter answers why the Iran–Iraq War was so impactful to the IRGC's development and how it shaped Iran's future and defense strategies.

Regime and IRGC stalwarts have written many books and articles since the inception of the Guards. As explained in the previous chapter, the IRGC-affiliated Holy Defense Research and Document Center[5] published a study on the Iran–Iraq War in 2014, outlining the purpose of the IRGC from their own perspective. The war was a critical moment as it not only allowed the IRGC to exercise broad authority and engage militarily but also to lay the groundwork for future diplomacy, economic integration, and further social intrusion. The authors of the study wrote that Western scholars and analysts have contorted the true meaning of the IRGC's existence. They argued that the Iran–Iraq War was not just about defending Iran but also about defending all Muslim countries, who should all unite behind Khomeini against Iraq.[6]

Per the principle of *velayat-e faqih*, the *Faqih*, or the jurist, is the most righteous man in the country who handles the people's moral well-being. The IRGC would safeguard this principle and enforce the law. The circumstances in Iran and the Middle East called on the Islamic Republic to define its defense strategy to meet their needs, and that began with the IRGC. A key figure in the development of the IRGC was Mohsen Rezaei. At the age of twenty-eight, he was both the defense minister and commander of the newly minted IRGC. Rezaei was "ruthless and powerful, a trusted servant for both Khomeini and his successor, Ayatollah Khamenei," and it was Rezaei "who transformed the Revolutionary Guard from a ragtag military into a sword for the Islamic Republic."[7] He was one of the more vocal leaders of the Guards who reinvented himself later in life with political ambitions. Rezaei's influence as a true Guardsman never really waned, but he found himself clashing with up-and-coming leaders who eventually pushed him aside.

But the Iran–Iraq War was the first major turning point for the IRGC. The fallout carved out a future for the Guards and a course for Iran's defense policy. Their defeat meant it was time to rebuild and pivot toward strategic efforts that would serve their domestic and international interests. Their only successful aspect was the large numbers of untrained so-called volunteers who were willing to "martyr" themselves for the revolution. This martyrdom for a cause was not traditionally known to be inherently Iranian, and it was the Iraqi army's major obstacle in their fight against Iranian soldiers. Iranian martyrdom was a byproduct of the Islamic Revolution in response to the Iran–Iraq War. The division among ranks and between the newly established IRGC and the Artesh made developing and executing a strategy futile. Many among the Artesh ranks either deserted, retired, or were purged, which left the armed forces weak. It became too burdensome to associate with this new ideology that pressed into military affairs.

From a policy perspective, Iran's Shah kept Iraq in check. Post-revolution Iran with an Ayatollah was markedly different. Both sides recognized each other as a threat and challenge to regional hegemony, but neither knew how to best approach it. Khomeini particularly viewed Saddam Hussein as being in the way of his revolutionary vision.

This chapter will not be a reevaluation of the Iran–Iraq War, nor will it serve as another summation of events. There is a wealth of widely available texts by scholars who have studied the war in depth, and their contributions are invaluable. Rather, this chapter will assess Iran's current defense strategy as a reflection of the war. The Iran–Iraq War was not only a lesson on strategic thought, but it is also educational for the United States in viewing linkages between the Islamic Republic's first hybrid conflict and its modern hybrid ones.

The purge

It is worthwhile to evaluate the Artesh purges as it would provide insight into the events that unfolded during the war and help us understand why the IRGC faced so many challenges. Khomeini's decision to immediately purge the security apparatus was deadly in practice and highly controversial. With hundreds of executions and incarcerations, Iran was paralyzed institutionally and so too was its existing infrastructure. The first wave struck before the creation of the IRGC, on February 15, 1979, with the execution of four generals.[8] This was part of Khomeini's vendetta against Shah loyalists and those who tried to resist the revolution. As the purges continued, new leaders emerged, including Mostafa Chamran. Chamran was a hardline Khomeini zealot and continued to purge Iran's military with a blend of lethality and ideological charge.

Subsequent results of these actions had wide-ranging unintended consequences on Iran's security infrastructure that ultimately contributed to the IRGC's power grab following the war. The Artesh was portrayed as ideologically and morally corrupt by the new Islamic standards in Iran. This empowered the IRGC to define itself as vanguards of the Islamic Revolution. The distrust of the Artesh further strained the already broken relationship. The IRGC lacked adequate artillery, and they had no qualification or expertise to put into use the ones they seized from the Artesh. Alternative courses of action often meant turning to external actors. Hossein Alaei,[9] a former senior member of the IRGC, authored a two-volume history of the Iran–Iraq War through the lens of the IRGC. Alaei alleged the IRGC obtained rifles from Yasser Arafat and also from the Democratic People's Republic of Korea (DPRK).[10] According to Alaei, other weaponry and alleged materiel were acquired from Austria and elsewhere. To conceal the countries of origin, official paperwork showed Sudan as the original purchaser;[11] the weaponry would be routed to the Port of Bandar Abbas for IRGC retrieval. Another former senior IRGC official, Mohsen Rafighdoost, authored a book on the IRGC's history. Most striking of Rafighdoost's claims of weapons purchases was that in 1984, Akbar Hashemi Rafsanjani and IRGC commander Mohsen Rezaei signed a deal with China for air-to-surface missiles, air-to-sea missiles, and other weapons from Muammar Gaddafi in Libya.[12]

Despite this, the IRGC still encountered heavy deficiencies in manpower and resources and lacked the ability to operate weaponry, vessels, and aircraft.[13] This suggested that Iran would need to adopt a strategy that optimized its forces and capabilities, however bleak they were, through a hybrid approach that brought out the greatest efficacy of each. As the Iran–Iraq War raged on, the IRGC wavered between successes and failures. Ultimately, in September 1985, Khomeini announced the creation of ground, naval, and air force branches of the IRGC, which expanded the Guards' responsibilities and stature.[14]

Ineptitudes in battle

From the Islamic Revolution in February 1979 to the outbreak of conflict in September 1980, Iran irrefutably faced significant organizational, ideological, and political challenges that directly affected the country not just during the war but also for decades to come. Considering that the IRGC was still in ideological and physical development, it suffered a series of inefficiencies that gave Iraq the strategic advantage at the onset of the war.

The IRGC lost access to tens of thousands of foreign military equipment technicians and faced an arms embargo from the United States and Great Britain. International isolation promptly followed. First, IRGC readiness efforts were compromised because of Iranian focus on political reliability as opposed to logistical support. The negative foreign perception, associated embargoes, and purges all forced the new Iranian regime to heavily prioritize its political footprint, neglecting readiness efforts from the very beginning of the war. Second, Iranian military training nearly came to a halt, while emphasis was placed more on indoctrination rather than conventional skills.[15] Training of new recruits focused primarily on ideological alignment instead of warfighting expertise. A declassified CIA report from January 1987 characterized the early IRGC as plagued by "inadequate organization, lack of training and discipline, and a chronic shortage of funds and equipment" that stymied their performance in battle.[16] The Artesh was forced to supply training and logistical support to make up for the IRGC's inefficiencies. The overlapping, interpretive language used to define the security role of the two arms of the military perpetuated this internal dynamic in the Constitution of Iran.[17] Because of this military shift, IRGC–Artesh tensions inflamed to where both sides refused to liaise and even started to ignore each other's orders.[18]

The IRGC was not trained or equipped to fight Iraq in conventional battle; there was no coordination at either the tactical or the operational level.[19] The war ultimately revealed the IRGC's flaws: religious fervor meant nothing if they did not know how to fight, which was a major lesson for the IRGC leaders and clerics back in Tehran.

Growth

Following Iran's incorporation of the IRGC into its security force structure, the Guards experienced rapid expansion in capabilities and influence as it institutionalized itself within the Iranian regime politically. This growth was most notable in four ways: organization of military units, recruitment of personnel, creation of command councils, and incorporation into Iran's Supreme Defense Council.[20] The establishment of combat units was crucial at the onset of the war. Iran needed to quickly defend its border with Iraq, and the organization of combat units became a part of the first line of defense.

This also helped with recruitment efforts as the war carried on. By 1982, the IRGC had roughly 50,000 fighters, which reached 450,000 by 1987.[21] The more Iran reorganized logistically, the more Iranian citizens took part as defenders of the revolution. Even with growing numbers, training and operational capacities were still significantly lacking. Men were sent to the front lines with no war-fighting experience, but they were committed to the cause.[22]

The IRGC's institutionalization supported its progress within the regime through its incorporation into key decision-making bodies, such as the Operational Area Command, the joint Command Council, and the Supreme Defense Council.[23] Each of these military centers worked to conjoin IRGC and Artesh leadership to establish a more unified cooperative in strategic planning. This resulted in centralized logistics and readiness while still allowing the IRGC to operate with autonomy. Membership brought desperately needed resources, while political and clerical leadership enjoyed legitimacy and prestige. At the Supreme Defense Council, the Guards "enjoyed representation and an influential voice in the highest military decision-making body."[24] Despite major obstacles and challenges, hardline volunteer fighters were a success for the IRGC as they could be capitalized on and used as strategic strength.

From conventional to asymmetric warfare

The IRGC was a conventional fighting force, but ideologically driven purges, international isolation, and deficiencies in war-fighting experience and weapons training proved otherwise. Iran's strategic calculation was to rely on the guerilla training that early IRGC architects had received in Lebanon and elsewhere that was experiencing internal strife. In terms of operational capabilities, Iraq significantly overpowered Iran's fighting force; Iran had just 500 operational Chieftain and Patton tanks, 300 functioning artillery pieces, and less than 100 fixed-wing aircraft compared to Iraq's 2,750 tanks, 4,000 other armored vehicles, 1,400 artillery pieces, and 340 combat aircraft.[25] A shortage of weapons led to some creativity and considerable effort on Iran's part. They bought much of their arsenal from the Soviet Union (such as tanks and artillery) as well as North Korea, China, Libya, and Eastern Europe.[26]

Only a quarter of Iran's conventional military was involved in early operations. However, Iran's air force was most effective; they leveraged their limited capabilities to their advantage. First, they conducted airlifts with the aircrafts they had at their disposal to move fighters to the front lines as part of their retaliatory strategy against Iraq's strike on Iranian airfields.[27] Iran's Air Force also successfully used Maverick missiles against Iraqi ground forces. Khuzestan was one of the first contested areas that proved to be a significant challenge for Iran to defend. The open land afforded Iraq's heavy artillery a distinct advantage against an IRGC force that was toiling to defend itself against Iraq's armor and artillery.

A clear shift toward irregular roots happened when the IRGC turned to urban areas to establish defenses with smaller arms. Through these defenses, moving in tandem with strategically called air strikes, Iran slowed Iraqi advances into urban areas and afforded themselves time to prepare. These strategic operations were the first signs of Iranian asymmetric military thinking and use of hybrid tactics to defend against a conventional force that would have otherwise overrun the Iranian military.

Human wave attacks were a part of the IRGC's strategy to return to guerrilla roots. The IRGC sent in its volunteer force, the Basij, to run toward Iraqi front lines to absorb the blunt of fire, clear mines, and breach obstacles for the ground forces to follow behind. The Basij were almost entirely composed of elderly men and boys as young as nine. The human waves served a dual purpose: attack Iraqi command centers to break the integrity of their lines of defense and rally IRGC forces around this "cult of martyrdom" and war of ideology.[28] Iran effectively blended the Artesh, the IRGC, and the Basij to conduct infantry attacks in waves that resulted in heavy casualties. This not only exhausted Iraqi ammunition and will but led to breaking Iraqi resistance.[29] If nothing else, the human wave as a tactic compensated for Iran's lack of conventional capabilities.

The Iran–Iraq War shifted in favor of Iran in 1982 as the regime finally regained control of the territories originally lost to Iraq through Operation Ramadan. This shift happened for two reasons: a change in strategy and a change in perception and focus. Strategically, the IRGC adopted a hybrid approach that gave it leverage in multiple domains over Iraq and its regional partners. In terms of perception, Iran successfully refocused the fight from one of national defense to promoting and exporting the Islamic Revolution beyond its borders.

Ultimately, the IRGC's guerilla and light infantry operations compensated for past conventional failures and inadequacies. Light infantry forces thrived on the maneuverability offered by smaller artillery and units. The IRGC, as a result, could maintain dynamic operations with a unique advantage by relying on the expertise of their own terrain—such as urban roads, marshes, and mountainous areas—coupled with poor weather under the cover of darkness.[30] This evolution of capabilities in operations favored Iran to develop a strategy that used its terrain, mobility, logistics, and minimal weaponry to its advantage.[31] Specifically, the IRGC brass polished their fighters' skills in subversion, their topographical expertise in marsh and mountainous terrain, as well as their ability to use the darkness of night to their advantage. This situational environment allowed the IRGC the concealment they needed for small-unit tactics while hindering Iraqi forces.[32] Light infantry and insurgent tactics were successful against a more technologically savvy adversary. The key takeaway here is not that Iraq won the war but that Iran understood what tactics worked against a superior adversary. Small gains through tactical advantages among other campaigns were sufficient lessons learned to be used as a platform for Iran's future defense doctrine. This was Iran's way of war that would be refined decades later.

This period during the war also showed Iran's experimentation with Shia partners outside of Iran's borders. The IRGC and Iranian-aligned Iraqi Shias formed the Supreme Council for the Islamic Revolution in Iraq (SCIRI) in 1982, followed by the Badr Corps in 1983. This was the earliest attempt by Iran to mimic the Lebanese Hizballah model in Iraq. Non-state partners brought deniability and had a strategic advantage in the conflict more directly, given Iran's exploitation of Shia groups. The use of non-state actors leveraged asymmetric maneuvers to gain an advantage over Iraq without conventional intervention, and, in identifying Iraq's ethnic and religious fault lines, it forced the Iraqi government to adjust defensively.[33]

The Tanker War

In 1984, for the first time since the Second World War, commerce came under attack in international waters.[34] Iran's strategy in the Gulf was "concealment in deception."[35] The IRGC's naval arm, the IRGCN, became the primary fighting force, executing tit-for-tat attacks to give Iran a strategic advantage in the Gulf. Iran bought a reasonable number of missiles and speedboats, and geographical strongholds aided its asymmetric approach at sea. Between 1985 and 1987, Iran was almost wholly reliant on Libyan clandestine transfers of Soviet Scud-B missiles.[36] The IRGCN's fleet comprised roughly 800 speedboats and 80 Swedish-made interceptor Boghammar craft, which were ideal for quick strikes against tankers and US ships.[37] Iran's F-6 and F-7 fighter aircraft and silkworm missiles were obtained from China.

The IRGCN used maritime geography to its advantage in the Gulf. They constructed headquarters at Farsi Island, with other bases on the islands of Hormuz, Sirri, Larak, and Abu Musa. The IRGCN exploited its strategic environment with greater flexibility. To achieve its strategy of "concealment in deception," the IRGCN used an early hybrid war-fighting technique to target Iraq and its partners at sea. This included missile launches, laying of mines, and a slew of retaliatory strikes, all of which helped develop an asymmetric strategy "based on avoiding direct or sustained confrontations at sea."[38]

Iran's use of mines was crucial during the Tanker War. Iran's mine arsenal was about 1,000 strong, mainly Soviet M-08s.[39] A heavy reliance on mines supported deniability. But when an Iranian mine damaged a US frigate, the United States responded with Operation Praying Mantis, effectively destroying two oil platforms and several surface vessels.[40] Following this setback, Iran focused its naval doctrine on a "layered defense and massing of firepower, integrating multiple sea, land and air-based weapons simultaneously to overwhelm and confuse adversaries."[41] The results from Operation Praying Mantis pivoted Iran's strategy toward the speed-based attacks it is known for today. The speed and agility of these small fighter boats offer maneuverability around large tankers and adversarial vessels. It also affords enhanced accuracy. Retaliatory strikes by the naval forces of the Revolutionary Guard were proportional and carefully controlled by Tehran, another clear definition of how war-related decisions were internally politicized. Attacks were most often conducted against crude oil tankers, as opposed to warships, to impose costs on other domains outside of combat, such as the regional economy.

The Tanker War reached its peak in 1987 as the Iran–Iraq War neared its end and Iran more fully embraced a hybrid approach that exploited the strengths of the IRGC against the weaknesses of Iraq and its regional partners. Vast changes in development and strategy reinvigorated Iran, even though they suffered in defeat. The practices employed in the Tanker War were revisited decades later.[42] Iran defines its defense strategy based on lessons learned and advances secured within its operational skills.

Lessons learned

Even though Iran was defeated,[43] it still found success that contributed to its strategic framework. Not only did the new regime garner political, theological, and regional influence, but it also groomed partner organizations to continue this work in the future. The West struggled to understand the new Iranian regime that rose to prominence in the aftermath of the Shah's ouster, and as a result, the Iranian threat was viewed as a conventional one. This is not a criticism, since there was nothing that paled in comparison up to this point, but the challenge led the West, notably the United States, to misinterpret the adversarial threat and the trajectory that it was on. The Gulf was the focus, and following the end of the Iran–Iraq War, Iran, let alone the IRGC, was more of an afterthought for the West. Many in Washington were deeply preoccupied with Iraq and Saddam Hussein, not realizing that the threat of the IRGC would loom large in the future.

After the Iran–Iraq War, Tehran strategically pulled political levers to maintain its power grab and establish a more permanent presence through exporting the revolution across the Middle East. The Iranian regime and the IRGC effectively mobilized a sub-conflict level campaign that blended a combination of hard and soft power to progress toward regional influence. Iran had, to some extent, effectively defended itself against Iraq through an asymmetric approach to conflict, yet the next phase of the Iranian revolutionary strategy required continued evolution of tactics to proliferate its influence outside of wartime.

One of the most effective strategies during the war was the IRGC's exercise of soft power. Iran cultivated a population loyal to its theocracy and with a willingness to volunteer for self-sacrifice in defense of the Islamic Republic. In terms of hard power, the greatest advantage was the institutionalization of the QF. The QF focused mainly on intelligence operations and external actions across the region, giving it significant control over the exportation of the revolution after the Iran–Iraq War.[44] The IRGC's legacy was fortified by the QF, given its strategic use of intelligence that continued to put Iran's ideological revolution into practice.

Khomeini and those around him firmly believed that "religious enthusiasm, engendered by their revolution, could replace military expertise, weapons systems and technology."[45]

In 1987, the CIA assessed that

> the regime intends the Revolutionary Guard to become the core of a new "army of the revolution" that will eventually replace the regular armed forces. The Guard's experience in the way with Iraq has made it a more effective military force. It has learned from its defeats, improved its operational skills, tightened its discipline and control, and assumed an increasingly significant role in planning war strategy. Despite many purges of the military and the creation of a political control apparatus attached to all regular armed forces units, the clerical leadership remains suspicious of the loyalty of the country's Ground Forces, Navy, and Air Force.[46]

Tehran's shift to asymmetric strategies during the war set the stage for future hybridity. This is attributed to the IRGC's ability to exploit the weaknesses of Iraq's conventional tactics while also turning the focus of the war from ideological export to national defense. The IRGC played into its strengths of light-infantry guerilla warfare, use of non-state actors, economic terrorism, and perception management. Once the IRGC secured prestige and political influence, it opened the doors to calculated manipulation, not just in Iraq but across the region. The Guards' ability to leverage asymmetric campaigns led to some of their greatest victories over the course of the war.

The legacy of the Iran–Iraq War is such that it continues to be of significance to the present study. Threat perception in the Middle East can be linked to various actors that have since spawned from the war and the deep animosity between pro-Iran factions in Iraq and their opponents. The IRGC deviated from a defensive to an offensive strategy through asymmetric tactics, which they found worked best against the Iraqi military. While the war was nearly a decade long, the IRGC was still a quick study even in its infancy. The shift in strategy became clear after it recaptured areas from Iraqi control. The Iran–Iraq War was the IRGC's first test, and it paved their way toward influencing Iran's defense doctrines and involving themselves in critical decision-making.

5

A Civil–Military Revolution in Post-War Expansion

Up to this point, we have established the creation of the IRGC and its foundational principles. Clerical oversight was crucial to the Guards' sustainability early on. The aftermath of the Iran–Iraq War revealed crevices among leadership as well as major vulnerabilities. The best options came from the executive level, but Guard ambitions created fissures in Iranian civil–military relations.

The IRGC was pulled into civilian control when Khamenei was inaugurated as Iran's supreme leader. The Guards were necessary for Khamenei's impetus for power and gradually became his Praetorian Guard. This muddled Iran's civil–military relations, which continued to widen the span of the IRGC's hybrid warfare capabilities. Immediately after its establishment, the Islamic Republic had to face the brutal Iran–Iraq War, followed by the death of Khomeini. Savvy political players such as Ali Akbar Rafsanjani saw an opportunity with Khamenei. Alongside Ahmad Khomeini, the late Ayatollah's son, Rafsanjani schemed to elevate Khamenei's stature and endorse his selection as Iran's next supreme leader. Khamenei did not have either the religious clout of Khomeini or his charisma and ambition, or so it seemed. Rafsanjani's plan portrayed Khamenei as a political pawn while attempting to keep the IRGC at bay. The civil–military line started with Khamenei[1] and has since developed into the model that we see today. Mohammad Khatami succeeded Rafsanjani and tried to similarly constrain the IRGC, but to no avail—the attempts only further mired civil–military relations. Khamenei capitalized on Khatami's weaknesses and helped promote the Guards' authority. Ultimately, this solidified their standing in Iranian politics and economy, and there was no reversing course.

This mishandling of civil–military relations has been a significant contributing factor to the IRGCs hybridity. No Iranian president has succeeded in constraining the growth and authority of the Guards, and they continue to become stronger with each regime. As a result, currently, Iran's foreign policy rests with the IRGC and not with the civilians in the Ministry of Foreign Affairs or elsewhere at the executive level. As Iran's priorities changed, so did the IRGC's role. The IRGC has essentially eliminated civil–military relations in Iran and contributed to the Guards' development as a hybrid actor. The blending of civil–military relations in the country was merely an accident that happened in the course of accounting for the regional shifts and responding to outside influences (such as sanctions and embargoes). According to Ali Alfoneh, "The bureaucratic politics of proxy warfare decision-making is complex due to dysfunctional civil–military relations, and as a function of parallel institutions with overlapping fields of responsibility."[2] Part of being a successful hybrid actor is adjusting and leveraging relationships. Khamenei pulled the IRGC into new areas, including foreign affairs, but it was not preferential; rather, it was done out of necessity for the new supreme leader to maintain authority, and for him to carve out his own legacy from Khomeini's shadow.

The IRGC's hybridity is due largely to its internal structure and hierarchical authority. Its link to the supreme leader magnifies its credibility and arguably allows it more authority than civilian decision-makers, including the Iranian president. This chapter examines how civil–military relations in Iran fostered an environment that constructed a political path for the Guards. In understanding the evolution of Iran's civil–military relations, we can better interpret the IRGC's continual rise as a hybrid actor.

Integrating Iran's civil–military relations within the study of hybrid warfare

In the immediate aftermath of the Islamic Revolution in Iran, there needed to be an honest and intellectual inquiry into this new ideology, the concept of a supreme leader and a set of new principles that Iran now claimed to stand for. While the West was slow to reach this understanding, soon enough, the rise and continual transformations of the IRGC changed the inquiries all over again. Iran's political leaders prioritized goals around the IRGC, which shifted the dynamics of control. This also created more questions within a burgeoning area of study.

Rafsanjani's and Khatami's failed attempts to bind the IRGC gave the supreme leader's military an appetite for expansion and wealth. Tehran's reactionary policies have bred a prime environment for the IRGC. While we in the United States think primarily long term (typically 15–25 years), Iran bases its decision-making on how to best respond to measured actions taken by the international community, which may be in the form of economic sanctions, military advancements, or even aids to Iran's Gulf adversaries. This reactionary process has facilitated the IRGC's metamorphosis, but it is also in part because of Khamenei's reliance on the Guards, which elevated their stature even as Iranian presidents tried to constrain them for the sake of the state's economy.

As such, Iran's civil–military relations are a part of the IRGC's development and ongoing hybrid war with the West. More importantly, it is precisely how hybrid warfare and foreign policy are interconnected relative to Iran: these relations endow it with the prime capacity to influence foreign policy decisions and be economic stakeholders. Civil–military relations scholar Risa Brooks, in a 2019 essay, recommended working toward normalizing the military's role in politics:[3]

> While the military's coercive power is important however, its political power is not reducible to it. In many respects, the military is akin to other powerful constituencies in the state in how it derives power and impacts distributional and policy outcomes. Neglecting these more routine dimensions of influence attenuates our understanding of the military as a political actor. It also creates an artificial division between the study of the military in authoritarian contexts and in democracies by obscuring similarities in the way the military can influence politics in both.[4]

The IRGC has essentially been "normalized" in Iranian politics, and it appears as though Iranian leadership has permitted this without reservation. This is important in identifying how Iran calculates decisions and how much the IRGC can shape policy. As Brooks notes, "normalizing the military's role in politics paves the way for analyzing how the organization and its leaders shape policy and distributional outcomes in states … Military actors may be able to affect elections or elite politics through conventional channels,"[5] which can further explain leadership mindset.

Despite the military's zeal, Khomeini wanted to keep them out of political affairs. He warned that "the involvement of the armed forces in politics would lead to disintegration of military effectiveness, open the military to manipulation by domestic politicians and machinations by foreign powers."[6] Khomeini believed that politics would undermine the Guards, and that all armed forces should avoid politicization, including law enforcement.[7]

As the IRGC was unwittingly embracing a hybrid model during the Iran–Iraq War, it was also unknowingly shaping Iran's civil–military relations.[8] The war was a sign of turmoil in civil–military relations in Iran and "is what most likely prompted Khomeini to include numerous references to what he believed would constitute the 'correct' foundations of civil-military relations,"[9] thus sparking the dawn of the Guards' hybridity.

By the war's end, Rafsanjani was appointed commander-in-chief of Iran's armed forces, and he called for

> a broad military reform plan that called for the creation of a single chain of command; a rationalization of the complex and unwieldy command system that had grown up around various subdivisions of the regular armed forces and Islamic Revolutionary Guard Corps; the development of national defense industries; and the acquisition of modern arms.[10]

Interestingly, Rafsanjani at this stage of his career identified that it was too difficult to process this new Islamic ideology that had forced its way into military affairs. He believed there needed to be a better approach that would separate this would-be conglomerate from political affairs.

Following Khomeini's death and Ali Khamenei's elevation to supreme leader, Rafsanjani was relieved of his duties as commander-in-chief. Khamenei swiftly brought all the armed and security forces under the control of the Supreme Leaders' Office (SLO).[11] During Rafsanjani's presidency, Khamenei strengthened the authority of the SLO by also assuming responsibility over the *bonyads*—or pseudo-charitable foundations—which fell under IRGC control. Khatami succeeded Rafsanjani and attempted to constrain the Guards like his predecessor. As Khatami's economic policy sought to restrict the IRGC's influence, Khamenei and the IRGC strengthened their relationship, which established the breadth of the supreme leader's support for the Guards.

Akbar Hashemi Rafsanjani

Rafsanjani served two terms as Iran's president from 1989 to 1997. As Ahmed S. Hashim, associate professor of strategic studies at Deakin University in Australia, notes, civil–military tensions were tense throughout both terms. Specifically, "early tensions stemmed from the fear of the IRGC' that its corporate interest, embedded in its sense of identity as separate from the regular army, was going to be threatened by the civilian authorities."[12] Rafsanjani played a large role in the Islamic Revolution and was a key confidante to Khomeini up to his death. He was arguably trying to preserve Khomeini's vision of keeping the IRGC out of politics. He also facilitated Khamenei's rise to supreme leader, which meant that Khamenei understood his indebtedness to Rafsanjani;[13] however, as significant as that was, it had an opposite effect on Rafsanjani's plans. The Guards and Khamenei built an alliance that overpowered the president's authority. According to Saied Golkar, assistant professor in the Department of Political Science & Public Service at the University of Tennessee, Chattanooga, under Rafsanjani, Iran "underwent a period of political reconstruction in which political elites less influenced by ideology took power while radical elites were marginalized."[14] Any pushback from Rafsanjani denigrated his image in Iran and hindered his economic agenda.

Rafsanjani empowered a new class of politicians who were less radical in their ideological belief and geared more toward self-sufficiency and advanced wealth among the elites. By boasting wealth and affluence and economic prosperity—at least Iran's version of prosperity—his economic policies were in subtle contradiction to the principles of the Islamic Revolution. As Golkar notes, Rafsanjani's economic agenda "precipitated a change in the priority of people's values from a revolutionary mindset to a less ideological and more materialist one."[15] Rafsanjani's style also showed that he may be open to relations with the United States and the West, at least economically.

In taking this approach, Rafsanjani was abating the IRGC's significance. He offered a "carrot" to the IRGC to secure some financial independence to help the country recover from the Iran–Iraq War. He encouraged the Guards to take on construction projects to physically repair Iran. But this was also a way for the Guards to integrate into the Iranian economy. Not only would this generate funds for the Guards but it would also preoccupy them and keep them from engaging in Iranian politics.[16]

Rafsanjani's government had appropriated several buildings and factories, which were then transferred to the IRGC. They in turn established several *bonyads* (or "charitable" foundations) to create more firms and shell companies in agriculture, engineering, construction, manufacturing, and transportation, among others. These foundations flourished because the IRGC benefited from no-bid contracts.[17] The IRGC's newly established engineering arm, Khatam al-Anbia Headquarters[18] (in Farsi, قرارگاه سازندگی خاتم‌الانبیا, "Seal of the Prophets"), operated these companies.[19] Khatam al-Anbia eventually spread into the oil and gas markets, which was the beginning of the Guards amassing wealth. Rafsanjani's argument was that the "IRGC has developed substantial engineering capacity during the war and could contribute to rebuilding the country, while also generating revenue to partially finance its military expenses."[20] Khatam al-Anbia was part of Rafsanjani's post-war reconstruction attempts to incorporate the Guards in Iran's development. It is a private entity that "often contracts out activities to other domestic and foreign companies."[21] More importantly, this new establishment was intended to drive the IRGC away from political aspirations.

Relatedly, Rafsanjani reopened Iran's stock market in 1989 to move the state toward privatization.[22] However, his economic plans were perceived as too Western oriented by religious zealots. Khamenei continued to paint himself as a "man of the people" and associated himself with Iran's poor, much as the IRGC did during this early period to garner support. This worked against Rafsanjani, whose family was notoriously known for its wealth. The narrative of Rafsanjani's political agenda went beyond just being "too Western," also portraying an affluent president working toward making the rich richer. Rafsanjani's reforms would also alter the IRGCs bonyads, which was one of the first signs of tension between the Guards and the president.[23]

Still, Rafsanjani's attempts to preoccupy the Guards with some economic influence had unintended consequences. The Guards' alliance with Khamenei coalesced around like-minded Iranians across religious circles, the military, and among the poor. In doing so, these Iranian conservatives passed "parliamentary bills favorable to their economic interests," but it also established the IRGC as "their own support base."[24]

Rafsanjani's second term was even more challenging as Khamenei had strengthened ties with Iran's poor and exerted authority in new ways.[25] According to Afshon Ostovar, associate professor of national security affairs at the NPS, "Rafsanjani and the modern right promoted policies aimed at modernizing Iran's economic and industrial sectors, while tempering its radicalism in the areas of social and foreign affairs."[26] Rafsanjani was pushing a privatization agenda that aimed to stabilize the economy following a disastrous war. However, this worked counter to the Guards' economic interests, which Rafsanjani had afforded them.

The economy was not Rafsanjani's only policy priority. As part of his political platform, Rafsanjani wanted to revitalize the armed forces, drawing from the expertise gained from serving as commander-in-chief. In 1989, he instituted formal military ranks, which was initially supported by the IRGC commander Mohsen Rezaei and other conservative military figures, but it conflicted with the original principles of the Guards that dismissed a ranking system in the military.[27] Indeed, Rezaei's military force was divided into five branches: ground, air, naval, Basij, and QF. Rafsanjani pulled the military into civilian affairs during post-war reconstruction through economic integration. He believed the IRGC would not only contribute to its own development independently but also to the economy as a whole, which included commercial, construction, and industrial developments.[28] Rafsanjani likewise incorporated the Guards under the newly established MODAFL.[29] The MODAFL combined the Ministry of Defense and the IRGC's Ministry under one umbrella organization. Mohsen Rezaei and another prominent figure, Ali Shamkhani,[30] were the IRGC's first leaders and arguably the most influential during the Guards' infancy. Both have been instrumental in shaping the IRGC's hybrid model. Shamkhani, in particular, has proven to be a pragmatic character who elevated the IRGCN when he served as its commander.

Ultimately, the IRGC enjoyed the fruits of Rafsanjani's labors during his first term. This regime gave them a boost to engage economically. But as Khamenei's support for Rafsanjani waned in his second presidential term, so too did the IRGC's support. In his second term, Rafsanjani introduced economic policies that curbed commercial pricing measures, which would affect the IRGC's newfound profit margins. Rafsanjani encouraged IRGC leadership to engage in the economy to become a self-serving entity. Being involved in the economy meant that the IRGC could finance its own activities without government aid. While Rafsanjani interlaced the IRGC into Iran's economy, the unintended consequences could not go unnoticed.

Seyyed Mohammad Khatami

Khatami succeeded Rafsanjani and likewise served two terms, from 1997 to 2005. The IRGC became even more involved in Iranian politics. Unfortunately for Khatami, he did not understand Rafsanjani's failures and subsequently made his own mistakes. But he was equally worried about the Guards' politicization when he affirmed, "Our armed forces should refrain from political tendencies and preferences and instead engage in the daily improvement of their scientific, organizational, and operational capabilities."[31] His policy platforms threatened the IRGC's "ideological and corporate interests" and also "endangered the IRGC's conception of national security and global orientation."[32] Having witnessed the IRGC's growth and potential under Rafsanjani, Khatami grew concerned with their politicization and stood firm on his stance that the Guards should stay clear of politics. By the time Khatami assumed the presidency, the IRGC had enough economic clout, particularly in construction projects, to deter the new president's encroachments.[33] The Guards threw their support behind conservative Iranian politicians to protect their interests.

During this time, the IRGC pressed for political participation with Khamenei's exclusive support as he wanted to prevent reform on the heels of the student protests of July 1999.[34] Throughout the summer of 1999, student protests erupted across Iran, and twenty-four IRGC senior leaders handed Khatami an ultimatum to suppress the protesters immediately or else the Guards would do so themselves.[35] This was among the first instances of the IRGC publicly displaying the potential vulnerabilities of an Iranian president; it was an indication that, institutionally, the Guards were willing to take action if the Iranian government was unwilling. This was not so much a show of independent force by the IRGC as a display of the extent of the supreme leader's support for the Guards and how much power they could hold.

By pushing them into Iran's economy, Rafsanjani's presidency offered the Guards sufficient leverage, which they used to gain political influence during

Khatami's tenure. Khatami's first attempt to constrain the Guards was the forced retirement of Mohsen Rezaei, who had served as their commander for sixteen years. Rezaei was adamant in the Guards' commitment to Khamenei and the vision of the Islamic Revolution. Of note, Rezaei claimed that "if the policies of the leader are implemented by the whole country, there will be no reason for enemy cultural combatants to profit from a cultural vacuum and permeate our society."[36] Khamenei replaced Rezaei with Yahya Rahim Safavi, who was considered a hardliner as Rezaei's deputy commander. As Ostovar notes, the change in leadership suggested "a new direction for the IRGC's political role and served notice that Rezaei's more cautious approach to the political activism was no longer favored by the Supreme Leader."[37] It was a signal of changing dynamics within the IRGC and their role within the Iranian regime's system.

Khatami ran on a platform of change, which resonated with ordinary Iranians and some in the security forces alike. His vision for Iran's economy was similar to that of Rafsanjani, in that he wanted to restructure the economy. But throughout Rafsanjani's eight-year tenure, the IRGC incrementally integrated itself into civilian affairs and the economic enterprise. Khatami could not undo what Rafsanjani inadvertently created, and this underestimation of Khamenei and the Guards ultimately resulted in both of them gaining more authority.[38]

The IRGC eventually even took over Iran's largest airport, Imam Khomeini Airport, and by the end of the civil–military revolution in 2005, the path was set for a hardline president, which will be discussed in a later chapter.

Has Iran's civil–military transformation impacted its strategic calculus?

Despite more than four decades, there is still very little understanding of Iran's political priorities and policymaking.[39] What is happening in Iran is unlike what happened in any other Middle Eastern country. It is certainly not what happened in Egypt with Abdel Fattah el-Sisi; there are enough IRGC officials without uniforms who are working behind the scenes and off the battlefield to secure their standing and authority in the country.

It is believed that Khomeini explicitly forbade the IRGC from political involvement. Hamid Ansari, Khomeini's biographer, claimed that Khomeini was against any politicization of the armed forces. According to Ansari, Khomeini declared,

> I insist that the armed forces obey the laws regarding the prevention of the military forces from entering into politics, and stay away from political parties, groups and [political] fronts. The armed forces [consisting of] the military, the police force, the guards, and the Basij should not enter into any [political] party or groups, and steer clear from political games.[40]

But Mohsen Rezaei interestingly used Khomeini's own logic in defense of the IRGC's expansion:

> Once someone asked Imam [Khomeini] as to why he lends so much support to the IRGC. The Imam had answered, 'why not?' and the interlocutor had warned him that it may result in staging a coup [if the IRGC became too strong]. The Imam answered, 'it stays in the family [if they stage a coup]; as they are our own guys.'[41]

As noted in the previous section, under Rafsanjani, the IRGC became a leading economic entity. He restructured the IRGC and redirected it toward economic activities to keep the Guards out of politics.[42] However, what resulted was a pathway to its politicization, which was achieved under Khatami. The civil–military power struggle affected the outcome of Iran's foreign policy. This struggle was in part due to the conflicting political views of politicians, especially during the earliest periods of the Iranian Revolution. As Michael Eisenstadt wrote in 1996, "The inconclusive nature of the struggle has often produced inconsistency and paralysis in Iranian domestic and foreign policymaking; thus, it frequently appears as if Tehran 'speaks to the world with more than once voice.'"[43] This affected the outcome of Iran's foreign and defense policies and placed a wedge between the IRGC and Iran's political leadership.

Ultimately, the role of civil–military affairs played a significant role in defining the IRGC's hybrid character. As will be addressed in the concluding chapter, the IRGC shapes the Iranian regime's foreign policy, which is expansionist, somewhat ideological, and aggressive. The civilian leaders are responsible for running a false narrative that is more of a façade for the international community's benefit. As the IRGC grew, it became the sole proprietor of the regime's foreign policy priorities. Iran's civil–military relations are not analogous to those of any other country, even though it is coup-proof—because the IRGC already executed the coup.[44] Civil–military relations are redundant in a state where the military controls the agenda.

6

The IRGC Economy

With civil–military relations now in favor of the IRGC, Iran elected Mahmoud Ahmadinejad for president in 2005 with help from the Guards. This marked a departure from Rafsanjani and Khatami, who had both tried to constrain the IRGC's expansion into Iranian politics. As discussed in the previous chapter, efforts by both Rafsanjani and Khatami to preoccupy the Guards economically resulted in unintended consequences. There was no way to foresee the Guards' ambition and foresight to forge monopolies within the Iranian economy. There is arguably no other institution, let alone military, that has integrated itself into a state's economy the way that the IRGC has in Iran. This chapter is not a commentary on the Iranian economy; rather, it is essential to the broader study of the IRGC's hybrid warfare model. Economic integration facilitated the means for the IRGC's ends.

Ahmadinejad, either intentionally or inadvertently, paved the way economically for the IRGC to achieve its ends. Economic clout aided the IRGC's successes both domestically and regionally. During the 2005 Iranian election, the IRGC viewed the atmospherics as "all politics is local." The Guards judged Ahmadinejad as a candidate they could support to deliver on self-serving agenda items. Iran's civil–military relations witnessed tectonic shifts, as noted in the previous chapter, and the election of Ahmadinejad was the ultimate power move that engrained the IRGC within the country's politics and foreign policymaking.

In 2005, an IRGC commander claimed that Ahmadinejad's election "was the result of two years of a multilayered and sophisticated strategy executed by the Pasdaran,"[1] and they were rewarded with various roles across the regime, including diplomatic posts.[2] Having steadily gained legislature seats, the 2005 election of Ahmadinejad allowed the unfettered flow of Guard members—active and former—to burrow into state security matters, intelligence, foreign policy, and the economy. It was Ahmadinejad's "apparent vision of his country becoming the dominant power in the region," which could expand its sponsored groups throughout the region, labeling Tehran as "the 'wild card' in the international system."[3]

The IRGC adopted a principle that political responsibilities were a part of its duties, thereby establishing itself into a security complex designed to promote a foreign policy that serves its interests. Ahmadinejad was the accidental architect of Iran's current defense posture, which affords the IRGC expanded roles in decision-making processes. As a result, the IRGC's enterprise cannot be undone and has only been further legitimized.

Iran's economy reimagined

Ahmadinejad was not a common household name in Iran. Even when he was elected mayor of Tehran, he was not a brand that was easily recognizable. Though he had a doctoral degree, Ahmadinejad was no intellectual like other senior Iranian officials. He came from modest beginnings that he worked to his advantage by posing as a man of the people. Additionally, he was a former Basiji who fought during the Iran–Iraq War, so the IRGC threw its weight behind him at the eleventh hour, handing him the victory in 2005. Other former IRGC members such as Mohammad Baqer Ghalibaf and Mohsen Rezaei also had IRGC support, but they did not have the support of the Basij, which was what secured Ahmadinejad's victory. He flooded his regime with IRGC members as a reward, appointing them to cabinet seats, ministry titles, and other powerful positions across Iran's provinces.[4] Ahmadinejad redefined the IRGC's political prestige. It was not uncommon for IRGC brass to occupy political positions in preceding regimes, but Ahmadinejad bought the IRGC's favoritism. More specifically, these institutional connections to the IRGC set him apart from Rafsanjani and Khatami, who had both acted deliberately to block the Guards' political ambitions.[5]

Khamenei had devised an economic strategy of privatization shortly before Ahmadinejad's election.[6] Considering his close relationship with the IRGC, this served a dual purpose. The supreme leader would implement economic policies that would benefit the Guards, and in turn, they will continue to protect the supreme leader and Iran's revolutionary ideals. The first change appeared with Article 44 of the Iranian Constitution, which originally stated,

> The state sector is to include all large-scale and mother industries, foreign trade, major mines, banking, insurance, power generation, dams and large-scale irrigation networks, radio and television, post, telegraph and telephone services, aviation, shipping, roads, railroads and the like; all these will be publicly owned and at the disposal of the state. The cooperative sector is to include cooperative companies and institutions involved in production and distribution that are established in urban and rural areas in accordance with Islamic percepts. The private sector consists of agriculture, animal husbandry, industry, trade, and services that supplement the economic activities of the state and cooperative sectors.[7]

In 2005, Khamenei amended Article 44 in favor of privatization, which subtly incorporated legalities under the IRGC's purview. The relevance of Article 44 is that it grants the regime control of "all large-scale industries, telephone companies, banks, insurance companies, utilities, and radio and television networks."[8] Ahmadinejad's election sold state assets valued at about $120 billion to the IRGC and its beneficiaries.[9] He further pushed for privatization as president, and the IRGC's influence broadened within Iran's legal institutions.

In 2006, the IRGC won a multi-billion-dollar gas pipeline contract. Khatam al-Anbia, the IRGC's largest engineering company, had completed over 1,200 projects by 2006 that included no-bid contracts for transport developmental projects and pipelines for oil and natural gas.[10] These were worth over $1 billion each and accounted for roughly 30 percent of the IRGC's industrial and budgetary capacity. On September 27, 2009, the IRGC purchased the majority share of Iran Telecommunications, which was valued at nearly $8 billion.[11] By 2010, former IRGC personnel held twelve of the twenty-one cabinet minister posts in Ahmadinejad's administration compared to the five posts the IRGC held in 1989.[12] With its newfound power in the government, the IRGC continued to grant more contracts to its own companies and subsidiaries, with no political restrictions. IRGC banks and financial institutions arguably hold the largest stakes in the Tehran Stock Exchange.[13]

Khatam al-Anbia

Khatam al-Anbia Construction Headquarters vaulted to prominence under Ahmadinejad. The company followed a "Look to the East" policy between 2005 and 2013 "in monopolizing the lion's share of economic and development projects in Iran."[14] It functions much like a private company that contracts and subcontracts to foreign and domestic entities.[15]

Reports suggest the National Oil Company[16] of Iran granted Khatam al-Anbia a contract in 2006 to begin plans for several phases of South Pars Gas Development (SPGD),[17] which was completed with no competing bids. Khatam al-Anbia is a part of many construction projects for Iran's ballistic missile[18] and nuclear programs, and they oversee subsidiaries.[19] It has the power to block other non-IRGC construction bids, and it continues to do so to this day. Open-source estimates suggest that the IRGC is linked to hundreds of companies and subsidiaries, controlling more than $12 billion in business and construction efforts.[20] They work with other nefarious entities to conduct business to either eliminate or deter competition. A prime example was when the IRGC used force in May 2004 to execute the sudden closure of Imam Khomeini International Airport because IRGC leadership believed that the Turkish company that was operating the airport was "a threat to Iran's security and dignity."[21] The Ministry of Oil, Transportation, and Energy also has several contracts with Khatam al-Anbia, with the projects completed by subsidiaries or private companies.[22] Two leading subsidiaries of the Headquarters are "Sepasad" and "Hara." Sepasad is contracted with many large transportation projects, while Hara is granted road and other major construction projects. Other companies are contracted with engineering projects and even hydroelectric projects spread across West Azerbaijan, Kermanshah, Ilam, Lorestan, and Khuzestan.[23]

Through Khatam al-Anbia, the IRGC became—and continues to be—engrained in Iran's oil and gas markets, despite sanctions.[24] For instance, following the successful completion of the SPGD contract, the company purchased the Oriental Kish company, which drills for oil and gas in several Persian Gulf oil fields. Given the size of Khatam al-Anbia, they have been lucrative throughout their development; moreover, they have their own in-house accounting firm, which found the company qualifiers for tax exemption, further maximizing profits.

The same Ahmadinejad who once "campaigned on the importance of moral purity and pledged to put an end to corruption in the Islamic Republic"[25] soon became the largest proponent of privatization in favor of IRGC companies. As a result, organizations like Khatam al-Anbia flourished from the political support of fellow guardsmen and the enactment of such economic policies. This exemplifies the IRGC's dual functionality as a paramilitary force, highlighting how it has consistently used coercion to achieve its economic goals.

Iran's nuclear program and sanctions as US policy

As international sanctions amassed against the regime, sanctions evasion became a part of Iran's foreign policy. It became an art form over time. Khatam al-Anbia eventually took control of almost all oil, gas, and petrochemical projects, which paved the way for the company's substantial stake in Iran's economy.[26] One example is Ghorb Nooh, which either owns or controls Hara Company, Omran Sahel, and Sahel Consultant Engineers.[27] The company reportedly has nearly a thousand affiliate companies, which makes it difficult to track.

Despite stringent economic sanctions, the company continues to thrive to this day. Prominent former Khatam chiefs such as Ghalibaf, Rostam Ghasemi, and Saeed Muhammad achieved personal successes for their roles in shaping Iran's economic policy through the company.[28] The Obama administration imposed the most rigorous sanctions against Iran, and later the Trump administration took it further. The Obama administration's sanctions policy notably targeted Iran's terrorist activities abroad through restrictions on its weapons of mass destruction (WMD) and nuclear program; the sanctions also addressed human rights abuses and other economically related constraints. While the Obama administration used sanctions as a tool of foreign policy, which is the intended purpose of sanctions, the Trump administration later used them as the foreign policy itself, which will be discussed in the following chapters. Nonetheless, both approaches had their flaws and successes.

But first, it is important to assess the Obama administration's sanctions policy. On WMDs, Executive Order (EO) 13382, "Blocking Property of Weapons of Mass Destruction Proliferators and their Supporters," was implemented on June 28, 2005.[29] This blocked the property of specially designated WMD proliferators and associates of affiliated networks, ultimately denying access to the US financial systems. EO 13438, "Blocking Property of Certain Persons who Threaten Stabilization Efforts in Iraq: Threats to Iraq's Stability," was implemented on July 17, 2007. Its stated objective is to reduce the flow of material support to insurgents and terrorists in the Iraq War. This includes those threatening the peace and stability of Iraq and those undermining efforts to support economic reconstruction and political reform in Iraq or to provide humanitarian aid to the Iraqi people, among other things.[30]

Targeted human rights abuse sanctions included EO 13553, "Blocking Property of Certain Persons with Respect to Serious Human Rights Abuses by the Government of Iran and Taking Certain Other Actions." On September 28, 2010, this EO implemented Section 105 of the Comprehensive Iran Sanctions, Accountability, and Divestment Act of 2010 (CISADA)[31] by sanctioning Iranians determined to be guilty of human rights abuses following the 2009 presidential election in Iran. EO 13572, "Repression of the Syrian People," blocked the US-based property of individuals believed to repress Syrian people. The QF, its commanders, and others have been sanctioned under this order from April 29, 2011. EO 13606, "Blocking the Property and Suspending Entry into the United States of Certain Persons with Respect to Grave Human Rights Abuses by the Government of Iran and Syria via Information Technology," implemented on April 22, 2012, sanctioned the following entities: IRGC, MOIS, General Command of the Law Enforcement (LEF), Datak Telecom. EO 13608, "Prohibiting Certain Transactions with and Suspending Entry into the United States of Foreign Sanctions Evaders with Respect to Iran and Syria," implemented on May 1, 2012, and EO 13622, "Authorizing Additional Sanctions with Respect to Iran," implemented on July 30, 2012, both targeted Syrian red lines that were associated with Iranian activities in that country.

More robust sanctions targeted the financial infrastructure of the IRGC. EO 13574, "Concerning Further Sanctions on Iran," prohibits any US financial institution from providing loans or credits to individuals sanctioned under the 1996 Iran Sanctions Act (ISA), any transactions in foreign exchange that are subject to US jurisdiction, and any transfers of credit or payment between financial institutions subject to US jurisdiction; additionally, it blocks all property and interests that the sanctioned entities might have in the United States as well as any links they might have to the United States, including to US persons.[32] EO 13581, "Blocking Property of Transnational Criminal Organizations," implemented on July 24, 2011, identified individuals and entities "threatening the stability of international political and economic systems."[33] Other targeted economic sanctions include EO 13590, "Iran Sanctions: With Respect to the Provision of Goods, Services, Technology or Support for Iran's Energy and Petrochemical Sectors,"[34] implemented on November 20, 2011, and EO 13599, "Blocking Property of the Government of Iran and Iranian Financial Institutions,"[35] implemented on February 5, 2012, which blocks US assets of entities determined to be owned or operated by Iran, which includes fraudulent practices by the Central Bank of Iran and other Iranian banks that mask transactions of sanctioned entities.

This is not a comprehensive list of sanctions, but it includes those that made the most substantial impact during Ahmadinejad's two terms as president. These sanctions were the catalyst for Iran and the United States agreeing to talks on Iran's nuclear ambitions. However, it can also be argued that sanctions have emboldened the IRGC. Sanctions evasion became common practice for both regime stability and survival. It was also essential to the IRGC's own survival and clutch on power. As the Guards studied sanctions and improved evasion abilities, they also created a dark economy, which unfortunately has been difficult to track and study.

"Introspection has never been Mahmoud Ahmadinejad's strong suit"[36]

Barbara Slavin interviewed President Ahmadinejad in 2005, which she details in her book *Bitter Friends, Bosom Enemies*. She interviewed him a second time in 2012 at what would be his final appearance before the United Nations General Assembly (UNGA). She asked him if Iranians were better off then than when he took office and if he would do anything differently. He claimed, "Certainly, people's conditions are better."[37] Recalling that Ahmadinejad essentially asserted that he would do nothing differently,

Slavin noted that Ahmadinejad is "the least reflective, thoughtful, contemplative person."[38] Ahmadinejad had a lasting impact on the Iranian presidency despite his character, having accelerated Iran's nuclear program and managed to frustrate the supreme leader. Moreover, while every single Iranian president except Khamenei has been marginalized after leaving office, Ahmadinejad continues to try to connect himself to popular culture.[39]

The Ahmadinejad years made IRGC companies increasingly susceptible to international sanctions. Nonetheless, they have benefited from these sanctions by tapping "into state funds, and its relatively vast independent resources have provided a decisive advantage."[40] Ahmadinejad's election in 2005 was a launching pad for the IRGC to gain control of Iran's "internal and national security organizations" as well as to receive increased governmental loans and contracts unopposed.[41] While sanctions from external governments were imposed rapidly on Iran and IRGC-affiliated companies, the Guards' security network in politics allowed for it to exploit national reserves and double down on its anti-Western messaging. Sanctions were effective in imposing costly consequences on global trade with IRGC-linked companies, but the Guards soon found other avenues to export both capital, such as illicit networks and smuggling, and revolutionary ideology.[42]

As an unintended consequence, international sanctions were a learning opportunity for the IRGC, specifically to expand its influence beyond economic activity into foreign policy as well. Despite harsh sanctions, including the maximum pressure campaign, which will be discussed later, IRGC-affiliated financial institutions and enterprises, including subsidiaries, continue to be lucrative and are the largest players across the Iranian stock exchange.

The Iranian clerics have not only used the IRGC as a tool to defend Iran's borders, prevent any rebellions, and export the revolution, they have also enabled it to act independently on the country's foreign policy. Iran believes it is the dominant Muslim country in the region; therefore, regional hegemony is imperative. The Guards' nefarious relationships with organized crime syndicates have permitted the IRGC to expand into foreign territory, like parts of Latin America and Africa. Under the guise of cultural and religious centers and diplomatic posts, the IRGC, QF, and even Hizballah partners maintain a deep footprint outside of the region. Not only does this offer Iran a cover for strategic and policy purposes, it is also a way for these groups to fundraise.

The IRGC's ability to seep into Iran's political and economic infrastructure has empowered the Guards to such an extent that it is virtually impossible to reverse their progress.

The IRGC was still coming into its own as a defense force, but with financial independence it achieved the success for which it had long pined. Ahmadinejad appealed to an Arab audience, particularly Palestinians. Lebanese Hizballah profited from IRGC expansion, specifically in 2006 during its war with Israel. Hizballah blended militia units, ATGM teams, modern information operations, SIGINT, operational and tactical rockets, armed UAVs, and anti-ship cruise missiles, all of which caught Israel by surprise.[43] Iran's actions and activities in Iraq happened despite Ahmadinejad. According to military historian Peter R. Mansoor, "They saw an opening in 2003, but when Ahmadinejad got elected in 2005, the IRGC was strengthened and emboldened because we were preoccupied with the insurgency in Iraq."[44] The IRGC-QF was already active in Iraq by the time Ahmadinejad became president. But with newfound wealth, resources, and authority, the IRGC made greater inroads in Iraq. Thus, Ahmadinejad was in large part responsible for the Guards' strength and resilience.

7

The Iranian Way of War

The United States' foreign policy toward the Middle East helped shape Iran's regional doctrine. The US invasion of Iraq in 2003 incited Iranian subversion out of fear that they might be next. While the United States was engrossed with deposing Iraqi dictator Saddam Hussein and later searching for WMD, the IRGC and QF took full advantage. Over the years, Iranian expansion spread across the Levant, while the United States was busy extinguishing other fires. Today's outcomes in the region are a culmination of US policy since 2003 as well as Iran's response. Before 2003, the IRGC was not given much—if any—thought at all. Iran and its quiet ambitions for regional influence were not looming over many analysts' horizon. After all, the attacks of September 11, 2001, were not plotted by Iranians, and as will be discussed in this chapter, Iran was not much of a factor in the Iraq War strategy.

Hybrid wars are long wars, and the IRGC's organizational structure is characterized by "layers and layers of hybridity."[1] Iran's regional strategy feeds into this hybrid model that has been in development since the Iran–Iraq War. Preceding chapters have focused on the IRGC as a whole; however, this chapter will introduce the QF ("Jerusalem Force," or سپاه قدس in Farsi) in more detail. The creation of the QF and its advancements with external partners are outcomes of the failures of the Iran–Iraq War. Iran's defense doctrine of the early 1990s established principles such as self-reliance and "holy defense," which was distinctively hybrid compared to its near peers.[2] But the United States has since drafted strategies and policies in direct response to QF activities in the Middle East rather than devising strategies that serve the region in its entirety.

The QF was formally established as an independent branch under the IRGC in 1988 following the Iran–Iraq War. The US Department of Justice defines the QF as a "branch of the IRGC that conducts sensitive covert operations abroad, including terrorist attacks, assassination, and kidnappings, and is believed to have sponsored attacks against coalition forces in Iraq."[3] Ahmad Vahidi, Iran's current minister of the interior, was its first commander, followed by Qasem Soleimani, who was the longest-serving commander, having held the post for nearly twenty-two years before his death on January 3, 2020, in a targeted strike in Baghdad. Esmail Ghani,[4] Soleimani's deputy, serves as the current commander, but he lacks his predecessor's magnetism that attracted Arabs to form the umbrella organizations that continue to pose a threat to US interests. Since taking over, Ghani has not wielded authority over Iranian-backed militants, but that may also be by design. Ghani may not view the militia groups as his responsibility as Soleimani did, and he may be directing efforts toward greater political influence in the region under President Ebrahim Raisi's new regime.

Since the end of the Iran–Iraq War, Tehran's strategy has been what the current secretary of the Iranian SNSC Ali Shamkhani once called "strategic deterrence."[5] From this standpoint, Iran focuses on maintaining a robust ballistic missile program, supporting naval forces that are adept in maritime situations that could potentially challenge commerce and violate maritime rules, and lastly, utilizing external militias.[6] Iran's way of war is focused not only on keeping its border tightly controlled but also on employing militias for plausible deniability. According to David Crist, senior historian to the Chairman of the Joint Chiefs of Staff, the US invasion in Iraq was an "opportunity to achieve what Iran could not achieve in eight years of bloody slaughter in the 1980s."[7] Iran undoubtedly represents a strategic problem. The hybridity that continues to be present in Iraq because of Iran's influence politically, economically, and militarily is a strategic challenge to US foreign policy. Iranian partnerships were iterations, and the Badr Organization was the first during the Iran–Iraq War. A new iteration of groups supported by Tehran in exchange for doing its bidding was ushered in with the US invasion of Iraq in 2003. The third iteration emerged as a response to ISIL in the form of the Popular Mobilization Forces (PMF), while the fourth iteration is currently unfolding following the death of Soleimani.

Ultimately, as addressed in this chapter, the lessons from the Iran–Iraq War influenced Iran's campaigns in Syria, Iraq, and Yemen, and these conflicts in turn informed Tehran's foreign policy. While the IRGC was originally intended to export the Islamic Revolution, regional events overtook that priority and turned into pockets of opportunity. Iraq continues to be an arena where episodic iterations of groups emerge as an avenue for Iran to project power in the region. As hybrid actors, the IRGC and QF fostered strategic relationships inside these operational environments that prolonged conflicts. Iran spent minimally to inflict higher costs on the United States and Coalition partners. Plausible deniability buttresses Iran's hybrid strategy as they work toward the result of reducing or eliminating a US regional footprint. Iran has mastered a strategy in which it roots influence in Syria and Iraq while distressing Israel through Lebanese Hizballah and Hamas on one side and Saudi Arabia through the Houthis on another.[8]

Iran has understood over time that terrorism is a tool of policy. Michael Eisenstadt wrote in 1996 that "Tehran resorts to terrorism because it has often yielded important policy successes without provoking military retaliation against Iran."[9] Regime leaders are aware of their military weakness and therefore prefer "ambiguity, indirection, and covert action over direct confrontation as means of dealing with enemies."[10] This is still true as of this writing, and arguably, Iran has perfected this way of warfare. Specifically, under Soleimani's leadership, the IRGC QF weaponized Shia populations abroad, which institutionalized hybrid warfare. While Lebanese Hizballah was a trial run turned successful, SMGs and the Houthis turned into patterns for the future.

This chapter surveys this hybrid defense strategy. The environment was habitable to Iranian forces with shared ideological identity and historic connections. Time showed transformative periods in Iran's defense doctrine. According to Eisenstadt, "the Islamic Republic's foreign and defense policy is anti-status quo. They want to shape the international environment to make it more conducive to their interests. But when it comes to the regime's military strategy, it's largely defensive—at least vis-à-vis the United States."[11] This has been continuous since the end of the Iran–Iraq War and especially since 2003.

Of note, this chapter is not a descriptive characterization of individual Iranian-backed groups in the Middle East. Rather, it is an assessment of Iran's overall hybrid strategy, and that includes the part played by such groups. Understanding Iran's approach to strategy serves as a better gauge for shaping US foreign policy toward Iran specifically and the Middle East more broadly.

Conflicts across the Middle East have been testing grounds for Iran and its militias, which help them improve tactically and operationally. This chapter will address how the IRGC and QF developed a structure in the Middle East that serves and protects Iran's interests and how it affects US foreign policy. Iran's military doctrine was strategically designed to face conventionally advanced militaries. They have employed a strategy that has increased both the human and economic costs to the United States. Interestingly, Tehran believes that Washington is in a hybrid war against Iran, and it "views this situation as short of armed conflict."[12]

Does Iran have its own hybrid war strategy?

On June 6, 2016, Iran's *Scientific Quarterly Journal of Defense Strategy* published a 32-page research paper on hybrid warfare. Titled "Developing Macro Strategies for Hybrid Warfare" (in Farsi, تدوین راهبردهای کلان جنگ ترکیبی), the paper assesses how to fight future wars with hybrid strategies.[13] As the Iranian authors note, hybrid wars have been playing out in Iraq and Syria, which they characterize as the "Resistance Front" (in Farsi, جبهه مقاومت). There are four key points that define Iran's hybridity, according to the Iranian authors: 1) elongated wars, such as the one between the United States and Iraq, and what follows; 2) wars that have no controlling authority, such as the current status of Iraq or the situation in Yemen; 3) irregular wars, such as the case in Syria with militia groups; and 4) sustaining influence within the state and from outside the state, such as in Lebanon and Iraq.

Likewise, the paper postulates that future wars will be regional and in the cyber realm. The Iranian authors suggest that Iran must think defensively, have more geographic, situational awareness to deter and surprise its adversaries, and fight directly and indirectly, with minimum ground forces, and use domestic militants, such as in Iraq.[14] One example of this is the IRGCN. The fact that it is better equipped compared to ground and air forces indicates that Iran has identified maritime as its strategic strength.[15] The IRGCN has routinely been accused of transporting weapons and other munitions to Syria and Yemen.[16] As the Iranian authors suggest, hybrid wars are not conventional wars, but they will use state and non-state sources.[17] Specific to Iran, the article identifies the following weapons of hybrid warfare: drones; electronic warfare, such as social media propaganda; ballistic and cruise missiles; and cyber warfare, which should include "SIGINT, satellites such as synthetic-aperture radars (SAR) and defense missiles."[18]

But there are challenges. Preventing domestic unrest was on the top of the list. Maintaining unity can help prevent civil disobedience, which poses a threat to the stability of the regime. Cyber and defense capabilities should be improved; specifically, the authors note that Iran should learn from Pakistan how to best develop its defense capabilities. The authors also write that from their vantage point, the US ground forces have vulnerabilities in an irregular campaign, and therefore, Iran should improve its irregular capabilities and develop urban war strategies. From a geopolitical theory standpoint, the authors also believe there is credence to the "Domino Theory" in warfare, which they posit can be implemented in Iraq and Syria. What follows naturally from this is the utilization of proxies and partners.

By all accounts, it appears that Iranian academics have thought this strategy through. Tehran practices strategic patience and has had the advantage of time since the Iran–Iraq War for Iranian defense leaders to adjust. As David Crist explained, "Iranians are smart and strategic thinkers. They have had a lot of time to analyze from the Iran–Iraq War forward and recognize the strategic imbalance of power."[19] Iran has arguably moved past the notion of exporting the revolution. It is now about projecting power. The rhetoric of the Islamic Republic's intent of exporting the revolution may still be alive; however, in practice, we are witnessing power projection in the form of capturing of key areas in the region through a network of influence. The IRGC and QF have established militia groups in the image of Lebanese Hizballah as well as political bodies and economic conglomerates to preserve the spirit of the ideology.

The IRGC's efforts in building Shia militias and its network of influence also lend toward its strategy to seamlessly weave insurgent and state powers together to maintain its internal security. Building militias that serve military and political purposes is one way in which Iran can exercise both hard and soft power. While external militants use hard power to achieve physical gains or influence, the IRGC and QF engage politically in the shadows to operationalize soft power through economic support.

Lebanon is a prime case study as Lebanese Hizballah and the IRGC grew into their own simultaneously, which lends credibility to Iran's hybrid strategy outlined above. Lebanese Hizballah is the most widely known and recognized terrorist organization affiliated with Iran. The 2006 war with Israel shocked the international community with how capable this terrorist organization really was when faced with a superior, conventional adversary. According to former US Ambassador to Iraq James Jeffrey, the IRGC at this time started emerging in two places: among the Shia militias in Iraq and then during Hizballah's campaign against Israel in 2006.[20] Iran cannot match the conventional superiority of the United States or Israel, but it can impose costs and lengthen conflict in the time and space, much like what we saw with Hizballah against Israel and what continued to play out in the Levant and Yemen. This is Iran's way of war. As Brian Michael Jenkins hypothesized in 1983, "local belligerents will mobilize foreign patrons,"[21] and Iran is the principal patron that saw potential in local militants.

While Hizballah is the most commonly known terrorist organization aligned with Iran, the country has a history with militants who have found refuge among guerillas in Somalia, with Palestinians, and with others elsewhere. Most notably, following the 1979 Revolution and the early years of the Iran–Iraq War, the IRGC enhanced its relationship with the Badr Corps, Iran's oldest-running Iraqi militia relationship. These groups have sustained their cooperative engagements through state sponsorship and have facilitated the creation of splinter groups in their image. The late QF commander General Qasem Soleimani is responsible for creating the most well-organized and lethal Badr and Hizballah offshoots in Iraq. His presence and experience made these groups what they are today, and his message still resonates with them even after his death.

Syria was a battleground for Iran to insert itself into to prevent the fall of Iranian ally President Bashar al-Assad. While Tehran was concerned about the longevity of one of its allies, it was mostly alarmed by the chaos potentially overspilling into Iranian territory. The Syrian War was Iran's first conventional conflict since the Iran–Iraq War, and it proved to be challenging. The conflict was not on the same scale or scope as what was happening nearby in Iraq. There were several unpredictable factors, including the various groups with ambiguous allegiances and the conflicting dynamics it produced.

Yemen, however, was an opportunity, not a strategic aspiration. The Houthis (also known as Ansarallah) have long had a relationship with the clerics in Tehran, and the crisis in Yemen posed a credible opening for Iran to insert influence along the border of its staunchest opponent: Saudi Arabia. While Iran has not garnered political influence in Yemen, it has facilitated a stream of weapons, including missiles and drones, as well as critical advisory personnel to the Houthis.[22] Since at least 2014, Iran has been aiding the Houthis in Yemen, and the aid has steadily increased with the intensification of the war over the years.[23] Iranian support is limited to baseline weaponry but sufficient to prolong conflict and endanger both Saudi Arabia and the UAE.

Whether in Lebanon, Iraq, Syria, or Yemen, Iranian partners[24] serve as plausible deniability, which blocks Iran from blame that may lead to conflict. According to Barbara Slavin, the Director of the Future of Iran Initiative at the Atlantic Council, Iran-backed groups in Iraq are partners rather than proxies because they all have their own agendas and circumstances. Each relationship is different. These groups cannot survive if they do not maintain some sort of relationship with Iran. Hizballah is the only true proxy, given its history with the Islamic Republic. Iran-backed groups in Iraq not only serve as militias but also engage in political influence on behalf of Iran. As will be discussed in this chapter, Qais al-Khazali's Asa'ib Ahl al-Haq (AAH) has long influenced Iraqi politics and been a champion of Iranian ideals, as have members of the Badr Corps. Both military and political elements have contributed to shape Iran's regional focus and development in Baghdad for the better.

The interweaving of state and insurgent supremacy contributes to Iran's power projection. Iran's goal is to perpetuate what it calls the "Axis of Resistance," which is its vision to build militants, economies, and political positions in its image. It also gives the IRGC QF strategic autonomy through access to operationalize its military and economic interests because it eliminates outstanding pressures from the West and the Gulf Cooperation Council (GCC) countries.[25] In developing Shia militias across Iraq and the Levant, Iran projects power through hybrid wars. According to Michael Connell, principal research scientist at the Center for Naval Analysis,

Hizballah and Iran are closely aligned on so many issues that there's no daylight between them. With all of these groups, sometimes the assumption is that it's like the flip of a switch that these groups will do what Iran says. But it's negotiated. They may receive Iranian support, but Iran has no control over what they do. Iran still must be sensitive to their interests.[26]

This is precisely the impact of the loss of Soleimani. He played a principal role in terms of finding the right balance: providing these militias what they needed and considering their interests while convincing them to pursue Iran's interests. Thus far, the issue is at the operational level because the strategic nature of those relationships must now be rebuilt.

The US invasion and Iran's emerging shadow network

War began on March 20, 2003, when President George W. Bush announced that US forces were conducting military operations in Iraq. The fall of Iraqi dictator Saddam Hussein was a critical moment in the Middle East because it outlined the future of the region.

The then secretary of state Condoleezza Rice said before the Senate Foreign Relations Committee on October 19, 2005, "Our political-military strategy has to be clear, hold and build: to clear areas from insurgent control, to hold them securely, and to build durable national Iraqi institutions."[27] Secretary Rice outlined a strong US strategy for Iraq:[28]

- Clear the toughest places—no sanctuaries to the enemy—and disrupt foreign support for the insurgents.
- We are working to hold and steadily enlarge the secure areas, integrating political and economic outreach with our military operations.
- We are working to build truly national institutions by working with more capable provincial and local authorities. We are challenging them to embody a national compact—not tools of a particular sect or ethnic groups. These Iraqi institutions must sustain security forces, bring the rule of law, visibly deliver essential services, and offer the Iraqi people hope for a better economic future.

What ensued was US involvement in the fight against insurgencies and terrorists between 2004 and 2021 while addressing an Iraq that has an overwhelming Iranian presence. The main flaw in Washington's strategy was its failure to factor Iran into the Iraq calculus. According to Peter R. Mansoor, the Bush administration ignored the history and culture of Iraq or the wider region, and there was a lack of understanding of Iraqi society.[29] Through the IRGC, Iran was preparing for what could happen next in Iraq and planning how to best approach the invasion. IRGC documents captured in Iraq in 2003 showed exactly that. The Badr Corps was at the center of the IRGC's plans in the event of a US invasion of Iraq and an influence campaign at the political, economic, and social levels within the country.[30] Indeed, the IRGC's plans were used, especially following the removal of Iran's main obstacle in Hussein.

Tehran viewed a US–Iraq alliance as a threat to its own security. A piece of its strategy was to force influence within Iraqi politics, forge alliances with sympathetic militias and grow their power socially, maintain economic clout, and eventually force the United States out of Iraq and the region. By creating internal instability within Iraqi governance and society and installing pro-Iranian politicians, Iran flipped the narrative against the United States and plausible deniability proved to be a strong strategy.[31]

The United States' strategy transitioned from containment to deterrence in Iraq over time, largely because of Iranian activities since 2003. The IRGC and QF are localized. Though vastly spread across the Middle East, Iran still has limited aim. What changes are its capabilities and capacities over time. According to a senior DoD official, Iran, however, is an adversary that does not play by the rules and that refuses to be deterred the way combatant commands want them to be deterred. Deterrence is not an end state but a constant state.[32] Iran-backed groups operating in the background since 2003 altered their strategy in tandem with the United States. Priorities shifted with each passing conflict in the region. The United States has been in a state of perpetual deterrence regarding Shia militias, as fighting terrorists and insurgents were threatening US interests.

The 2007 "Surge" was a successful strategy in Iraq, though there were many challenges.[33] It purged insurgents from key areas and prevented further proliferation. And the United States finally understood the importance of incorporating the Iraqi people in order to try to gain an understanding of the culture. This progress concerned Iran. As a result, Tehran tried to bridge diplomatic ties when Ahmadinejad visited Baghdad, which was the first time an Iranian president visited Iraq since the 1980s. A steady US presence with Iraqi control over territorial security was a working strategy. The narrative shifted with President Obama's election in 2008. On February 1, 2009, President Obama announced plans to remove combat brigades by August 2010; a transitional force of 35,000 to 50,000 soldiers and marines would remain to train, equip, and advise Iraqi security forces. On June 30, 2009, the Status of Forces Agreement (SOFA) between Iraq and the United States required US combat troops to withdraw from Baghdad and other Iraqi cities. Finally, on August 31, 2010, the United States ended its combat mission in Iraq. President Obama addressed the nation, remarking that, "in the end, only Iraqis can resolve their differences and police their streets."[34] Failing to secure a SOFA on a residual force led to troops leaving Iraq on December 18, 2011.

The border between Iran and Iraq was the first entry point. Former US Ambassador to Iraq Ryan Crocker stated on February 7, 2004, that there is no border policy and even if there was one, the United States lacked the ability to enforce it: "The Iranian regime was exploiting this policy and enforcement vacuum, sending agents and businessman into southern Iraq to garner influence and lay the groundwork for larger elements and capabilities to arrive."[35] Militia groups were carefully curated to exploit weaknesses in a country that had been dominated under a dictatorship.

Throughout all of this, the IRGC and QF developed a shadow network in Iraq. Iran-backed Shia militia groups in Iraq and any splinter groups have become iterations. Transformative periods over the last four decades have spawned new factions to serve strategic purposes. US foreign policy has been a deciding factor. Iranian allies helped place wedges between the West and Iraqi politicians. Every move made by Iran since the US invasion of Iraq in 2003 has been meticulously crafted and calculated. Defense planners, however, did not factor in Iran when strategizing Saddam Hussein's removal. According to Crist, "That was a huge strategic blunder because we did not look at what opportunities this might give Iran. Today, it is clear that we cannot look at Iran without looking at the SMGs."[36] While the United States supported a new government, Iran was looking for crevices to leak through.

After all, Iran sought to keep Iraq weak, and that strategy required cooperation by a variety of militia groups.

Badr (بدر)

As previous chapters indicated, Iranian involvement in Iraq dates back to the 1980s during the Iran–Iraq War. Iraqi-born cleric Ayatollah Hashemi Shahrudi[37] developed the Badr concept while living in Qom. Shahrudi and other early Badr leaders relied on Iraqi prisoners of war and defectors who found refuge in Iran to fight alongside Iranians against Saddam Hussein. While Iran was on the defensive for most of the war, it rallied support from Iraq's Shia populations. Since its inception, Badr has maintained unrelenting loyalty to Iran. Led by Hadi al-Amiri, Badr has benefited from Iranian sponsorship through funding, training, and weaponry. However, the group went underground following Iran's defeat, fearing Hussein's retaliation. It was not until the US invasion of Iraq in 2003 and the fall of Hussein that Badr resurfaced. The fight to secure Iraqi freedom was, and continues to be, a hard-fought challenge. Badr rallied around IRGC and QF in Iraq and targeted not only US and Coalition forces but also Sunnis. It was these sectarian tensions that the IRGC exploited, justifying Iran's return to Iraq in 2003, following the US overthrow of Hussein, and Badr was the first Iranian ally to assist with exploiting Iraq's security situation.[38]

Iran's gateway to Iraqi politics was also through Badr. Tehran and Badr "played a key role in shaping the 2005 constitution and Iraq's nascent political institutions" while consistently trying to influence successive Iraqi parliamentary elections through funding and advising efforts.[39] Hadi al-Amiri even became the minister of transportation under former Iraqi Prime Minister Nouri al-Maliki, and Mohammed Ghabban, another Badr leader, served as Iraq's interior minister in 2014.[40] Badr is ideologically aligned with Iran's supreme leader and has a view of Iraq in the image of Iran's brand of Islam. The group expanded and created a separate political entity. Known as the Fatah coalition, or the Fatah Alliance, it was Badr's way of collecting additional seats in Parliament to influence Iraqi politics to be favorable toward Iran.

Asa'ib Ahl al-Haq (عصائب اهل الحق)

In 2006, Qais al-Khazali split from Muqtada al-Sadr's Mahdi Army[41] and formed Asa'ib Ahl al-Haq (AAH). The group enjoys Iranian sponsorship in the form of weapons, funding, and training. AAH is also ideologically aligned with Iran and works closely with the IRGC, having worked mostly with Soleimani until his death. Iranian IED have been a staple of the country's strategy as used by its Iraqi partners.[42] These are responsible for the most US casualties in Iraq, and the SMG most aligned with its use is AAH.[43]

Much like other Iran-backed groups, AAH formed political wings to influence Iraqi politics in Iran's favor. In AAH's case, this happened in 2011 following US troop withdrawals. Qais al-Khazali and his brother Laith al-Khazali were captured on March 20, 2007,[44] in Basrah on evidence that they and AAH had killed US military advisors in Karbala in January 2007.[45] In May 2007, General Petraeus wrote to Secretary of Defense Robert Gates:

> The five-page Qais Khazali sworn statement, made last week and marked with his inked fingerprints, is an unequivocal indictment of Iranian interference. His statement, along with those of his brother and other detainees, provides incontrovertible evidence that Iran is arming, funding, training, equipping, and advising Shia extremists operating in Iraq ... The statements of those interrogated are buttressed by dozens of documents taken from the captured laptops.[46]

Khazali's group remains committed to Iran and the supreme leader, and Khazali himself continues to be outspoken on his preferred alliance with the Islamic Republic. According to Hamdi Malik, an associate fellow at the Washington Institute for Near East Studies, Khazali "keeps trying to portray himself as a strategic ally of Iran, not a proxy," and had also claimed to have told Ghani "not to ask him to stop attacks on US forces in Iraq."[47] This lends Khazali authority in the country, given Iran's silence on the matter.

Kata'ib Hizballah (KH) (كتائب حزب الله)

Kata'ib Hizballah (KH, "Brigades of the Party of God") was created in 2007 and was formerly led by Abu Mahdi al-Muhandis, the militant leader who was believed to be a loose cannon and who died in the same targeted strike that killed Soleimani.

Muhandis was not just a soldier; he was Soleimani's soldier. They had a strong bond, and it was no surprise that KH was the most trusted Shia militia group in Iraq. They remain the strongest force in Iraq that poses a significant challenge to US interests. KH is reportedly behind the series of attacks against the Green Zone and elsewhere against US troops in Iraq since the 2019 protests. Muhandis's close relationship with the IRGC and with Soleimani facilitated the flow of training, weapons, and funding. Kata'ib Hizballah also established smuggling routes to transfer Iranian weapons and personnel to Iraq. Lebanese Hizballah was first to facilitate smuggling routes, but operations have since been taken over by KH in Basra, Maysan, Wasit, and Diyala provinces.[48] IRGC and QF forces supported these activities using "unmanned aerial vehicles, helicopters, visual surveillance, signals intelligence, and gunfire to intimidate and chase off Iraqi border patrols."[49]

KH may likely still be the most powerful Iran-backed group in Iraq despite the death of both Soleimani and Muhandis. Militarily, KH has been responsible for "some of the most lethal attacks against US and coalition forces throughout the [US-led war in Iraq]," according to Ali Khedery.[50] KH targets went beyond the US and Coalition forces; they targeted ISIL and Iraqi Sunnis. But Soleimani exported the group to Syria to help fight ISIL, which reveals not only their capabilities but also the fact that they earned his trust to conduct operations outside Iraq's borders.

Kata'ib Sayyid al-Shuhada (KSS) (كتائب سيد الشهداء)

Kata'ib Sayyid al-Shuhada is a younger group, established in 2013. Allegedly, the group was formed by KH and Badr to fight in Syria.[51] While they predominantly fought in Syria, KSS made its way into Iraq to fight ISIL under the PMF banner.

There is plenty of uncertainty surrounding the group in terms of leadership and size, but what is known is that Iran sponsors them, particularly as they operate under the PMF. They have openly affiliated themselves with Iran's supreme leader, but little is known about their political motivations. Given the limited data and availability of information, it can be inferred that the group is heavily integrated into the PMF, unlike KH, AAH, and Badr, which still operate independent of the PMF. As one research indicates, KSS "is not a mass political movement but remains primarily a militant group trading off the caché of its Iranian ties."[52]

Harakat Hizballah al-Nujaba (HaN) (حركة حزب الله النجبا)

In 2013, former AAH and KH members formed Harakat Hizballah al-Nujaba (HaN) to fight in Syria. Formed by Ahram al Kaabi, it was a collective of Shias in Syria that fought under Soleimani's banner. Another lethal Iran-backed group, they are closely aligned with Lebanese Hizballah and loyally fought in Syria to protect the Assad regime.[53] They are ideologically aligned with Iran and have pledged allegiance to Iran's supreme leader.

Additionally, HaN is one of the groups responsible for violently putting down protesters in Iraq. In 2015, Kaabi admitted that "technical and logistical support comes from the [Iranian] Islamic Republic" and that HaN "received military and logistical support from the Republic [of Iran] in continuing form and according to the needs of the fronts."[54] Kaabi also explained in a January 2019 interview that HaN receives "all levels of training, arming and the provision of advice through the presence of leaders and field advisors from the brothers in the Quds Force of the Revolutionary Guards" and Hizballah.[55]

Popular Mobilization Forces (الحشد الشعبي)

The PMF, also known as Hashd al-Shaabi, is an umbrella organization that houses Iran-backed militias. The significance of the PMF is its autonomy in Iraq. On November 26, 2016, the Iraqi Parliament formally institutionalized the PMF by passing the "Law of the Popular Mobilization Authority."[56] Under this law, the PMF is a subset of the Iraqi armed forces. Despite being institutionalized under Iraqi law, Iran-aligned factions within the PMF continue to receive resources and funding through Iranian sponsorship.[57] Many Iraqis interpreted the PMF as an "Iraqi Basij,"[58] modeled after Iran's Basij forces. Institutionalization afforded the PMF political legitimacy. Many leaders and senior PMF officials hold political office, blurring the lines between military and political responsibilities.[59]

In 2014, Iran-backed militias fought ISIL under the PMF and QF authority. Iran's strategy to bring militia troops to border-region conflict zones is one that presents itself across its military interventions of the 2000s, demonstrating how it prioritized territorial markers, land grabs, and internal security. Its focus on border regions was ultimately a hybrid approach, as Iran supplied more than just fighters to these areas. A military imperative for the QF was to regain control of Mosul from ISIL. Power projection takes its truest form when influence goes beyond just militias and bleeds into a state's citizenry. Iran assessed that taking back control and reinstating security of Iraqi citizens would significantly improve its chances of establishing a lasting presence. Much of Iran's hybrid strategy has strengthened over time, especially since the Iran–Iraq War, but this strategic priority remains constant. A chaotic Iraq is an ideal scenario for Iran. Iraq would continue to be dependent on Iranian resources, namely energy, which is sufficient for Iran to sustain a foothold in its neighboring country.

Through Iran's propagation of the PMF as a multifaceted blend of insurgent and state power during each of these offensives, Iraq's Shia militias also seized power politically. In some way, Iran formulated a functional shadow government in Iraq that operates with relative autonomy and poses a significant threat to Western interests and international security.

Lebanon and Syria

There was a civil war in Lebanon prior to the Islamic Revolution in Iran.[60] Between 1975 and 1990, Lebanon's turmoil led thousands of Lebanese to immigrate elsewhere. The Islamic Revolution in Iran and the ensuing Israel–Lebanon conflict in 1982 spurred Hizballah's rapid ascension. Early IRGC figureheads were responsible for Hizballah's development. One such figurehead was Mohsen Rafighdoost, an early IRGC commander who had previously trained in Lebanese refugee camps in the 1970s.[61] Another prominent IRGC leader was Hossein Dehghan, who later became Iran's minister of defense, between 2013 and 2017, as well as Khamenei's senior military advisor.[62] Early IRGC leaders and Hizballah militants traded experiences to enhance their war-fighting capabilities. Both sides were ideologically driven, which bolstered the need to further develop their skills. In bolstering Hizballah within Lebanon's government through political appointments and sponsorships, the IRGC can promote policies that favor Iranian interests.[63]

Lebanese Hizballah is the IRGC's success model, having grown into a powerful force both within Lebanese politics and society as well as internationally. Hizballah has developed into a vast global network. Considering how Lebanese Hizballah has pledged allegiance to Iran's supreme leader and follows the Iranian ideology of *velayat-e faqih*, they commit these acts in the name of the Islamic Revolution; therefore, they are a true Iranian proxy.

As previously mentioned, Hizballah's success during its war with Israel in 2006 was unexpected. They defended themselves against the IDF for over a month, which garnered international attention.[64] But Hizballah's success could also be attributed to the IDF's failure to prepare for a hybrid threat.[65] Hizballah had an unpredictable advantage over the IDF. Iran and Syria continuously built up Hizballah's arms, using Iranian 747s to "routinely offload arms in Syrian airports."[66] Its leader, Hassan Nasrallah, organized the terrorist organization to function like a state.[67]

Hizballah owns thousands of short- and intermediate-range rockets and missiles. During the 2006 war, Iranian advisors from the QF were present with Hizballah for tactical support. The battle between the IDF and Hizballah in southern Lebanon uncovered Israeli weaknesses. Using IEDs and EFPs proved efficient as they pierced the IDF's armored vehicles. These are easy to manufacture and inexpensive and were later widely used by Iran-backed groups, most prominently in Iraq.[68]

Several years later, the IRGC delegated Hizballah as its primary fighting force in Syria. This was an added experience with a new adversary in ISIL, and they even coordinated on the ground operations with Assad's forces and air operations with Russia.[69] Their experience working closely with the Russian military is unique to Hizballah because; they can call in airstrikes and serve as liaisons for intelligence and reconnaissance. They also use "artillery cover more effectively," drones and "improv[e] logistical operations to support big offensives."[70] Hizballah's evolution through Iranian sponsorship is indicative of hybrid threats on the rise.

State sponsorship aided Hizballah; the blending of insurgent and conventional tactics proved to be a successful strategy to support the Iranians' goal of keeping Assad in power.[71] Syria also serves as an important land bridge for Iranian oil sales, economic activity, and human smuggling. The IRGC's role in Iran's foreign policy involves circumventing sanctions, particularly through oil smuggling across Iraqi and Syrian borders.[72] The Syrian land bridge serves as a physical loophole for the Iranian regime, allowing them to forego the logistical challenges associated with international sanctions. With Syrian territory and Lebanese militias on its side, the IRGC has sidestepped international pressures by creating new pathways for economic transfers. The IRGC recognizes how important logistics and flow of money and resources are for meeting its military and political objectives. Throwing its strongest militia into these operations is a critical component of the Guards' overarching strategy in Syria and is incredibly telling of how Hizballah is interwoven into the inner workings of the IRGC.

By training and equipping other Shia militias, the IRGC secures itself a larger network through which it can project power.[73] These relationships allow it to cast their net further into the Middle East and solidify their role as both the shadow government and military force of Iran, all the while indirectly dictating areas of Iran's foreign policy.

Senior Iranian cleric Mehdi Taeb[74] claimed, "If we lose Syria, we cannot keep Tehran."[75] This has set the tone for Iranian forces and militias in Syria since civil war ensued in 2011. Politically, Syria represents a forward base against Israel and a physical buffer zone. Economically, the country offers considerable opportunities for oil sales and sanctions evasion.[76]

The Guards' primary fighting force in Syria is Lebanese Hizballah, considering its proximity and its prestige as the most developed Iranian proxy. Hizballah is used in Syria to operationalize Iran's hybrid strategy. Iraqi partners have also joined the Syrian fight, and while they are active in theater, they are most influential in disseminating propaganda in favor of IRGC interests through various social media platforms.[77] Violent videos documenting battlefield action spurred recruitment and promoted widespread support for Iran-backed groups.

Religious undertones are critical in furthering the IRGC's defense strategy because it enables them to recruit more broadly. According to Ambassador Jeffrey, "Religion is still a factor because [Iran] doesn't have conventional power. What they can do is feast on the rot internally of all these countries and play on them. That requires them to bring the religious element to this because they take the side of the Shia."[78] This has been a supporting component to developing partners in Iraq and across the Levant to enhance Iran's border defense and foreign policies.

Yemen (انصار الله)

Iran needs to feed chaos.[79] Freedom of movement deters its adversaries and lengthens conflict. Engulfed in chaos for years as a war-torn state and riddled with violence, humanitarian crises, and economic failure, Yemen is Iran's latest victim. Iran saw an opportunity in Yemen to support the Houthis—also known as Ansarallah—to project power in the Gulf. Contrary to common belief, the Iran–Houthi relationship is not new. In fact, it dates as far back as the 1990s. The Houthis are Zaydi Shias who follow the Fifth Imam, which is closer to Sunni Islam than Iran's Twelver Shia.

Conflict broke out in 2004 when President Ali Abdullah Saleh faced rising tensions in the country. In September 2004, Yemeni security forces killed Hussein Badr al Din al Houthi, which intensified the conflict.[80] Saudi Arabia intervened militarily in November 2009 when reports confirmed that the Houthis were being supported by Iran, which the Kingdom perceived as a direct threat to its security. Through Iranian support in the form of weapons and advisors, the Houthis made steady progress across Yemen, and at one point in September 2014, they seized Sana'a with help from an unlikely ally—Saleh, who had returned from exile.[81] Iran's similar strategic aim prompted it to exploit the turmoil. Yemen was a strategic area for the IRGCN to capitalize on asymmetric tactics using speedboats for swarming operations and explosive-laden drone boats.[82]

Houthi advancements incrementally endangered Saudi security, and the threat of instability led to the formation of a Saudi-led coalition on March 25, 2015, which was supported by Washington. Overall, Yemen became a strategic piece in Iran's hybrid war in the Middle East with marginal political commitment. Instability is a key factor in Iran's decision-making. Iran has a way of embedding itself in chaos and finding militants to challenge the status quo in opposition to the West. However, Yemen is not a priority. It was an opportunity that Tehran seized upon while committing limited resources. While Iran does not have political influence in Yemen as it does in Iraq and the Levant, it is advancing the turmoil and fueling instability. Tehran does not directly control the Houthis or their operations. The Houthis are recipients of Iranian resources, but they are not beholden to Iranian directives. After all, the conflict in Yemen is not international but domestic and contained to its near peers.

Yemen quickly became the pinnacle of Iranian maritime strategy and asymmetrical warfare. A maritime presence would be beneficial to the IRGC and its economic conglomerates. This strategy would work to properly counter Saudi forces to maintain security, project power against its regional adversaries, and even attempt to garner support from unlikely partners such as the United Arab Emirates (UAE).[83] Hence, though the conflict in Yemen is a domestic conflict over power,[84] Iran's limited influence through training and equipment is still impactful.[85] According to Ambassador Jeffrey,

> Iran needed a religiously oriented expeditionary force to expand its influence in face of a conventionally far more powerful and rich Arab states and their Western allies by playing on internal weaknesses of these states, such as the fate of Shia populations, certain Islamic groups, or oppressed populations like the Houthis and Palestinians. Without that strategy, Iran had no clear path to regional dominance. The strategy and its implementing tool—the IRGC—are inseparable.[86]

Since 2003, but especially since the US withdrawal in 2011, the IRGC and QF have intimately been involved with Iran's foreign policy. Elaborate smuggling schemes keep the flow of finances and personnel that directly benefits Tehran's widespread influence. As Barbara Slavin explained, "It is unknown if the Houthi's will stop fighting even if the Iranians told them to because they're doing well as a result of the war and have positioned themselves favorably."[87] Much like other Iranian partners, the Houthis are better at irregular tactics, but the overall outcome of the Yemeni conflict remains unclear.[88]

Iran's strategic investments and US policy

While Iran is tactically disadvantaged compared to an advanced Western military, it is in fact strategically advantaged in the region due to its practice of inflicting costs inexpensively. In some ways, we have facilitated the current outlook. During the early years of the Iraq War, the United States made little effort to prevent Iran and Syria from facilitating fighters' movement into Iraq, largely through Syria. While the US forces fought these fighters on Iraqi territory, the question remains as to why they were not prevented from arriving—especially why no effort was made to stop them from using Syria as a transit point.[89]

The IRGC and QF are vastly influential in the Middle East but mostly in Iraq. It is difficult to roll back these gains without a strategy that incorporates the region in totality instead of individual policies for each state. When this author asked former US Secretary of Defense James Mattis in an interview if there was a need for a regional strategy, Mattis answered, "There absolutely needs to be a regional strategy. The United States does not have one, and the Middle Eastern countries are too connected globally to leave them outside of our strategic interests."[90] Compartmentalizing would allow Washington policy and strategic planners to devise doctrines that incorporate each adversarial threat while reflecting on our vulnerabilities to make necessary adjustments. Iranian influence across the Middle East requires a reassessment of how to work with US allies and partners to better measure its threat from policy and defense perspectives.

Indeed, Operation Inherent Resolve (OIR) continues to fight ISIL remnants. Over the course of the nearly eight-year operation, it had no authority to counter Iran-backed activities. US Central Command (CENTCOM) was already stretched thin in conflicts across Iraq and Syria with the ISIL fight. It would have been a burden to "devote resources to monitor and deter Iranian activity" as it would take away from fighting ISIL. According to the 2021 lead Inspector General (IG) Report to Congress on OIR, the Defense Intelligence Agency (DIA) assessed that "Iran-aligned militias trumpeted the US departure from Afghanistan and the subsequent Taliban takeover as evidence of the United States' weakness as a security partner and the ineffectiveness of its training missions."[91] An Iranian and SMG assessment of the US withdrawal from Afghanistan is that military pressure can force a departure.[92] In line with Secretary Mattis, a senior DoD official noted,

> The strategy needs to focus on the address: Tehran. Any strategy would have to take into consideration the strategy of Iran. When it comes to Iraq, a successful sovereign Iraq that is squarely in the Iranian regime's camp would not represent a threat to Tehran. They may have 80 percent control of the militias.[93]

But the official continued, "A sovereign, prosperous, democratic, Western-leaning Iraq would stand in stark contrast to the Iranian regime's multiple failures over the decades to either deliver for the Iranian people or play a constructive role on the world stage," and this would pose the regime an existential threat.[94] Any strategy should recognize that the regime's leaders have a higher threshold than we might think because they have learned from their own experiences.

But US policy toward the region has neglected to factor in Iran across the board. It has tried to treat the Iran problem as mutually exclusive. In September 2018, the United States temporarily closed its consulate in Basra, Iraq, and it remains closed as of this writing. The then Secretary of State Michael Pompeo cited security threats from Iran and Iran-backed groups in Iraq following a barrage of rocket and mortar attacks in the general vicinity.[95] The unintended consequence of this has been a surge of Iran-backed attacks. Increased attacks led Pompeo to issue an ordered departure of non-essential personnel from the US Embassy in Baghdad in mid-May 2019.[96] While staff reductions ensure the safety of US personnel, adversarial actions should not dictate US strategy. Given the turmoil and rising anti-Iranian sentiment, this was an opportunity for the United States to strengthen ties with its Iraqi counterparts through diplomacy and counterterrorism measures. Indeed, reductions damaged not only diplomatic efforts but also critical humanitarian and defense measures that support broader operations, effectively eroding the United States' strategic objectives in Iraq.

From a counterterrorism perspective, we may have made the same mistake of withdrawing too early, which left a vacuum for ISIL to fill. According to terrorism expert Daveed Gartenstein-Ross, one difference is that the United States is not actively targeting the SMGs except for when they target us: "They can gain as much ground as they want to, but we're kind of hands off."[97] For that reason, an American presence on the ground is not serving as any kind of bulwark against SMG advances. "This is an example of the general inability of the US to execute strategy of any kind," Gartenstein-Ross said, though he added that it would be difficult to forge a US policy to prevent SMG gain without it posing unacceptably high risks to US forces.[98] This raises the question of whether our status quo is sustainable. Our adversaries have evolved, but it does not seem as though the United States is evolving at the same rate.

Relatedly, attacks continued and intensified. On December 27, 2019, a KH rocket attack killed a US defense contractor and wounded four other US military personnel in Kirkuk, Iraq.[99] A few days later, on December 31, 2019, KH and some PMF elements breached the US Embassy in Baghdad, starting fires and breaking fortified glass.[100] Tehran and its partners identified that increased attacks will ultimately pressure the United States and force a departure, setting a dangerous precedent for the future. Iranian power projection in Iraq aimed at consistently advocating for US withdrawal. An extensive US presence meant rising costs as the IRGC QF and its partners had to reinforce attacks.[101]

Circumstances for the region changed on January 3, 2020, when Soleimani and Muhandis were killed in a US-targeted strike in Iraq. What followed was a crowd of enraged protesters storming the US Embassy in Baghdad, trying to breach the compound again.[102] Many across the international community, including the United States, feared intense retaliations, but that has not been the case so far. Iran is patient, not impulsive. However, the unintended consequences include a notion that militia groups lack the cohesiveness that Soleimani provided. Soleimani was the glue that kept the groups together, but he also served as a check on any independent ambitions. He was heavily involved with their development, met with their leaders regularly, and "became an international symbol of the IRGC's effectiveness and power."[103]

The SMGs share an Iranian allegiance, but following the death of Soleimani and Muhandis, these groups have not only splintered but presented diverging interests. Indeed, the SMGs "all owed their potency—and even existence—to the Iranian regime's Quds Force and its powerful commander, Qasem Soleimani."[104] But this is counterfactual, given that today's operational environment, coupled with US strategy for the region, reveals indicators of factionalism among alliances and an Iran that has no interest in controlling the SMGs if they are imposing costs on the United States and maintaining some level of influence in Iraq. As described in this chapter, most of these organizations were Soleimani's creations in his vision. According to Crist, "Soleimani was the indispensible man. He provided unity in action and synchronization. Without him that goes away. They are more independent, but in some cases less effective. This creates the potential for them to operate more independently against us. So the conundrum is, do you hold Iran responsible?"[105]

In Iraq, Iran is playing both defense and offense. IRGC QF and the SMGs deny access and operability while also finding opportunities to strike below the threshold of kinetic activity. But it is no longer just a campaign because the "objective is as much political as it is military in operational terms."[106] What we are seeing today is that political leadership in Iraq is too intimidated by the PMF and Iran-backed groups. Any political pushback from the Iraqi establishment is responded to with some form of violent retaliation. Beyond Soleimani's killing, Muhandis' killing, according to Ali Alfoneh, "had a disastrous impact on the less institutionalized PMF."[107] Alfoneh indicated that his research showed that "Soleimani's killing did not have any greater impact on the IRGC QF, which, after all, is a highly institutionalized organization."[108] "The IRGC QF," Alfoneh continued, "has embraced the factionalism of Iraqi militias and even encourages inter-militia rivalry rather than pursue a Lebanese Hizballah model."[109]

As of this writing, the fate of the Middle East's future rests on the US policy toward Iran and whether Washington can deliver a regional strategy that incorporates Tehran as a part of the whole. Iran's influence is further proliferated through its exploitation of sectarian tensions. By way of funding, training, recruitment, and weapons transfers, the IRGC and QF provide extensive military and political support to its various partners to strengthen its regional foothold. What secured internal security in Iraq soon became one of Iran's greatest tools of power projection across the Middle East. Badr, Asa'ib Ahl al-Haq, and Kata'ib Hizballah are brand names in Iraq synonymous with Iran and the QF. As the authors of the 2019 volume, The US Army in the Iraq War, articulated, "In terms of geostrategic consequences, the war produced profound consequences. At the time of this project's completion in 2018, an emboldened and expansionist Iran appears to be the only victor."[110] And this is still true as of this writing. Having a steady presence in Iraq to curb these militias is important, but equally important is a presence that will have meaningful political impact and drive out all Iranian influence. One way to accomplish this is to build up the Iraqi security forces to resist the PMF, which would push back individual Iran-backed forces.[111] The Shia nature of the organizations would need to diminish for the Iraqi forces to instill discipline in them, which will in turn encourage the Iraqi populace.

8

Rouhani and the Shadow Government

The transition from Ahmadinejad to Hasan Rouhani was openly welcomed by most ordinary Iranian citizens. Iranians seemingly had had enough of the turbulence, and Rouhani's promise was to provide a sense of normalcy through engagement and the hope of economic prosperity. Yet, the same could not be said for hardline and IRGC officials. When Rouhani was elected, the IRGC was already so ingrained in Iranian politics that he was the first Iranian president to inherit such a dominant organization that spanned across all Iranian sectors.

At the time of Rouhani's election in 2013, both the Artesh and the IRGC were enduring mass casualties in Syria in support of Bashar al-Assad, who repeatedly crossed red lines.[1] Meanwhile, contrary to the IRGC's experiences in Syria, they were thriving in a post-US Iraq. That is until the rise of ISIL, as discussed in the previous chapter. The Syrian campaign and ISIL were the first post-Iran–Iraq War challenges that the IRGC faced. Rouhani was soon a quasi- "war-time" Iranian president. Amid all this conflict, the JCPOA was passed in 2015.

The IRGC's foreign and defense policies revealed themselves under Rouhani. That is not to say that Rouhani allowed this to happen; rather, divisions among the Iranian president, his inner circle, and the IRGC, who had the full support of the supreme leader, further strengthened the Guards. The concept of civil–military relations discussed earlier ceased to exist; it is difficult to see where the line of civilian control over policy matters begins and where it ends as it is so blended with the IRGC. Moreover, the IRGC Intelligence Organization burgeoned under Rouhani, presumably with the supreme leader's blessing. Under the authority of cleric Hossein Taeb,[2] who has a close friendship with Khamenei's son, Mojtaba Khamenei,[3] the intelligence unit sowed division among the MOIS and ingratiated itself within defense and foreign policy. Having a direct line to the supreme leader through this special friendship facilitated this with ease.

While already empowered, the hybrid model of coercion and applying pressure hit home with the JCPOA. Rouhani prioritized opening Iran's economy to international markets, and a compromise with the United States was the way to do this. However, the IRGC's financial portfolios were heavily tied to the Iranian economy in a variety of facets that a nuclear deal would either expose, limit, or eliminate all together. Rouhani was forced to make a series of concessions with the Guards to achieve a nuclear deal. Beyond this, Khamenei pressed on the notion of an Iranian "resistance economy" that further enabled the Guards, despite the JCPOA. Both before the JCPOA and following the subsequent US withdrawal, the Guards masterfully circumvented US and international sanctions, further empowering their economic aptitude. The Guards evaded sanctions under Rouhani unlike ever before, and it has since become a defining part of their hybrid war against the United States and the West. With the supreme leader's support, the IRGC's hybridity grew unfettered. The Guards' role in foreign policy matters is not advisory; rather, the IRGC comprises actual, legitimate stakes in decision-making authority and influence, which has caused serious tension among Iranian senior leadership.

"The diplomatic Sheikh"[4]

Rouhani was no stranger to revolutionary zeal. His rhetoric, writings, and leadership roles were all a reflection of his time and experiences during the Islamic Republic's infancy following the 1979 Revolution. But he embarked on an intellectual trajectory through Western education and moderate views. He surrounded himself with like-minded advisors and largely avoided controversy.

In 2003, he became Iran's chief nuclear negotiator and held the post through 2005. Vastly different from his predecessors, Rouhani was an academic, so to speak. Much like some Iranian elected officials, Rouhani is Western educated. He received a PhD in law from Glasgow Caledonian University in Scotland[5] and has consistently espoused a more moderate[6] viewpoint on relations with the international community. He frequently wrote academic articles and painted himself as a reformist, though still revolutionary in spirit. To bolster his academic stature, he led Iran's foreign policy think tank, the Center for Strategic Studies. Between 1989 and 2005, Rouhani was secretary of the SNSC, which is akin to the United States' NSC. He also helped found the SNSC.[7] Rouhani simultaneously served as deputy speaker of Iran's Majles (the parliament) from 1996 to 2000.

Steven Ditto analyzed a series of Rouhani's articles leading up to his presidential election and discovered a telling line, that the next Iranian president should be a "crisis manager ... who has the power to negotiate with the world."[8] And crisis manager he was—or at least he tried to be. As president, Rouhani facilitated a shift in responsibility on nuclear negotiations.[9] He stripped the SNSC of its authority and handed it to the Ministry of Foreign Affairs, with the foreign minister Mohammad Javad Zarif in the lead. However, Rouhani appointed a shrewd moderate to head the SNSC, Ali Shamkhani, both a former IRGCN leader and former defense minister. Rouhani's legacy has a dual modality characterization. His first term brought the JCPOA, while his second term saw US withdrawal from the JCPOA and Iran's subsequent economic decline, which he was largely blamed for by the Iranian public. The Covid-19 pandemic that ravaged Iran, the most hard-hit country in the Middle East, also damaged Rouhani's image.[10]

It is important to understand the type of leadership style that tried to once again place a check on the IRGC. Rouhani publicly vowed to contain the IRGC, specifically its economic enterprises, in favor of Iran's private sector.[11] While analysts of Iran and Middle East policy alike continue to evaluate former president Rouhani's legacy, the IRGC's involvement in the two-term president's regime has thus far gone largely unnoticed as it was almost entirely overshadowed by the JCPOA. While Iranian presidents attract attention from the media, it is easy to forget that the supreme leader is the ultimate deciding authority. Overall, Rouhani failed to achieve his policy goals, despite the JCPOA, because of his regime's tension with the IRGC. It is difficult for any Iranian president to govern and execute whatever policy goals they may want when the IRGC is this empowered. The IRGC was already too big to fail when Rouhani inherited it, and it essentially created a shadow government that had independence and dominion over Iranian foreign and defense policy.

The IRGC under Rouhani

When Rouhani was elected president in 2013, it was commonly believed that the election of a so-called moderate would usher in a new era of Iranian foreign policy. While that may be an appropriate interpretation in theory, in practice it did not turn out quite as Iran and the international community expected. Rouhani had a complicated relationship with the IRGC; at times, he even clashed with the then QF commander, General Qasem Soleimani, and while Rouhani can claim credit for the JCPOA, he is also blamed for its loss. Over time, Rouhani lost his grip on the country, and the IRGC is responsible for it. The IRGC thrived—though not without tough early losses—in Syria, Iraq, and Yemen, while Rouhani watched and sang their praises, not that he had any choice in the matter.

Rouhani also made several attempts to constrain the IRGC. At his first press conference, he vowed to dismantle monopolies and bolster the private sector.[12] It is important to note that Iranian presidents are essentially the supreme leader's pawns. There is no policy directive that can be pursued or accomplished without the supreme leader's support and guidance. Rolling back any IRGC gains thus proved to be impossible. Rouhani was a moderate president who sought improved relations with the West for the sake of the regime's economy. Interestingly, both of Rouhani's cabinets were IRGC light compared to his predecessor's. Rouhani's cabinet members were mostly like-minded academics with a Western education. Rouhani's minister of interior for both of his terms was an academic, Abdolreza Rahmani Fazli. Rouhani even departed from the longstanding tradition of filling the minister of defense role with an IRGC brass and replaced Hossein Dehghan with Brigadier General Amir Hatami (2017–21), the first Artesh defense minister. Another academic, Bijan Namdar Zangeneh, was confirmed as Iran's minister of petroleum in 2013. Zangeneh reappointed "Western-friendly oil experts" to boost foreign investment and oil prices.[13] Zangeneh also canceled contracts that originally belonged to the IRGC. In response, the Guards showed the weight of their authority and turned to Tehran's mayor Mohammad Bagher Ghalibaf, obtaining $7 billion worth of development contracts[14] as a show of force and authority.

Even Rouhani's foreign Minister, Zarif, knew that there needed to be some IRGC element present to begrudgingly appease the institution. Zarif appointed an Ahmadinejad figure, Hossein Amir-Abdollahian, as the deputy foreign minister for Arab and African Affairs. Amir-Abdollahian has "always been considered the lookout of the generals at the foreign ministry,"[15] and as of this writing, he is serving as Iran's minister of foreign affairs. Amir-Abdollahian, was known to be close with Soleimani, but Zarif removed him from his team after the signing of the JCPOA. A lighter IRGC footprint in Rouhani's cabinet signaled a desire for change and fewer political and economic responsibilities for IRGC elites.

But while Rouhani was playing the diplomatic game through the negotiations that led to the JCPOA, he concurrently endorsed the IRGC's operations in Syria and reinforced efforts in Iraq, as explained in the previous chapter. However, he did not have any choice in either case. Soleimani overshadowed Rouhani in many ways. The tense relationship was most noticeable during the chaotic period following the Arab Spring and subsequent Iranian involvement in Syria. Soleimani had a direct line to the supreme leader on operations as Rouhani was trying to be the "diplomat in chief."

This is notwithstanding that every Iranian president must act on the orders of the supreme leader, and Rouhani was certainly no exception. Rouhani used rhetoric to convey to the Iranian people that he would take economic measures that would constrain the IRGC, but it was never direct. His reluctance to take them on directly is indicative of the fact that an Iranian president can only go so far with the Guards. Rouhani tried to shape the Iranian economy within a framework that was not entirely exclusionary of the IRGC but to no avail. As Mehdi Khalaji of the Washington Institute for Near East Studies noted, "Rouhani and the Supreme Leader seem to view the reduction in the IRGC's economic role as more of a practical move than a political maneuver."[16] After Ahmadinejad's tumultuous tenure, there was a level of understanding between Khamenei and the so-called moderates that the economy needed to be repaired not necessarily for the Iranian people but to alleviate any civilian tension and prevent protests, which may pose a threat to regime stability. However, the Guards were already in too deep economically and were gaining more ground.

An intelligence unit divides leadership

The IRGC's hybridity is advanced through irregular means and its intelligence apparatus, both of which are "essential component[s] in Iran's unconventional warfare capabilities overseas which rely on various foreign movements and proxies."[17] Military intelligence within the IRGC and the QF conduct clandestine operations, which includes "gathering intelligence, conducting the foreign policy of Iran in Lebanon, Iraq, Afghanistan, and in Gaza; and supervising Iran's relationship with surrogate groups and terrorist organizations such as Hizballah, Hamas, and the Taliban."[18] This has afforded them the opportunity to essentially be majority stakeholders in Tehran's foreign policy.

Sufficient literature is available on Iran's MOIS that a reasonable assessment of its role in Iran can be conducted. However, there is very little research available on the MOIS's counterpart, the IRGC Intelligence Organization, which Khamenei established in 2009 following protests in opposition to Ahmadinejad's election. Khamenei founded the subunit within the IRGC because he feared that increased protests would threaten the Islamic Republic's legitimacy. Its creation flew under the radar, and it has benefited them in such a way that they operate with complete autonomy under the protection of the supreme leader himself. While the IRGC's intelligence apparatus has been functioning since Ahmadinejad's second term, its relation to the Rouhani regime is most important. As one Chatham House report indicated, "Under Rouhani, the agency [IRGC Intelligence Organization] has even more reasons to engage in parallel activities to those of the ministry."[19] The unit created divisions among leadership, and its secretive nature exacerbated policy efforts. As a result, it contributed to the overall establishment of the shadow government in Iran.

However, the little information that is available on the Guards' intelligence apparatus is significant to the present study on the IRGC's hybridity. As one author wrote in 2015,

> Khamenei retains direct control of the IRGC Intelligence Organization as a check on potentially dissenting forces within the government. Meanwhile, the IRGC has grown into a potent political force itself, using its intelligence capabilities to gain control over the internet, telecommunications, and key economic sectors. As a result, the IRGC is arguably the most powerful force

in Iranian politics with its own interests, which are, for the time being, mostly aligned with those of the clerical regime and the Supreme Leader.[20]

The establishment of an intelligence unit within an already powerful conglomerate "solidified the IRGC's control of Iran's intelligence apparatus and weakened the government's ability to challenge the IRGC's authority and to impede its activities in cracking down on dissenters."[21] This not only undermines the MOIS, but it delegitimizes a portion of its authority and appropriated oversight under its own jurisdiction.

Having done so, the Guards' subunit has clandestinely expanded its prerogative powers within the state through its involvement in both domestic and international operations:

> Foreign operations are usually directed at the United States and its allies in the Middle East, principally Israel and Saudi Arabia, or to preserve or expand Iranian influence in the region ... The IRGC also has a history of conducting targeted killings of individuals seen as particularly harmful to the clerical regime. Underpinning all of these operations and capabilities are the vast economic resources of the IRGC, which it generates through its involvement in the Iranian public and private economy.[22]

This means that the IRGC furthered its stake in foreign policy matters.

The Joint Comprehensive Plan of Action (JCPOA)

Extensive literature is available on the JCPOA. There are countless debates and arguments by proponents and opponents of what is commonly known as the nuclear deal. As such, this chapter will not serve as an in-depth analysis into the contents of either side. Rather, it focuses on how the implementation of the JCPOA in 2015 affected the IRGC.

As explained in Chapter 6, the IRGC thrived economically when it became a national enterprise. With private and public entities involved in IRGC affiliations, there was no rolling back the gains. Rouhani ran on a platform to improve Iran's economic capacity, and to achieve this goal, the IRGC needed to face some limitations. Interestingly, the JCPOA was a way to curb the IRGC's economic activities, though it was not a reasonable excuse in defense of the agreement. Because the IRGC's firms were so entwined with public entities, they were easy targets for sanctions. Sanctions relief from the JCPOA were designed for the IRGC to pull back on its economic practices[23] to allow the regime to abide by the deal, which meant that it would limit profits and require the IRGC to become more creative.

The IAEA continued its inspections of Iran's nuclear facilities, and even as of this writing, it issues reports of its verifications or lack thereof. Reports during the nuclear talks concluded that Iran was abiding by its commitments. Between October 28 and 29, 2013, all parties met in Vienna, Austria, and negotiated terms toward a deal. A joint statement was released by the then IAEA director general Yukiya Amano and Iran's then deputy foreign minister Abbas Araghchi, announcing Iran's proposal on "practical measures as a constructive contribution to strengthen cooperation and dialogue with a view to future resolution of all outstanding issues."[24] A nuclear deal was officially signed in July 2015.

However, the IRGC endured sanctions. The Ahmadinejad regime was a lessons-learned case study for the IRGC in sanctions policy. Since private companies in Iran could no longer use international financial institutions, foreign companies also had to leave Iran, and IRGC-affiliated companies filled the void.[25] This eliminated market competition and fostered domestic competition, however, the only competition in Iran were IRGC-affiliated companies, which meant that the profits would only benefit one entity. More importantly, the IRGC improved its ability to circumvent international sanctions while increasing their profits.

But what did the JCPOA mean for the IRGC and Iran's regional activities with its proxies and partners? Or more generally, what did the JCPOA mean for the IRGC as a whole? For one, Abbas Araghchi made it a point that the JCPOA would have no bearing on these activities: "We told [Kerry and the P5+1 negotiators] that we cannot cease providing weapons to Hizballah, and we would not make Hizballah the victim of our nuclear program."[26] Indeed, the IRGC did not let the nuclear agreement prevent it from assisting Iran-backed groups. Hizballah continued to receive weapons and other necessary resources to maintain Iran's support in Syria. In Iraq, the IRGC facilitated weapons smuggling to Shia militia groups. Sophisticated smuggling routes through the Gulf of Oman were utilized to deliver arms shipments to the

Houthis in Yemen. Nothing was going to stop the Guards from fueling their power projection in the region.

US withdrawal from the JCPOA

Despite sanctions relief from the JCPOA, there were still ongoing conflicts in the Middle East with obvious Iranian regime fingerprints, specifically in Syria. Iran's defense budget faltered as the IRGC scrambled to fund its proxy wars. Rouhani was partially successful in scaling back IRGC political activities following the implementation of the JCPOA. Khatam al-Anbia, for instance, was no longer the major entity that was awarded grants and other deals, which further strained the IRGC's profits. The signing of the JCPOA canceled two contracts of the IRGC and Khatam al-Anbia, totaling over $27 billion.[27] Rouhani's criticism of the IRGC's economic prowess was emphasized in his May re-election bid: "We handed our economy to a government that has guns, media, and many other things, and no one dares to compete with them."[28]

The IRGC did not take this criticism lightly, and they pushed back. IRGC commander Major General Ali Jafari said, "We believe that the government, which does not possess guns, could be humiliated by the enemy and surrender."[29] But Rouhani's re-election showed that he had the supreme leader's support. While Rouhani was focused on improving Iran's economy, the IRGC was still working on external operations in Syria, Iraq, and Yemen.

However, Iranian foreign and domestic policies took a turn in an unexpected direction when the United States withdrew from the JCPOA on May 8, 2018. The Trump administration would also reimpose pre-JCPOA sanctions beginning in November 2018. Waivers also ceased with the announcement of the maximum pressure campaign in 2018.

The Trump administration argued that the US withdrawal was to renegotiate a better deal that would address other concerns, including ballistic missiles and regional activities. The earliest statement came from the then NSA Michael Flynn, who had famously put Iran "on notice" following a missile test.[30] The goal of the maximum pressure campaign, according to Trump administration officials, was to curb Iran's malign influence, but the flaw in the strategy was the belief that Iran could be strong-armed into renegotiating a new nuclear deal. Instead, E3 signatories attempted to maintain the JCPOA, but Iran took advantage of the United States' withdrawal and began enriching uranium and installing previously banned centrifuges. While the Trump administration consistently maintained that the maximum pressure campaign was working, Iran was seamlessly getting closer to its nuclear goals, which had been previously restricted under the terms of the JCPOA.

The "resistance economy" and FTO designation

Before the maximum pressure campaign, Iran touted a "resistance economy." In 2014, Khamenei reasserted this concept, which has since become a principal tenet of Iran's central strategy to circumvent sanctions. Khamenei announced the general policies of this strategy in accordance with Article 110 of the Iranian Constitution, which states, "The scientific and indigenous model of revolutionary and Islamic culture will cause the defeat and retreat of the enemy in the imposed economic war against the Iranian nation."[31] The full text of the communique is lengthy, but the one line that stands out is, "Monitoring sanctions programs and increasing costs for the enemy."[32] This is the fundamental element of the Iranian regime's strategy. And the IRGC is the primary entity responsible for circumventing sanctions and increasing costs for the United States and the West.

Some may argue that the Iranian regime is ignorant or unaware of how its adversaries operate. However, in relation to sanctions, this is a mistaken outlook. In fact, the Iranian regime is well versed in US and international sanctions policies. It is not as though they are experts in all sanctions, but they are experts in sanctions that apply directly to Iran. Having a solid understanding of how sanctions and designations impact their bottom line, the Guards have been students of sanctions. To survive, the Islamic Republic has learned to live with sanctions. But to function at a high rate, avoid collapse, and even accumulate profit, the IRGC had to become experts. Sanctions circumvention became an art form, and this should be important to the Western understanding of its adversary. Circumventing sanctions is indeed a part of the IRGC's hybrid war against the United States and the West. Iran's survival wholly depends on it.

The IRGC has gone as far as to criticize Rouhani's economic strategy and the implementation of the JCPOA because in their view both violate the principles of the "resistance economy." To appease the Guards, Rouhani was forced to include Khatam al-Anbia and several associated entities and subsidiaries in oil and gas transactions following sanctions relief as a result of the JCPOA. While it seemed that Rouhani compromised with the IRGC to meet its economic concerns post sanctions relief, it was in effect a series of unwelcome concessions from having no other viable alternatives to facing an entity that seemingly was not accountable to the regime, only to the supreme leader.[33]

Even a foreign terrorist designation was not going to stop the IRGC. In fact, it further emboldened them. On April 8, 2019, the United States designated the IRGC as a Foreign Terrorist Organization (FTO).[34] President Trump said that the designation would "significantly expand the scope and scale of our maximum pressure on the Iranian regime" and if anyone is conducting business with the IRGC, then they are "bankrolling terrorism."[35] The Trump administration argued that this action would hurt the IRGC's financial arm and, as a result, reduce its footprint in the region. Iran's Majles in turn declared US CENTCOM and any affiliated forces in the region as terrorists. While this may seem insignificant, it is indeed an action that publicly puts a larger target on the backs of US personnel.

The US designation of the IRGC and the maximum pressure campaign escalated tensions.[36] The United States heavily sanctioned Iran in 2019, in addition to ceasing waivers to countries seeking extensions to purchase Iranian oil. This was the Trump administration's attempt to bring Iranian oil exports to zero, which is mathematically impossible. Every US action against the regime was met with a reaction from the IRGC and its affiliates. As previously stated, such reactions led to drawdowns of non-emergency personnel from US diplomatic posts in Iraq, specifically in response to the threat from Iran-aligned groups on May 15, 2019; furthermore, the United States widely suspected that Iran-backed groups were responsible for firing a missile into the "Green Zone" in Baghdad on May 19, 2019.

A flurry of tanker attacks and seizures in the region only made matters worse. Eventually, Rouhani announced to the international community that Iran would no longer abide by JCPOA obligations regarding its stockpiles of low-enriched uranium and heavy water.

There is no status with Iran

As much as his regime intended to curtail the Guards' economic capacity, Rouhani was unsuccessful. It is important to remember that the IRGC answers only to the supreme leader. Therefore, whatever policy Rouhani wanted to implement that opposed the Guards would have been difficult since Khamenei would likely not have approved them. To appease the IRGC, given their stance on the JCPOA, Rouhani doubled their defense spending, which included Khatam al-Anbia.[37] Following the implementation of the JCPOA, hardline officials and the IRGC perceived the economic gains from the international markets as threats and initiated harsh attacks against Rouhani's regime. A major component of this strategy was a series of operations by the IRGC that included "arresting dual citizens, businesspeople, and journalists [and] accusing them of being part of an espionage network to undermine the state."[38] This was part of the larger strategy to deter foreign investment and maintain an anti-Western position.

Iraq was always the prize for Iran, and the maximum pressure facilitated a piece of that prize. Economically, it is difficult to wean Iraq off Iranian goods. Reports indicate Iraq is still Iran's leading export destination, amounting to billions of dollars annually.[39] It is important to consider that Iraq actually wants an economic presence other than Iran. There is likely enough room to engage near-peers such as Saudi Arabia, Jordan, and Kuwait, among others, which would be in Iraq's interest. Maximum pressure also threatened US interests in Iraq. It swayed the Iraqi government toward Iran because, in many ways, maximum pressure also touches Iraq. Applying economic pressure overtly is something Iran uses politically. Meanwhile, the Iraqi government has been trying to stay neutral, but to survive, they need to side with Tehran instead.

A slew of sanctions was implemented in the final year of the Trump administration in 2020. The Treasury Department targeted dozens of individuals, entities, and companies that were believed to have supported designated terrorist groups' attacks on US forces in Iraq. Specifically, sanctions were imposed against Katai'ib Hizballah and Asaib Ahl al-Haq, which Treasury officials argued would "call attention to Tehran's activities."[40] But these sanctions were only symbolic and arguably weakened their efficacy. To be fair, the maximum pressure campaign started strong with targeted sanctions that had teeth. Whether or not maximum pressure has been successful has been debated on both sides. Ultimately, sanctions should be used in coordination with other concepts and other countries. An effective tool within sanctions policy is the prevention of "U-Turn" transfers; these are transactions that transfer funds from a foreign bank, which then that pass through a US financial institution before being transferred to another foreign bank.[41] On November 10, 2008, the Department of the Treasury launched Iranian Transactions Regulations to prohibit "U-Turn" transfers.[42] According to Samantha Ravich, chairman of the Foundation for the Defense of Democracies' (FDD) Center on Cyber and Technology Innovation and its Transformative Cyber Innovation Lab and the principal investigator on FDD's Cyber-Enabled Economic Warfare project,

> U-Turn sanctions were the biggest success because we have the technology to enforce such transactions. Other major sanctions, like gas and oil, are not set it and forget it; they need to be constantly massaged. They maintain their importance, but if there's no rigorous oversight and management of those sanctions, including new technology to disrupt anti-sanction movements and a coalition, then they won't be effective.[43]

From a policy perspective, the FTO designation of the IRGC was purely symbolic and only bound the United States diplomatically. The 2007 designation of the QF was far more meaningful and impactful. The United States lawfully issued a designation for a military institution though traditionally only non-state threats had been the targets of such designations. In setting this precedent, the United States has paved the way for Iran and any other adversary to do the same against the US military and the militaries of other Western countries.

Interestingly, in October 2015, the then Iranian foreign minister Zarif admitted that Iran's Syria policy was "not in the hands of the Foreign Ministry in Tehran."[44] In a leaked audio from April 2021, Zarif said, "In the Islamic Republic, the military field rules."[45] While this confirmed the longstanding suspicion among Iran watchers, it was a rare piece of insight from a sitting Iranian foreign minister. The IRGC created greater divisions among the rank-and-file senior leadership in Rouhani's regime. In successfully doing so, they attained more power and showed that sanctions were not having the desired effect. The IRGC has consistently overpowered senior leadership through their relationship with the supreme leader.

Certainly, Rouhani was a strategic president and found ways to fulfill his campaign promises while allowing the IRGC to continue down its own path.

In doing so, Rouhani was picking the battles he wanted to fight against the IRGC. However, he did not foresee US withdrawal from the JCPOA, which ultimately shattered his legacy. The Covid-19 pandemic enabled the IRGC to establish a narrative that they are going to help save Iranians rather than the regime's politicians. All the while, the IRGC was dictating Iran's broad foreign policy toward the region, and the Foreign Ministry's only claim to fame was its stake in the JCPOA. In effect, Rouhani was unsuccessful in rolling back the IRGC in the way he had hoped. If anything, his strategy bore the brunt of the unintended consequences, which further emboldened the Guards. According to Henry Rome, the deputy head of research and a director covering global macro politics and the Middle East at the Eurasia Group,

> From a public diplomacy standpoint, having someone like Rouhani was important in terms of making a credible case in Washington. While [current] president Raisi doesn't use language as abhorrent as former president Ahmadinejad, he's still a dark figure to have as president, and that is just another barrier on top of many towards making progress with Iran.[46]

Influence in foreign policy matters. Shaping Iran's foreign policy and moving it toward the Guards' preferred direction is a part of the hybrid war that the United States and Iran have been engaged in, and with the Guards in charge, diplomacy will not have a fighting chance.

An Iranian Cyber Command?

When it comes to cyber activities and capabilities, Iran is not as sophisticated as the United States, China, or Russia. Iran is often compared to the DPRK, or North Korea, but that comparison also has its flaws. DPRK's cyber activities are economically targeted. The aim of its ransomware activities is to secure the quickest way to steal funds from private entities. Iranian activities are primarily geared toward espionage. Over the last decade, Iranian cyber capabilities have steadily improved, but they are still not as sophisticated as other cyber adversaries. However, that should not be viewed as a reason to underestimate the challenge posed by Iran in this area.

A survey of literature on Iranian cyber capabilities since 2010 shows that the research has heavily focused on successful Iranian cyber attacks and attempted attacks. This chapter builds on extant research by exploring the new information that is available in open source. More importantly, it aims to show that cyber is a critical component to hybrid warfare. As has been stated throughout this book, hybrid warfare is not a new concept, and any component of warfare that is a continued blend of modalities is attributable to it. After all, experts such as John Arquilla and David Ronfeldt warned of netwars in the 1990s.

What is evident is that Iran has weaponized cyberspace for espionage and to threaten the critical infrastructure of an adversary. As a DIA report on Iran's military assessed, cyber operations are tools of "statecraft and internal security," and Iran is continuing to improve its cyber capabilities because it is a "low-cost method to collect information and retaliate against perceived threats."[1] While TTPs may differ depending on the intended target, Iran has continuously fused cyber threats into its ongoing hybrid approach to the global environment. The Stuxnet virus was a wake-up call to the Iranian regime as it identified a critical vulnerability in its infrastructure. Since then, Iran has worked toward research and development to strengthen its domestic capabilities while developing models for targeted foreign intelligence collection.

Stuxnet

Stuxnet was a sophisticated malware that Iranian leadership believed to be a glitch at first glance. Iran hired a Belarusian company to investigate the matter, which ultimately exposed the malware. Stuxnet destroyed at least one thousand centrifuges at one of Iran's nuclear facilities in Natanz. The malware caused the centrifuges to self-destruct by spinning out of control. Stuxnet was likely installed by an unwitting Iranian with a USB drive that was transferred across computer systems within a local area network (LAN). It traveled undetected, spreading throughout the network and duplicating itself without attaching to specific files while reprogramming integral systems. The damage and overall international humiliation caused by Stuxnet led the regime to explore ways to upgrade its cyber capabilities and practices. Heavy investments poured into research and development, both at the academic level and within Iran's defense apparatus.[2]

A common pattern among Iran-related cyber attacks has been the preference toward the financial sector, though not to steal monetary assets but to signal the international community that it has reach. In some ways, it is also a response to US and international economic sanctions against the regime. For instance, in 2012, Iran was believed to be behind Saudi Arabia's Aramco and Qatar's RasGas malware attacks, which wiped data from company computers.[3] Known as Shamoon, the malware not only wiped data but also stole passwords and other valuable information. Also in 2012, Iranian actors hit the US banking systems[4] with a distributed denial of service (DDoS) attack, specifically targeting Bank of America, US Bancorp, Fifth Third Bank, Citigroup, PNC, BB&T, Wells Fargo, Capital One, and HSBC. The attack was known as Operation Ababil; hackers flooded banking websites and prevented users from accessing accounts and other information. In 2016, seven individuals linked to the IRGC were indicted for their involvement by the Department of Justice.[5] In 2013, an IRGC-linked attack was conducted against the Bowman Dam in Rye, New York. Attackers remotely took control of the dam's supervisory control and data acquisition (SCADA) systems, which compromised its functioning.[6] In December 2014, a DDoS attack wiped network data from the Sands Casino in Las Vegas.[7] According to open sources, this attack was believed to be in response to Sheldon Adelson's comments on detonating a nuclear bomb in Iran.[8]

DDoS attacks escalated to espionage. In September 2013, an alleged Iranian actor accessed the United States Navy's unclassified computer network.[9] Government personnel are certainly the most-prized targets for Iranian actors. In November 2015, a spear phishing campaign for espionage compromised DoS officials' social media accounts.[10] Each attack is presumed to be conducted by the IRGC's cyber arm. Over time, the attacks became more blatant. In 2018, Twitter revealed that they had removed over 2,600 Iran-linked accounts that were "engaging in malicious activity."[11] A year later, Facebook (now Meta) announced that it had removed countless Iran-linked accounts, including on Instagram.

Capabilities and networks

Before Hossein Salami was promoted to IRGC commander, he claimed that Iran is "in an atmosphere of a full-blown intelligence war with the US and the ... enemies of the Revolution and the Islamic system ... This atmosphere is a combination of psychological warfare and cyber operation, military provocations, public diplomacy, and intimidation tactics."[12] While the vast majority of the Iranian regime rhetoric is meaningless, there are times when true intentions reveal themselves, as is the case with Salami. The IRGC collects intelligence domestically and across the region to thwart domestic opposition.[13] But it is also actively targeting the West for espionage.

The IRGC controls Iran's leading internet service provider, bringing the Guards that much closer to civilian control. Following the 2009 privatization of the internet sector, the IRGC bid for a controlling stake of the Telecommunications Company of Iran through one of its shell organizations.[14] The IRGCs ability to track and monitor internet and other domestic activity of ordinary Iranians is due to its majority ownership of Iran's Telecommunication

Company and its subsidiaries.[15] Surveillance of Organized Crime, and the Working Group for Determining Criminal Content, the IRGC monitors and tracks internet activity to collect domestic signals intelligence. Just as they operationalize cyber threats against foreign adversaries, the Guards assert dominance over the Iranian population in every aspect of life.

But since Stuxnet, Iran has pivoted toward cyber defensive and offensive capabilities from a strategic standpoint. Their development has not been the most successful, but they have exhibited signs of improvement, specifically in advanced persistent threats (APT). These are Iran's most powerful cyber tools because they are targeted and effective. Iranian actors seek specific targets of opportunity to either gain leverage, steal funds, or collect foreign intelligence. This requires the technical know-how on specific, targeted systems.[16]

Iranian APTs have been active as far back as the early 2000s, but it was only as the size and scale of the attacks advanced that they were paid more attention. APT 33, for instance, which is also known as Elfin Espionage Group or Refined Kitten, was active across the United States, Asia, and the Middle East, seeking exploitation vulnerabilities. Specifically, APT 33 targeted engineering, chemical, research, energy consultancy, finance, IT, and healthcare sectors.[17] The most recent common vulnerability and exploit (CVE) by APT 33 struck in February 2019, known as CVE-2018-20250 in WinRAR. According to a report by the US software company Symantec (Gen Digital), WinRAR is a

> widely used file archiving and compression utility capable of creating self-extracting archive files. The exploit was used against one target in the chemical sector in Saudi Arabia. If successfully exploited on an unpatched computer, the vulnerability could permit an attacker to install any file on the computer, which effectively permits code execution on the targeted computer.[18]

APT 33 primarily uses malware for exploitation through spear phishing. They used fake job descriptions against the civilian and military aviation, energy, and petrochemical industries. Cybersecurity firm FireEye assessed that

> the targeting of multiple companies with aviation-related partnerships to Saudi Arabia indicates that APT 33 may possibly be looking to gain insights on Saudi Arabia's military aviation capabilities to enhance Iran's domestic aviation capabilities or to support Iran's military and strategic

decision-making vis-à-vis Saudi Arabia ... APT 33 may have targeted these organizations as a result of Iran's desire to expand its own petrochemical production and improve its competitiveness within the region.[19]

APT 34[20] is another Iranian threat actor that specifically targets global financial, energy, government, chemical, and telecommunications sectors for espionage. APT 35, also known as Charming Kitten, Newscaster, Rocket Kitten, Phosphorus, and Saffron Rose, was last seen in 2022.[21] APT 35 shows the trajectory of Iranian cyber cases in their willingness to push the envelope. This threat uses "watering hole" attacks and fake online profiles to bait US government personnel for espionage. But academics, human rights groups, and journalists are also targets. A threat actor linked to the Iranian government unsuccessfully attempted to break into former president Trump's re-election campaign, according to open sources.[22] Rocket Kitten is believed to be linked to the IRGC.[23]

APTs ultimately fall, for the most part, under what cyber expert John Arquilla describes as "strategic crime" because of their focus on intellectual property theft and industrial espionage. According to Arquilla, a key concern is the unknown future: Will every state power have its own APT, or will they form alliances with others? And what happens to those powers who decide that the United States is their enemy?[24] There are fundamental new dynamics that go beyond just the economic component. APTs are ideal cyber tools that can be used to wage political warfare, and Iran has consistently been using APTs globally.

Hybridity in practice

Iran's need to develop a cyber strategy grew out of its recognition that the regime's critical infrastructure was vulnerable and wide open to threats. Hybrid cyber developments are included in a 2016 academic report from Iran, which has been previously cited in this book. It shows that Iran is aware of its vulnerabilities and is engaged in adjusting them.

One of the most significant lessons learned by Iran as it transformed its cyber capabilities into an offensive hybrid threat is that cyber conflict is effective because of the anonymity it provides. There is very little the international community can do if the targeted country chooses not to act or respond because of the deniability the offender possesses. This concept gave Iran the freedom and range to confront adversaries it may otherwise not have confronted, allowing it to redefine its asymmetric approach to global dynamics. Examining cyberwarfare in the context of Iranian history offers some explanation to its broader cyber strategy, where there is very little clarity. Iran has no official cyber doctrine, but historical events provide insight into Iran's thought processes and strategic goals that explain how it conducts attacks today.

According to Arquilla, Iran is, overall, more defensively oriented in cyberspace because of concerns about the threat posed to regime stability by civil society movements that involve much networking online.[25] The aim is to detect, track, and disrupt activities like the Green Movement and prevent any domestic unrest that would threaten the regime. Ultimately, the inequity in capabilities will cause Iran to continue preparing for cyber threats while conducting operations to monitor the critical infrastructures of the United States and the West. Offensive cyber operations (OCO) offer significant benefits to Iran's strategic environment, such as cyber weapons, force protection, anonymity and ambiguity, and homogeneity with other unconventional operations.[26] Cyber weapons (worms, viruses, and malware, for example) are much more easily attainable and require less maintenance and resources than conventional weapons. They also secure force protection for the IRGC since cyber warriors operate from remote, protected locations and hijack the target's ability to detect the attack. For Iran, this means significantly fewer casualties compared to the onslaught of destruction it had experienced in physical conflicts in the past. As mentioned earlier, anonymity and ambiguity are also hallmarks of cyber threats, specifically OCO, as they permit Iran to act in coordination with external forces that provide additional deniability. These characteristics make it difficult to prove that the aggressor acted on orders from the Iranian government and thus allow Iran to avoid retaliation that may lead to unwanted conflict. Perhaps the greatest benefit of OCO in Iran's hybrid strategy is its homogeneity with other tactics as it facilitates multiple tactics to be used in tandem to support one unifying operation.[27] This is hybridity at its finest and the key to Iranian strategic success over the last several decades. Operationalizing multiple tactics simultaneously is not a new concept, especially in Iran. Cyber capabilities simply offer another avenue through which the IRGC may operate.

Iran views cyberwarfare as a zero-sum conflict fought on a cultural battlefield. Its hybrid threats online are swift, blunt, and ideologically focused. The IRGC, being the governing body of Iran's cyber threat, has evolved its tit-for-tat strategy from the Tanker War so that it may be employed in cyberspace as well. This approach is centered on adaptability and dynamic responses to geopolitical tensions regionally and internationally. Some cyber attacks may be responses to geopolitical events, while others are geared toward foreign intelligence collection. There is a methodical strategy to collect relevant information for both policy purposes and kinetic actions. Should Iran deem geopolitical tensions as a threat to its cultural or political foundations, it would adapt its cyber strategy to inflict targeted, quick responses to the threat. Minimal intrusion and maximal consequences are key to Iranian attacks in cyberspace to inflict the greatest damage with as little accountability as possible. Similarly, the tit-for-tat approach gives Iran the flexibility to target states it would be more hesitant to confront in physical conflict. Many of Iran's cyber attacks have been against its biggest adversaries: the United States, Israel, and Saudi Arabia. In conventional conflict, Iran would not be able to compete with the military prowess of these powers, but the dynamic nature of cyberspace allows it to attack rapidly and without the constraints of inferior weapons, artillery, or human capital.

Cyber as a tool for hybrid wars

To understand Iran's SIGINT capabilities and where the military plans to use them in the future, there are a couple of steps the United States and its allies should take. First, it would be beneficial to track with whom Iran develops contracts on cyber-related transactions. Data on cyber-related transactions may provide information on whether Iran has developed a metadata collection mechanism or other related capabilities. Second, it is important to know if other countries act as intermediaries for Iranian cyber threats; if so, it is imperative to identify these countries. Should the West seek to confront Iran in cyberspace, having a better understanding of its transactions and intermediaries would be key, and this begins with a stronger partnership with the private sector.

During Rouhani's first term, Iran's security budget increased by 1,200 percent,[28] leading to a variety of investments in cyber capabilities that show the regime's commitment toward a broader hybrid strategy. With its vast investment in the cyberspace as a domain of strategic intent, Iran has simultaneously worked to establish strategic imperatives and targeted operational approaches. Iranian APTs are still functioning, namely APT 35, which continues to be a credible threat against US government personnel, academics, and journalists, though it is not limited to the United States. In 2019, Microsoft revealed that it had identified members of APT 35, or Phosphorous, who had targeted current and former US government personnel, journalists, Iranians living abroad, and potential 2020 US presidential candidates with over 2,700 attempts to identify email accounts and 241 successful attacks.[29]

Iran's cyber capabilities are not limited to cyber vandalism, theft, or foreign intelligence; they also have the potential to be a mechanism for sanctions evasion through cryptocurrencies and digital currencies.[30] Iran's economy has been crippled in recent years because of external factors such as sanctions and international isolation as well as internal factors such as corruption. With these limitations, cyber capabilities would provide an outlet for Iran. Cyber economics is also a way to work with China. Chinese proprietors have flooded into Iran since 2018 to take advantage of the inexpensive Iranian electricity to mine for Bitcoin and other digital currencies. Although the West has effectively isolated Iran from international trade and global markets, Chinese involvement in Iran's cyber sector could prove to be a way for it to circumvent these problems and provide defensive security through a diversified economy. This is a part of what Samantha Ravich calls cyber-enabled economic warfare. It is the use of cyber tools to undermine an adversary's economic wherewithal to curtail their political, military, and strategic options. Shamoon was a cyber-enabled economic attack, according to Ravich, because Iran attacked Saudi Arabia's key economic asset.

This hybrid war is escalating in cyberspace, and it will probably continue for years to come. We should be more concerned about how Iranians are getting more aggressive in the cyber domain than in the conventional battle domain. Cyber activities afford Iran the ability to operate with more deniability in areas that are in turmoil, including Iraq, Syria, Yemen, and other places where governing institutions are fragile. As Arquilla explained, the priority for the time being will be regime protection.

From a policy perspective, the United States must understand how little effect sanctions have had on Iran, especially during the period of maximum pressure. From a strategic perspective, we must then recognize that cyber is the most usable tool we have against Iran. Since sanctions are no longer having the desirable effect, we must turn to our own cyber capabilities. Cyber is a usable, viable option and should rise as a policy option for the United States and the West. A "cyber missile," so to speak, is a meaningful response that will make the regime incur immeasurable costs. It can deter Iran and disrupt any potential actions against the United States and our allies. The United States must also work toward strengthening its defensive capabilities to prevent Iranian intrusion, protect critical infrastructure and intellectual property rights, and identify vulnerabilities open to strategic crime.

As of this writing, Iranian hardliners are in power, and, given their ideological fervor, they are more open to increased offensive cyber operations. Cyber may be a more usable tool for Iranian hardliners, and the IRGC is best suited to take on the additional role. Iran's cyber capabilities may not be ranked high, but it does not mean that they should be underestimated. The United States must realize that it has capabilities other than kinetic, diplomatic, and economic, and it is important to be better prepared. In an interview, Arquilla explained his concept of a worst-case scenario:

> The stars are aligning with this hardline government that's not afraid to act. A nightmare scenario is that Iran takes the sort of Stuxnet variants they have been playing with and aims them at Saudi Arabia's energy sector. Iran's politics suggests a willingness to contemplate these sorts of acts, and the fact that they've shown a willingness to target Saudi Arabis's oil industry [implies that they] will no doubt be willing to continue in a more sophisticated, cyber way. A strong Russo-Iranian dark alliance could be formed as a result of the war in Ukraine, and other clandestine cyber alliances could spring up. As a result, fresh global vulnerabilities will emerge, and their consequences will play out in increasingly troubling ways.[31]

To borrow a concept from Arquilla, the deepest concern is arguably "cybotage."[32] What types of capabilities do the Iranians have in terms of sabotaging military defense systems? More importantly, according to illicit-finance expert John

Yaros, "the US is vulnerable, but they [Iran] are more vulnerable and that is a major factor in cyberspace."[33] The United States should consider the cyber threat from Iran a credible one and adopt a warlike mindset to devise targeted strategies to identify its capabilities, prepare for operations, place a greater emphasis on deniability and disruptions, and incorporate these within the policy debate. For these strategies to be successful, we must assume that the Iranian regime is refining its cyber capabilities.

10

A Modern Foreign Policy in the Age of Hybrid Warfare

Often when it comes to policymaking, political motivations impede what it is we should actually achieve, whether it be toward a state or a regional issue. This is, of course, a natural way of going about policy and is a characteristic that is embedded within our institutions. Who is to say what is right and what is wrong? We all have different opinions. However, the danger to this is that groupthink and staunch political will can sometimes get in the way of real strategic thought, which ultimately defines the outcome of a policy, for better or worse.

Unfortunately, with the Middle East, the United States has employed a one-size-fits-all strategy. While our adversaries are pulling plays from various playbooks, the United States pulls from just one. There are other factors that have gone overlooked, such as culture and language. A sound, competitive strategy needs to campaign back at opponents who are actively working against US interests and influence in any part of the world. Conventional methods are waning against an adversary that is opting to use hybrid methods. We should be fighting hybrid with hybrid since our adversaries do not view modalities in terms of dichotomies like the United States. The United States is either in peace or at war because it is encoded bureaucratically. For the Iranian regime, however, it is much clearer. According to Mahnken, "For our adversaries, there is much more direction to what they do."[1]

When the United States was preparing for the Iraq War in 2003, Iran was noticeably absent from our calculus. The significant impact of an Iranian influence in Iraq was discovered much later and yet was still largely unheeded as we had to focus efforts on al-Qaeda in a post-Saddam Iraq. By that time, it was too late; Iran had already executed a series of campaigns for influence in Baghdad. Remarkably, US and Iranian leaders actually met in Iraq in 2007, which was the first time officials from the two countries had met since the 1979 Islamic Revolution.

The IRGC has complicated how the United States goes about its foreign policy toward Iran. It is not just a state military institution, but as this book has argued, the IRGC is also an economic player and, most importantly, a foreign-policy hand. The Guards play a leading role in Iran's foreign policymaking, and US policymakers must take that into account before attempting to devise a strategy on how best to approach Iran both from a strategic military standpoint and a diplomatic one. According to Michael Eisenstadt,

> The IRGC has played a major role through its deterrent/warfighting triad, which consists of precision-strike forces (the missiles and drones of the IRGC-AF); a guerrilla navy (IRGCN); and proxy forces (its so-called Shiite foreign legion, controlled by the IRGC QF). Moreover, the US is limited and constrained by its laws and the laws of armed conflict, although it is also a hybrid actor. But the United States is constrained in how it employs its hybrid methods and capabilities. The IRGC is not.[2]

Eisenstadt gets to the fundamental issue at hand. The IRGC should not be treated like an ordinary state, for instance, or even a non-state threat. It is an institution in itself, and the United States must find ways to loosen its own constraints when addressing an adversary capable of adjusting to challenges.

Foreign policymaking is more complicated in the age of hybrid wars than, for instance, during the Cold War. According to a senior DoD official, the difference between now and forty to fifty years ago is that "events have caused US policy to shift in the Arab world … have informed adversarial actions. The adversarial mindset is that if they keep going long and hard enough, the US will leave."[3] And this is a strategy that Iran has employed in Iraq. The DoD official further explained, "We can stay in places like Iraq and Afghanistan with a small footprint to maintain influence. If our goals have not changed, then we must decide what our risk threshold is, and to do that, we need to get to the bare bones of military and diplomacy."[4] As such, this concluding chapter will assess the most recent foreign policy decision made by the United States, notably the Trump administration's maximum pressure campaign. Sanctions are the United States' most powerful foreign policy tool, and maximum pressure is a prime example of the overuse of sanctions and how that could be dangerous for future policymaking. The region continues to be volatile and unpredictable due to its hybrid nature. Strategic concepts and policies should begin with what the United States wants as an end-state, and in answering that question, we must anticipate the adversaries' steps and reactions.

The unintended consequences of maximum pressure and the influence of the militant networks

The United States instigated the rise in tension with Iran with the maximum pressure campaign. There is no doubt that the JCPOA was a flawed deal. Subject matter experts who understand Iranian language and strategy will argue that the corruption within the regime and the IRGC would have revealed some violation that would have triggered snapback sanctions per the JCPOA. But this requires time, as do sanctions. The Trump administration chose not to continue with the JCPOA, and that is certainly within the realm of a president's prerogative. The United States withdrew from the JCPOA on May 8, 2018, bewildering the international community and, more particularly, leaving the E3 countries scrambling to hold on to what they could from the deal. The crux of the Trump administration's argument was that US policy toward Iran aimed to curb Iran's malign influence and deter it from reaching nuclear status. While those are constructive policy points that absolutely should be worked toward, withdrawal from the JCPOA proved counterintuitive. Iranian malign influence increased, and Tehran's nuclear progress expanded. As of this writing, Iran has enriched at 60 percent and installed centrifuges that were banned in the original nuclear agreement. According to Peter R. Mansoor,

> Since US prestige is on the line, we need a new agreement. The nuclear program can be negotiated. The problem is that neither side trust[s] each other on maintaining an agreement and on what each side's vision or goals are for the Middle East. Iran is creating leverage. The real issue isn't the nuclear program. It's the nature of the Iranian government.[5]

Without a new deal or a clear path forward, the United States and the region should expect continued retaliatory measures by the Iranian regime. The nature of the regime is preventing the United States from creating any off-ramps.

For instance, on June 20, 2019, Iran shot down a $130 million US drone. The Global Hawk surveillance drone was flying over international waters when Iran shot it down with surface-to-air missiles, claiming that the drone had entered Iranian airspace.[6] The United States chose not to respond, which spurred diverse arguments from both sides of the aisle. On the one hand, if the United States reacted, a military response would have been the only option, which would almost certainly have escalated toward war. But on the other hand, the lack of response, as it has been argued, meant that the United States left the door open for further attacks. Either way, it is a lose–lose situation.

According to David Crist, "If the Iranians' intent is to kill Americans, then inaction doesn't help our case."[7] The United States is not waiting on the Iranians to respond with conventional attacks. Indeed, the targeted killing of Soleimani was a high-magnitude earthquake. But as previously explained in this book, strategic patience is the regime's virtue. They may not retaliate immediately, or in the near future, but retaliation must be expected. As Crist explained, "They don't respond at the same time and space as the event. It's hard to link an action with a precipitating action. Patience is a strength, which means that vengeance could be years from now."[8] The unpredictability is the threat. In the age of hybrid wars, patience is a characteristic that will pay dividends in the long run. Iran's past behavior should show the international community that responding on impulse is not their style; rather, Iranian attacks have become a kind of a guessing game. They are predictable in the sense that there will be a response, but when and where (either physically or in cyber space) are not as easily identifiable. A level of planning and organization, as well as timeliness, all play a part. A major issue across Iran policy experts in the United States is that we tend to believe that Iran is just as compartmentalized as the United States. This false thinking has led us to continually miscalculate the IRGC and its strategic doctrine. It is precisely because past sanctions have proven harmful to the IRGC's interests that they have repeatedly reinvented themselves for survival. Compartmentalization is characteristic neither of the IRGC nor of Iran's political hierarchy. It must be perceived as a single entity with the supreme leader and his office at the top, from where everything trickles downward.

It can be argued that with each sanction imposed on the Iranians under maximum pressure, Tehran indirectly responded with low-impact reaction through its partners in the region. The IRGC—through its partners and proxies—conducted a flurry of attacks particularly in 2019 as sanctions were heavily imposed against Iran. At some point, however, the sanctions became ineffective. Symbolic sanctions have no impact, and they only nudge the adversary toward a response, which usually happened in Iraq. Overall, the maximum pressure campaign further isolated Iran; however, while that was deserving of the greatest state sponsor of terrorism, it also had grave unintended consequences for the United States and the international community.

From an illicit finance standpoint, the IRGC's role grows in the face of sanctions because they have external forces such as the QF, proxies, and partners. They continue to operate on an elevated scale since they can rely on countless front and shell companies to finance their operations and get their people paid. There are so many such companies that even if some are identified and sanctioned, it does not faze the IRGC; there are others to choose from, or they can simply create more. According to John Yaros, "Officials from the Central Bank of Iran have used intermediary banks in Iraq and elsewhere to fund and facilitate the operations of Iranian terrorist proxy groups such as Lebanese Hizballah."[9] Yaros also explained the use of correspondent banking, which is essentially banking for banks. Many financial institutions do not know the customers of their counterparties as well as they should, which enables nefarious actors like Iran to move funds throughout the financial sector. Unfortunately, the United States often lacks the access to real-time information and resources to shut down these operations and transactions before the payments are processed. A similar situation exists within the shipping industry. Iran uses flags of convenience and forged documents to take advantage of oversight weaknesses within the shipping industry.

With approximately 90 percent of global trade occurring via shipping lanes, documenting due diligence and compliance can be difficult in the shipping industry. The large size and global nature of shipping combined with legal loopholes for shell companies and flag registrations make it an extremely tough industry to oversee. This also makes it rather simple to find negligent partners or facilitators within the industry willing to accept payouts and conduct operations on behalf of bad actors. Shipping is a significant problem because there are no ideal solutions or tools for shutting down trade-based money laundering, and our adversaries are aware of it. This makes global trade an attractive avenue for illicit activity, even for bad actors under sanctions. The IRGC has demonstrated a particularly high level of sophistication in this arena, such as changing the bill of lading where a ship is docked or changing how it is flagged. Yaros defined this concept as "trade-based illicit finance."[10] This includes ship-to-ship transfers[11] because the IRGC largely has advanced procurement networks comprised of shell and front companies. The IRGC uses these companies for getting what it needs for its various programs and defense systems as well as for securing other items. The Guards have been known to use commodities such as gold as cash substitutes.[12]

The Biden administration hoped to revive the nuclear deal, but as of this writing, there is still no deal and Tehran had been stalling through numerous rounds since Biden took office. And now there is the added element of a tightening relationship between Tehran and Moscow since Russia invaded Ukraine in February 2022. The question we should ask is, why would the Iranian regime want a nuclear deal that constrains its enrichment and centrifuge installations when it has already surpassed the enrichment levels of the original deal? Iran appears to be getting what it wants, despite being under heavy sanctions. We should know by now that, after more than four decades, Iran is adaptable. The IRGC has studied sanctions to circumvent them for its own advantage and survivability. It has weathered the harshest sanctions ever imposed, which leads one to deeply question if the sanctions have failed and if Iran is a case study on how not to impose sanctions. David Crist observed that "the Iranians have found interesting ways to circumvent sanctions and promote their economy through the IRGC's control," which, as a result, has driven them back to self-sufficiency and pushed them toward China and Russia. "Isolation is counterproductive," Crist continued, adding, "They don't like the West, but they need it, and that was the whole point of JCPOA. We have driven them long term in accommodation with some of our adversaries."[13] If the Iranians are not dependent on us, then we have no leverage. The Iranian regime has pushed enrichment levels as leverage and are arguably in a better position at the negotiating table compared to the United States and E3. There is very little the United States can offer Iran that would convince them to return to the nuclear deal. As long as they are willing and able to weather economic sanctions, there is no reason for a hardline regime to acquiesce to any Western deals.

From a policy perspective, we must also consider that the problem is not enriched uranium but the warhead design and delivery. What is lacking in the analysis and literature covering the JCPOA is the fact that Iranians do not have the delivery ability,[14] which is arguably the most critical factor. The flaw of the JCPOA was its failure to recognize this and the fact that the more imminent threat came from Iran's ballistic missile capabilities. As the Iranians have made significant progress and advancements in their ballistic missile designs, production, and use, this is the field in which Iran is likely researching and developing avenues for a nuclear warhead delivery mechanism. Limiting Iran's ballistic missile program should have been the first step.

Policy concepts and strategic thought

The IRGC and the supreme leader are entwined, and they both have strategic interests in maintaining this relationship. The aging Khamenei will eventually need a replacement, and the next supreme leader will be even more powerful if the IRGC gets a stake in his selection. For the time being, the IRGC has supremacy over military, intelligence, and foreign affairs. Internal disputes among the rank and file, as well as various organizations such as the MOIS and other domestic elements, have declined over time as the IRGC's vast apparatus grew in strength and superiority. Henry Rome noted that the IRGC will not face any pressure at all under Ebrahim Raisi, Iran's president as of this writing Rome correctly observed that Raisi does not have very developed views or experience in the realm of foreign policy because he does not have a clear worldview: "The challenge for Raisi is when he actually has to govern on a variety of issues. The supreme leader gives broad guidance, but it is up to the government to actually implement it."[15] Rome added that "Raisi hides behind vague comments by the supreme leader, so there is likely going to be a heavy reliance on advisors."[16]

When it comes to Iran and the IRGC, what usually surprises policy analysts and advisors at the DoS is the extent of Iranian support for proxies and partners and what they are trying to achieve. From a policy perspective, the DoS is not looking at it through that lens. There is an obvious disconnect between DoS and DoD, and we must first deal with the severity of this problem.

In a discussion with the author, former Ambassador Jim Jeffrey articulated this very point:

> The State Department is the institution along with the NSC that should put together all the elements of strategy and operational plans worldwide to carry out our global mission, and that is our global collective security system. This should be managed by civilians and diplomats, not the Department of Defense.[17]

This is a critical point because, over time the DoS has pushed itself to become an alternative to hard power foreign policy. The problem is institutional. The latest intelligence and strategic concept thoughts should drive foreign policy, but it is largely coming out of the DoD as opposed to the DoS. Diplomacy is the tool to achieve foreign policy ends. And until those changes occur institutionally, there will not be much change in terms of policymaking.

The United States could have negotiated for a better deal. The sunset clauses, for instance, were too early. But the sanctions were punishing the Iranian economy more severely during that time compared to the maximum pressure campaign that followed or even the time of this writing. The Obama administration used targeted sanctions that largely attacked Iran's protectionist policies. We need to acknowledge that Iran will not concede certain core values they believe are vital to their interests. The Iraqi militia groups are prime examples of this. We also need to be realistic in identifying what is in the realm of possibility. Missiles will never be a part of any nuclear deal, no matter how much they should be or should have been from the beginning. Iran developed its missile arsenal, given its experience in the Iran–Iraq War. It is its version of deterrence and is integrated within its defense strategy.

From a strategic perspective, the IRGC's hybrid warfare is restricted to the region. They have limits, but they will continue to be a major player in the Middle East. Crist calls this "competitive control for influence in the region."[18] There is a kind of Cold War competitiveness with Iran for influence.

Washington's policy of deterrence toward Iran is not traditional. Rather, it is what a senior DoD official calls "contested deterrence," which tries to prevent Iran from lashing out militarily or even thinking it can successfully lash out militarily.[19] So far, there have been the Abraham Accords, which with time, should prove positive. Unity among the Arab nations could theoretically curb Iran. In their own way, the Abraham Accords account for the impact of allies and partners, and they should continue to be utilized. As former defense secretary Jim Mattis explained,

> There are ways to make this work, but we Americans want it more than the Arabs do. There is always going to be a certain level of heat on the region and that level of heat can go up quickly and it will just breed more discontent. Arab unification would be good to block the Iranians, but it would fail right now because the Arab states are unwilling to unify at the level necessary. The Arabs must want to get together, but they have a long memory of discontent between them.[20]

Integrating Arab partners within the Iraqi economy is another way to deter Iran's hybrid warfare strategy in that country.

Overall, Barbara Slavin's point on differentiating between partners and proxies, as noted earlier in this book, is accurate and fitting in the general context of hybrid wars and the current need to shift away from the notion that Iran is compartmentalized. The IRGC's preferences vary depending on the group, even though they share common views. In Iraq, for example, there is a mixture of groups, including some that are almost entirely dedicated to the Iranian ideology and others whose members are travelers. According to Michael Eisenstadt,

> We have a limited ability to shape the dynamics that will influence the long-term prospects of these groups. Moreover, we're focusing more on the Indo-Pacific region now. That means the United States will have fewer military resources at its disposal in the Middle East. On the other hand, a lot of these militias, their status is due to Iran's largesse. If the Islamic Republic ceased to exist tomorrow, what would happen to these groups? Would they disappear or not? They're so imbedded in the politics and economics of Iraq that who knows? Iran faces a lot of long-term challenges, however, so we can't assume anything in terms of the longevity of the Islamic Republic. But, if and when the IRI goes, do its proxies have the ability to ensure their own survival?

Will the demise of the Islamic Republic take the wind out of their sails and discredit their ideology? We can expect that the members of these groups will probably try to reinvent themselves to survive in a new era.[21]

And indeed, the SMGs in Iraq have been repackaging themselves following the Soleimani strike. The Houthis in Yemen constitute a different form of partner with minimal commitment on both sides. The relationship is mostly economical in terms of providing financial and logistical support. Iran, through the IRGC QF, has been good at not pushing groups outside of their comfort zones to keep them on their side. A whole-of-government approach is ultimately needed to address these issues.

The same cannot be said of near peers. Oman, for instance, has been known to play both sides. They have consistently shown that they can serve as a back channel. The UAE is hardline, though evidence suggests that there is a vast Iranian network operating in the UAE with Abu Dhabi's knowledge. Qatar leans in Iran's favor, particularly because of natural gas, but as of late, Doha has shown that it wants to play a larger diplomatic role in the region. After all, Qatar hosted the "Doha Talks" between the United States and the Afghan Taliban and has also hosted a round of nuclear talks between Iran and JCPOA signatories. Regardless of Arab involvement thus far in negotiations, there have been no off-ramps, and this has arguably weakened US leverage and deprived Washington of political levers.

The future of foreign policy

The IRGC will continue to conduct Iran's real foreign policy for the foreseeable future. It is both expansionist and aggressive. Iran's foreign policy does not rest with its civilian leadership. According to Elliott Abrams, "Iranian presidents are PR figures. The decision about SMGs were made by Khamenei and Soleimani."[22] Additionally, the IRGC is coup-proof. They have solidified their role as Iran's prime decision-makers with unsurmountable influence. Iran is not analogous to any other country in the world in terms of how decisions are made and who really is in control.

One of the biggest questions to consider in terms of policy and even defense is who will replace the supreme leader when he eventually dies. This author argues that the next supreme leader will be even more powerful than Khamenei. In the interim, the United States should continue to foster relationships and build on existing policies such as the Abraham Accords. Regardless of whether or not they were controversial, the Abraham Accords established the building blocks for bringing the region together based on collective security. As Barbara Slavin explained, "We have to try to solidify relationships in the region and convince the people that we're not going to cut and run, especially after Afghanistan."[23] The Abraham Accords can be useful in this effort because Arab countries are not focused on Israel as a threat but more as a security ally. It also includes the benefit of having a presence in Iraq to maintain some foothold in the region. There is a counter argument to this, according to another senior DoD official. Basic policy in the Middle East should be containment, and the United States should be "trying to expand normalization agreements, but we need to let [regional] countries do that on their own time."[24]

For either of these to work, however, we need partners and allies. Withdrawing and then relying on regional actors is not the solution to the problem. The United States must act as a committed partner and avoid the sense of abandonment that was felt during the Afghanistan withdrawal. According to Michael Connell, an expert at the Center for Naval Analysis, Arab states are now "much more distrustful of us and engaging in hedging. China and Russia are playing a bigger role in the region and the US less so over time."[25] Connell added, "Part of the solution is to understand the consumers of the intelligence and the products better because there is a tendency on the part of authors of those products on adversaries to not make it relevant to consumers of that information. We must make it relevant and therefore need to understand the customer base better."[26] Connell's point is applicable across all facets of foreign policymaking. However, specific to Iran and the IRGC, it most notably applies to our understanding of the Iran-backed groups. There was a lack of calculus prior to entering the Iraq War in 2003 regarding Iran's influence, and there arguably still exists a lack of understanding on how deeply rooted these groups are in the region.

Overall, Iran has mismanaged its economy. But maximum pressure has vastly weakened the efficacy of sanctions. Most states have recognized that if they have a proper infrastructure in place and can brace for sanctions, then they have a chance of survival and can use it to their benefit. There are always going to be ways to circumvent sanctions because adversaries will keep finding new loopholes. Specific to the maximum pressure campaign, the United States overstated its success and set unreasonable expectations; the IRGC is a parallel entity to the Iranian government itself and will continue to find ways to adjust, such as by expanding ties to Arab states.

The United States is a global power, but that does not mean that all regions should be treated equally and that our interests are of equal value.[27] As the IRGC's hybrid war against the United States persists, we should assess how capable regional actors are and what can be done to boost their deficits. A regional strategy for the Middle East that incorporates the study of hybrid warfare could help future policymaking. With regard to Iraq, as a senior DoD official noted, it is important to the United States but "not existential, given other competing national security challenges and priorities, [and] this disparity in intensity of interests is important."[28]

What is certain is that today's conflicts are shaping foreign policy instead of the policies preventing conflicts to begin with. As Peter R. Mansoor explained, "We're going to see this with Russia soon enough. Hybrid warfare is a tool, and it is one of many in a toolkit."[29] It is not a concept that can only be applied to Iran's IRGC; it is equally applicable to other adversaries, especially Russia. Adversaries learn from each other. The United States should consider integrating the complexities of hybrid warfare in foreign policy and continually evolve. We may have the geographic advantage of being physically away from conflicts, but that does not mean we can ignore our influence abroad. This helps maintain our image and standing in the global security collective. After all, US national security depends on both our military and our diplomats.

Notes

Chapter 1

1 von Clausewitz, Carl, *On War*, ed. and trans. Michael Howard and Peter Paret. Princeton, NJ: Princeton University Press, 1976. Page 606.
2 Ibid.
3 Author interview with a senior Department of Defense official.
4 Author interview with a senior Department of Defense official.
5 Mattis, James N. and Frank Hoffman, "Future Warfare: The Rise of Hybrid Wars," *Proceedings Magazine*, United States Naval Institute, Vol. 132, November 2005. www.milnewstbay.pbworks.com/f/MattisFourBlockWarUSNINOV2005.pdf.
6 Author interview with Gen. (ret.) Jim Mattis.
7 Mansoor, Peter R., "Introduction: Hybrid Warfare in History," in *Hybrid Warfare: Fighting Complex Opponents from the Ancient World to the Present*, Williamson Murray and Peter R. Mansoor (eds.), New York: Cambridge University Press, 2012. Page 1.
8 Ibid. Page 2.
9 Ibid. Page 3.
10 Ibid. Page 7.
11 Author interview with Thomas G. Mahnken, President and Chief Executive Officer of the Center for Strategic and Budgetary Assessments.
12 *The Lexus and the Olive Tree: Understanding Globalization*, from 1999 is derived from Friedman's "Golden Arches Theory" from a 1996 *New York Times* article, "Foreign Affairs Big Mac I," https://www.nytimes.com/1996/12/08/opinion/foreign-affairs-big-mac-i.html. Friedman addresses globalization and how the world is facing two struggles. The first is represented by the "Lexus," prosperity, while the second is the "Olive Tree," or the sense of identity.
13 A special thanks to Ambassador James Jeffrey for providing his thoughts in a conversation on foreign policy.
14 Findlater, Euan, "Islamic Republic of Iran's Strategic Culture and National Security Analysis," *Small Wars Journal,* January 19, 2020. https://www.smallwarsjournal.com/jrnl/art/islamic-republic-irans-strategic-culture-and-national-security-analysis.

15 Farver, David, *Taken Hostage*. Princeton, NJ: Princeton University Press, 2005. Page 183.
16 Douville, Alex, "The Iran-Contra Affair," Case Studies Working Group Report, Richard Weitz (ed.), Vol. 2. Strategic Studies Institute, US Army War College, Carlisle Barracks, PA. 2012. Page 88.
17 See: Tower, John, Edmund Muskie, and Brent Scowcroft, *The Tower Commission Report*, joint publication of Bantam Books, Inc., and Time Books, Inc., New York, February 1987. https://archive.org/details/towercommission00unit/page/n5/mode/2up?ref=ol&view=theater.
18 Ibid. Page 102.
19 Ibid.
20 See: Hoffman, David, "Bush Offers 'Goodwill' if Hostages are Freed," *The Washington Post,* August 10, 1989. https://www.washingtonpost.com/archive/politics/1989/08/10/bush-offers-goodwill-if-hostages-are-freed/953ab824-67de-4a3f-a69f-4a77874ab9b7/.
21 For a brief review of the Gulf War, see: Freedman, Lawrence and Efraim Karsh, "How Kuwait Was Won: Strategy in the Gulf War," *International Security*, Vol. 16, No. 2, 1991. Pages 5–41. *Project MUSE.* muse.jhu.edu/article/447278.
22 See: Crist, David, *The Twilight War: The Secret History of America's Thirty-Year Conflict with Iran*. New York: Penguin Press, 2012. Pages 380–97.
23 For a detailed insiders account, see: Paul Wolfowitz, "What Was and What Might Have Been—the Threats and Wars in Afghanistan and Iraq," *Strategika*, Issue 76, Hoover Institution. https://www.hoover.org/research/what-was-and-what-might-have-been-threats-and-wars-afghanistan-and-iraq.
24 See: Gibson, Bryan R., "The Long Road to Tehran: The Iran Nuclear Deal in Perspective," London School of Economics, 2015. Page 6.
25 "Fact Sheet: Iran and the Additional Protocol," Center for Arms Control and Non-Proliferation, July 14, 2015. https://armscontrolcenter.org/factsheet-iran-and-the-additional-protocol/.
26 "Implementation of the NPT Safeguards Agreement in the Islamic Republic of Iran and Related Board Resolutions," *IAEA*, August 11, 2005. https://www.iaea.org/sites/default/files/gov2005-64.pdf.
27 Ibid.
28 "Security Council Imposed Sanctions on Iran for Failure to Halt Uranium Enrichment, Unanimously Adopting Resolution 1737 (2006)," United Nations Security Council, Press Release December 23, 2006. https://www.un.org/press/en/2006/sc8928.doc.htm.

29 "Security Council Toughens Sanctions against Iran, Adds Arms Embargo, with Unanimous Adoption of Resolution 1747 (2007)," United Nations Security Council, Press Release March 24, 2007. https://www.un.org/press/en/2007/sc8980.doc.htm.

30 "Security Council Authorizes More Sanctions against Iran over Nuclear Issue," United Nations News, March 3, 2008. https://news.un.org/en/story/2008/03/251122-security-council-authorizes-more-sanctions-against-iran-over-nuclear-issue.

31 "Joint Statement on a Framework for Cooperation," IAEA, November 11, 2013. https://www.iaea.org/sites/default/files/gov-inf-2013-14.pdf.

32 See: "Statement by IAEA Director General on Geneva Agreement," IAEA, November 24, 2013. https://www.iaea.org/newscenter/statements/statement-iaea-director-general-geneva-agreement.

33 For full details, see: "Status of Iran's Nuclear Programme in Relation to the Joint Plan of Action," IAEA, January 20, 2014. https://www.iaea.org/sites/default/files/govinf2014-1.pdf.

34 See: "Director General's Statement on the Announcement by the E3/EU + 3 and Iran on the Agreement of the Joint Comprehensive Plan of Action," IAEA, July 14, 2015. https://www.iaea.org/newscenter/pressreleases/director-generals-statement-announcement-e3/eu-3-and-iran-agreement-joint-comprehensive-plan-action.

35 See IAEA Report to Board of Governors: "Status of Iran's Nuclear Programme in Relation to the Joint Plan of Action," IAEA, July 20, 2015. https://www.iaea.org/sites/default/files/gov-inf-2015-15.pdf.

36 See: Katzman, Kenneth, "Iran: Internal Politics and US Policy and Options," Congressional Research Service (CRS), updated May 30, 2019. https://crsreports.congress.gov/search/#/?termsToSearch=RL32048&orderBy=Relevance. Page 19.

37 See: "After the Deal: A New Iran Strategy," an interview with Mike Pompeo at the Heritage Foundation, May 21, 2018. https://www.heritage.org/defense/event/after-the-deal-new-iran-strategy.

38 See Keshavarz, Alma, "The United States Needs an Iran Strategy, not a Campaign," The Atlantic Council: https://www.atlanticcouncil.org/blogs/iransource/the-united-states-needs-an-iran-strategy-not-a-campaign/.

39 Douville, Alex, "The Iran-Contra Affair," Case Studies Working Group Report, Richard Weitz (ed.), Vol. 2. Strategic Studies Institute, US Army War College, Carlisle Barracks, PA, 2012. Page 110.

40 The GAO analysis of DoD military concept and briefing documents and academic writings. United States Government Accountability Office (GAO), "Hybrid Warfare." September 10, 2010. Page 17. https://www.gao.gov/assets/gao-10-1036r.pdf.
41 Ibid.
42 Ibid.
43 Ibid. Page 11.
44 von Clausewitz, Carl, *On War*, Michael Howard and Peter Paret (eds.). Princeton, NJ: Princeton University Press, 1976. Page 87.
45 Keshavarz, Alma. "Hybrid Warfare: The Islamic State, Russia, and Iran's Islamic Revolutionary Guard Corps (IRGC) Threats, Challenges, and US Policy Response." PhD diss., Claremont Graduate University, 2018.
46 Glenn, Russell W., "Thoughts on 'Hybrid Conflict.'" *Small Wars Journal*. 2009. https://smallwarsjournal.com/jrnl/art/thoughts-on-hybrid-conflict.
47 See: Cordesman, Anthony H., "Preliminary 'Lessons' of the Israeli-Hizballah War," Center for Strategic and International Studies, September 11, 2006. Page 19.
48 Author interview with Gen. (ret.) Jim Mattis.
49 Keshavarz, Alma. "Hybrid Warfare: The Islamic State, Russia, and Iran's Islamic Revolutionary Guard Corps (IRGC) Threats, Challenges, and US Policy Response." PhD diss., Claremont Graduate University, 2018.
50 Ibid.
51 Ibid.
52 Ibid.
53 Ibid.
54 Ibid.

Chapter 2

1 Jenkins, Brian Michael, "New Modes of Conflict," RAND Corp., prepared for the Defense Nuclear Agency, 1983. Page v. https://www.rand.org/content/dam/rand/pubs/reports/2006/R3009.pdf.
2 Ibid. Page vi.
3 Ibid. Page 8.
4 Ibid.
5 van Creveld, Martin, *The Transformation of War*. New York: Free Press, 1991. Page 57.
6 Arquilla, John and David F. Ronfeldt, "The Advent of Netwar," RAND Corp., 1996. Page vii.

7   Ibid. Page vii, 1.
8   Ibid. Pages 1–2.
9   Arquilla, John, David Ronfeldt, and Michele Zanini, "Networks, Netwar, and Information-Age Terrorism," in *Countering the New Terrorism*, Lesser, O. Ian, Bruce Hoffman, John Arquilla, David Ronfeldt, Michele Zanini, and Brian Michael Jenkins (eds.). RAND Corp., 1999. Page 41.
10 Nemeth, William J., "Future War and Chechnya: A Case for Hybrid Warfare," Naval Postgraduate School, Master's Thesis, 2002. Page 2.
11 Ibid. Page 3.
12 Ibid. Page 61.
13 Ibid. Page 69.
14 Ibid. Page 76.
15 *National Defense Strategy of the United States of America*, Department of Defense, March 2005. Page 2. https://history.defense.gov/Historical-Sources/National-Defense-Strategy/.
16 Hoffman, Frank G., "Conflict in the 21st Century: The Rise of Hybrid Wars," Potomac Institute for Policy Studies, 2007. Page 8.
17 Ibid.
18 Ibid. Page 14.
19 Ibid. Page 58.
20 Hoffman, Frank G., "Hybrid Warfare and Challenges," *Joint Force Quarterly*, Issue 52, 1st Quarter, 2009. Page 35.
21 Kilcullen, David, *Accidental Guerrilla*. New York: Oxford University Press, 2009. See also, *Hybrid Warfare and Transnational Threats: Perspectives for an Era of Persistent Conflict*, Paul Brister, William H. Natter, III, and Robert R. Tomes (eds.). Council for Emerging National Security Affairs, 2011.
22 Glenn, Russell W., "Thoughts on 'Hybrid Conflict,'" *Small Wars Journal*, 2009. https://smallwarsjournal.com/jrnl/art/thoughts-on-hybrid-conflict.
23 McCuen, John J., "Hybrid Wars," *Military Review*, March–April 2008.
24 Glenn, Russell W., "Thoughts on 'Hybrid Conflict,'" *Small Wars Journal*, 2009. https://smallwarsjournal.com/jrnl/art/thoughts-on-hybrid-conflict.
25 Bowers, Christopher O., "Identifying Emerging Hybrid Adversaries," *Parameters*, US Army War College, Spring 2012. Page 39. https://press.armywarcollege.edu/parameters/vol42/iss1/3/.
26 Ibid. Page 41.
27 Ibid.
28 Ibid. Page 45.
29 Ibid.

30 Ibid. Page 40.
31 Hammes, Thomas X., *The Sling and the Stone: On War in the 21st Century*. St. Paul, MN: Zenith Press, 2006. Page 2.
32 Lind, William S., Col. Keith Nightengale, Capt. John F. Schmitt, Col. Joseph W. Sutton, and Lt Col. Gary I. Wilson, "The Changing Face of War: Into the Fourth Generation," *Marine Corps Gazette*, October 1989. Page 23.
33 Ibid. Page 23.
34 Ibid.
35 Ibid. Page 22.
36 Ibid. Page 24.
37 Hammes, Thomas X., *The Sling and the Stone: On War in the 21st Century*. St. Paul, MN: Zenith Press, 2006. Page 2.
38 Ibid. Page 14.
39 Hammes, Thomas X., "War Evolves into the Fourth Generation," *Contemporary Security Policy*, Vol. 26, No. 2, 2005. Page 206.
40 Ibid.
41 Bunker, Robert J., "The Transition to Fourth Epoch War," *Marine Corps Gazette*, Vol. 78, No. 9, 1994. Page 22.
42 Ibid.
43 Ibid.
44 Ibid.
45 Ibid. Page 24.
46 Ibid.
47 Manwaring, Max G., "The New Global Security Landscape," in *Networks, Terrorism and Global Insurgency*, Robert J. Bunker (ed.). New York: Routledge, 2005. Page 30.
48 Ibid.
49 Ibid. See also: Bunker, Robert J., "Battlespace Dynamics, Information Warfare to Netwar, and Bond-Relationship Targeting," in *Non-State Threats and Future War*, Robert J. Bunker (ed.). London: Frank Cass, 2003. Page 97–107.
50 Manwaring and Hammes offer different definitions for 5GW. Manwaring believes that 5GW is in the realm of information and technology, while Hammes believes it is biological and chemical warfare. This is what Manwaring believes may be sixth-generation warfare (6GW): "elaborated on all the previous generations but emphasizes biological and informational methods to achieve desired ends." Examples of 6GW may include cyber attacks or the use of biological weapons in populated areas: "willingness to use 'unethical' bio-informational technology to disrupt, control or destroy an enemy. Thus, the lines between civilian and

military and lethal and nonlethal are eliminated, and the 'battlefield' is extended to everyone, everything and everywhere." See: Manwaring, Max G., "The New Global Security Landscape," in *Networks, Terrorism and Global Insurgency*, Robert J. Bunker (ed.). New York: Routledge, 2005. Pages 30–1.

51 Friedman, Thomas, "Beyond Fourth Generation Warfare," *ROA National Security Report*, September 2007.

52 Reed, Donald J., "Beyond the War on Terror: Into the Fifth Generation of War and Conflict," *Studies in Conflict & Terrorism*, Vol. 31, No. 8, August 14, 2008. Page 692.

53 Ibid.

54 Ibid. Page 705.

55 Ibid.

56 Katzman, Kenneth B., "Iran's Islamic Revolutionary Guard Corps: Radical Ideology Despite Institutionalization in the Islamic Republic." New York University, Dissertation, 1991. Page iii.

57 Ibid. Page iv.

58 Cordesman, Anthony H., "Iran's Military Forces: 1988–1993." Center for Strategic and International Studies (CSIS). September, 1994. Pages 30–1.

59 Ibid. Page 53. On 12 January 2016, ten US servicemen were detained by the IRGC Navy during a trip from Kuwait to Bahrain when the US ship neared too close to the Persian Gulf's Farsi Island, where Iran has a military installation. See: Lamothe, Dan, "Navy: 'Poorly Led and Unprepared' Sailors Were Detained by Iran after Multiple Errors," *The Washington Post,* June 30, 2016. https://www.washingtonpost.com/news/checkpoint/wp/2016/06/30/navy-poorly-led-and-unprepared-sailors-were-detained-by-iran-after-multiple-errors/.

60 Arjomand, Saïd Amir, *After Khomeini*. Oxford: Oxford University Press, 2009. Page 152.

61 Wehrey, Frederic, Jerrold D. Green, Brian Nichiporuk, Alireza Nader, Lydia Hansell, Rasool Nafisi, and S.R. Bohandy, "The Rise of the Pasdaran: Assessing the Domestic Role of Iran's Islamic Revolutionary Guard Corps," RAND Corp, prepared for the Office of the Secretary of Defense, 2009. Page 8. https://www.rand.org/pubs/monographs/MG821.html.

62 Ibid. Page 56.

63 Crist, David, *The Twilight War: The Secret History of America's Thirty-Year Conflict with Iran*. New York: Penguin Press, 2012. Page 6.

64 Sinkaya, Bayram, *Revolutionary Guards in Iranian Politics: Elites and Shifting Relations*. London: Routledge, 2016. Page 1.

65 Groh, Tyrone L, *Proxy War: The Least Bad Option*. Stanford, CA: Stanford University Press, 2019. Page 29.

66 Mumford, Andrew, "Proxy Warfare and the Future of Conflict," *RUSI Journal*, April/May 2013, Vol. 158, No. 2. Page 40.
67 Ibid.
68 Krieg, Andreas and Jean-Marc Rickli, *Surrogate Warfare: The Transformation of War in the Twenty-First Century*. Washington, DC: Georgetown University Press, 2020. Page 7.

Chapter 3

1 See: Ward, Steven M., *Immortal: A Military History of Iran and its Armed Forces*. Washington DC: Georgetown University Press, 2009. Page 226.
2 Author interview with Michael Eisenstadt, Kahn Fellow and director of The Washington Institute's Military and Security Studies Program.
3 Mostafa Chamran earned a Ph.D. in Physics from UC Berkeley. He taught at Berkeley and also worked at NASA's Jet Propulsion Laboratory (JPL) but returned to Iran to participate in the Iranian Revolution. He was the father of Iran's irregular warfare doctrine and had a particular interest in Lebanon. He died fighting in the Iran–Iraq War. For a contemporary reading of Chamran, see: "Revolutionaries for Life," by Maryam Alemzadeh in *Global 1979: Geographies and the Histories of the Iranian Revolution*. Cambridge: Cambridge University Press, 2021. Pages 178–210. See also: Crist, David, *The Twilight War: The Secret History of America's Thirty-Year Conflict with Iran*. Penguin Press, 2012. Pages 91–2.
4 Zabih, Sepehr, *The Iranian Military in Revolution*. New York: Routledge, 1988. Page 122.
5 Author interview with Barbara Slavin, Director of the Future of Iran Initiative and nonresident senior fellow at the Atlantic Council.
6 Hovsepian-Bearce, Yvette, *The Political Ideology of Ayatollah Khamenei: Out of the Mouth of the Supreme Leader of Iran*. Routledge, 2016. Page 54.
7 Ibid. Pages 150–1.
8 "Islamic Republic of Iran's Constitution of 1979 with Amendments through 1989," https://www.constituteproject.org/constitution/Iran_1989.pdf?lang=en.
9 Ibid.
10 Alexander, Yonah and Milton Hoenig, *The New Iranian Leadership: Ahmadinejad, Terrorism, Nuclear Ambition, and the Middle East*. Westport, CT: Praeger Security International, 2008. Page 19.

Notes

11 Alaei, Hossein, *Analytical History of the Iran-Iraq War,* Vol. 1, 2016. Farsi edition.

12 See: Cordesman, Anthony H., "Iran's Revolutionary Guards, the Al Quds Force, and Other Intelligence and Paramilitary Forces," Center for Strategic and International Studies (CSIS), August 16, 2007. https://www.csis.org/analysis/irans-revolutionary-guards-al-quds-force-and-other-intelligence-and-paramilitary-forces.

13 *The Quarterly Studies of the Iran–Iraq War,* Vol. 3, No. 9, Spring 2014, Research and Review at Sacred Defense, *The Holy Defense Research & Document Center.* Pages 124–30. Farsi edition.

14 Ibid.

15 Ibid.

16 Ibid.

17 See: Nadimi, Farzin, "Who is Iran's New Armed Forces Chief of Staff?" The Washington Institute for Near East Policy, July 5, 2016. https://www.washingtoninstitute.org/policy-analysis/who-irans-new-armed-forces-chief-staff.

18 See: Ministry of Defense Armed Forces and Logistics (MODAFL), Iran Watch, https://www.iranwatch.org/iranian-entities/ministry-defense-armed-forces-logistics-modafl.

19 See also: Wehrey, Frederic, Jerrold D. Green, Brian Nichiporuk, Alireza Nader, Lydia Hansell, Rasool Nafisi, and S.R. Bohandy, "The Rise of the Pasdaran: Assessing the Domestic Roles of Iran's Islamic Revolutionary Guard Corps." RAND Corporation, 2009. Pages 8–9. Rand.org/pubs/monogrpahs/MG821.html.

20 See: Sofaer, Abraham, D., *Taking on Iran: Strength, Diplomacy, and the Iranian Threat.* Stanford, CA: Hoover Institution Press, 2013.

21 Edelman, Eric S. and Whitney Morgan McNamara, "Contain, Degrade, and Defeat: A Defense Strategy for a Troubled Middle East," Center for Strategic and Budgetary Assessments, 2017. Page 51. https://csbaonline.org/research/publications/contain-degrade-and-defeat-a-defense-strategy-for-a-troubled-middle-east.

22 Ibid.

23 See: Carl, Nicholas, Kitaneh Fitzpatrick, Zachary Coles, and Frederick Kagan, "Iran Crisis Update," Critical Threats Project (CTP), November 17, 2022. https://www.criticalthreats.org/analysis/iran-crisis-update-november-17.

24 O'Hern, Steven, *Iran's Revolutionary Guard: The Threat that Grows while America Sleeps.* Dulles, VA: Potomac Books, 2012. Page 72.

25 Alfoneh, Ali, *Iran Unveiled: How the Revolutionary Guards is Turning Theocracy into Military Dictatorship.* Washington, DC: AEI Press, 2013.
26 See: Cummings, Michael and Eric Cummings, "The Costs of War with Iran: An Intelligence Preparation of the Battlefield," *Small Wars Journal,* August 31, 2012. http://smallwarsjournal.com/jrnl/art/the-costs-of-war-with-iran-an-intelligence-preparation-of-the-battlefield.
27 Congressionally Directed Action (CDA), "Unclassified Report on Military Power of Iran," April, 2010. https://man.fas.org/eprint/dod_iran_2010.pdf.
28 Bunker, Robert J. and Hakim Hazim, "Are We Prematurely Designating Iran's Revolutionary Guards as Criminal Soldiers?" *Small Wars Journal,* September 5, 2007. http://smallwarsjournal.com/blog/are-we-prematurely-designating-irans-revolutionary-guards-as-criminal-soldiers.
29 State Sponsors of Terrorism Overview, Bureau of Counterterrorism, Country Reports on Terrorism, US Department of State. https://www.state.gov/j/ct/rls/crt/2014/239410.htm.
30 Sofaer, Abraham D., "Taking on Iran: Strength, Diplomacy, and the Iranian Threat," Hoover Institution Press, 2013. Page 30. See also, *Brewer v Islamic Republic of Iran,* 664 F. Supp. 2d 43 (DC Cir. 2009), http://docs.justia.com/cases/federal/district-courts/district-of-columbia/dcdce/1:2008cv00534/130417/20/0.pdf.
31 Ibid. See also, *Welch v Islamic Republic of Iran,* https://www.gpo.gov/fdsys/pkg/USCOURTS-dcd-1_01-cv-00863/pdf/USCOURTS-dcd-1_01-cv-00863-1.pdf.
32 For additional information on the Marine barracks bombing, US Embassy annex in Beirut, the AMIA attack and the Khobar Towers bombing, see: Levitt, matthew, *Hezbollah: The Global Footprint of Lebanon's Party of God.* Washington, DC: Georgetown University Press, 2013.
33 See, "An Open Letter: The Hizballah Program," *The Jerusalem Quarterly,* No. 48, Fall, 1988. https://web.archive.org/web/20060821215729/http://www.ict.org/il/Articles/Hiz_letter.htm.
34 Rafighdoost, Mohsen, *Baraye Tareekh Megooyam (For History),* 2015. Farsi edition.
35 Congressionally Directed Action (CDA), "Unclassified Report on Military Power of Iran," April, 2010. https://man.fas.org/eprint/dod_iran_2010.pdf.
36 Ibid.
37 Ibid.
38 Katzman, Kenneth, *Iran's Influence in Iraq,* CRS Report RS73938, September 29, 2006, http://fpc.state.gov/documents/organization/73938.pdf; see also, 2009

report: Kenneth Katzman, *Iran–Iraq Relations,* CRS, Report RS22323, August 13, 2010, http://www.fas.org/sgp/crs/mideast/RS22323.pdf.

39 O'Keefe, Ed and Joby Warrick, "Weapons Prove Iranian Role in Iraq, US says," *Washington Post,* July 5, 2011, http://www.washingtonpost.com/world/war-zones/weapons-prove-iranian-role-in-iraq-us-says/2011/07/05/gHQAUnkmzH_story.html.

40 See, "US Concerned Iran Providing Weapons to Iraq Militants," Reuters in *Haaretz,* July 11, 2011, http://www.haaretz.com/news/middle-east/u-s-concerned-iran-providing-weapons-to-iraq-militants-1.372670.

41 Congressionally Directed Action (CDA), "Unclassified Report on Military Power of Iran," April, 2010, https://man.fas.org/eprint/dod_iran_2010.pdf.

42 See: Felter, Joseph, and Brian Fishman, "Iranian Strategy in Iraq: Politics and Other Means," Combating Terrorism Center at US Military Academy, West Point, October 13, 2008, http://www.ctc.usma.edu/wp-content/uploads/2010/06/Iranian-Strategy-in-Iraq.pdf.

43 See: Harari, Michael, "Status Update: Shia Militias in Iraq," *Institute for the Study of War,* August 16, 2010; Knights, Michael, "The Evolution of Iran's Special Groups in Iraq," Combating Terrorism Center (CTC) at West Point, Vol. 3, Nos. 11–12, November 2010; and Smyth, Phillip, "From Karbala to Sayyida Zaynab: Iraqi Fighters in Syria's Shia Militias," Combating Terrorism Center (CTC) at West Point, Vol. 6, No. 8, August 2013.

44 Rubin, Michael, "Iran's Basij Recruiting for Syria Fight," American Enterprise Institute (AEI), March 1, 2016, https://www.aei.org/articles/irans-basij-recruiting-for-syria-fight/.

45 "Fact Sheet: Designation of Iranian Entities and Individuals for Proliferation Activities and Support for Terrorism," US Department of the Treasury, October 25, 2007, https://www.treasury.gov/press-center/press-releases/Pages/hp644.aspx.

46 Ibid.

47 Ibid.

48 Katzman, Kenneth, "Iran, Gulf Security, and US Policy," Congressional Research Service. Washington DC, May 28, 2015. Page 32.

49 Ibid. Page 34.

50 See: Mansuri, Javad, *Oral History of Establishment of the Islamic Revolutionary Guards (Tareekh-e Shafaee Tasees-e Sepah-e Pasdaran),* Markaz-e Asnad Enqelab-e Eslami (Center for Islamic Revolutionary Documents), June 2014. Page 15. Farsi edition.

51 Ward, Steven M., *Immortal: A Military History of Iran and its Armed Forces*. Washington, DC: Georgetown University Press, 2009. Page 226.
52 O'Hern, Steven, *Iran's Revolutionary Guard: The Threat that Grows while America Sleeps*. Dulles, VA: Potomac Books, 2012. Page 11.
53 Author interview with Michael Eisenstadt.
54 Alfoneh, Ali, *Iran Unveiled: How the Revolutionary Guards is Turning Theocracy into Military Dictatorship*. Washington, DC: AEI Press, 2013. Page 17.

Chapter 4

1 Bowers, Christopher O., "Identifying Emerging Hybrid Adversaries," *Parameters*, US Army War College, Spring 2012. https://press.armywarcollege.edu/parameters/vol42/iss1/3/.
2 Ibid.
3 Katzman, Kenneth, *The Warriors of Islam: Iran's Revolutionary Guard*. Boulder, CO: Westview Press, 1993. Page 85. See also: Zabih, Sepehr, *The Iranian Military in Revolution and War*. New York: Routledge, 1988.
4 See: Razoux, Pierre, *The Iran–Iraq War*, trans. Nicholas Elliott. Cambridge, MA: The Belknap Press of Harvard University, 2015.
5 Archival material from Iran's Holy Defense Research and Document Center can be found here: https://www.persianarchive.com/publisher/holy-defense-research-document-center/.
6 "The Quarterly Studies of Iran–Iraq War," Vol. 3, No. 9, Spring 2014. Research Review at Sacred Defense, The Holy Defense Research and Document Center. https://hds.sndu.ac.ir.
7 Crist, David, *The Twilight War: The Secret History of America's Thirty-Year Conflict with Iran*. New York: Penguin Press, 2012. Page 122.
8 See: Rose, Gregory F., "The Post-Revolutionary Purge of Iran's Armed Forces: A Revisionist Assessment," *Iranian Studies*, Vol. 17, No. 2/3, 1984. Page 183.
9 Hossein Alaei is believed to be the founding commander of the IRGC Navy and one of its key strategists. See: Haghshenass Fariborz, "Iran's Asymmetric Naval Warfare," The Washington Institute for Near East Studies, Policy Focus #87, September 2008. Alaei is also a professor at the Imam Hossein University and frequently writes for the *Scientific Quarterly Journal of Holy Defense Studies*, https://hds.sndu.ac.ir/?lang=en.
10 Alaei, Hossein, *Analytical History of the Iran-Iraq War*, Vol. 1, 2016.

11 Ibid.
12 Rafighdoost, Mohsen, *For History* (in Farsi, گویم می تاریخ برای) 2015.
13 See: Ward, Steven R., *Immortal, Updated Edition: A Military History of Iran and its Armed Forces*. Washington, DC: Georgetown University Press, 2014.
14 "Iran's Revolutionary Guard: Armed Pillar of the Islamic Republic," Central Intelligence Agency (CIA), January 1987. Declassified in Part—Sanitized Copy Approved for Release 2012/05/08. Page 11. https://www.cia.gov/readingroom/document/cia-rdp06t00412r000606580001-5.
15 See: Alfoneh, Ali, "Eternal Rivals? The Artesh and the IRGC," *Middle East Institute*, November 15, 2011. https://www.mei.edu/publications/eternal-rivals-artesh-and-irgc.
16 "Iran's Revolutionary Guard: Armed Pillar of the Islamic Republic," Central Intelligence Agency (CIA), January 1987. Declassified in Part—Sanitized Copy Approved for Release 2012/05/08. Pages 7–8. https://www.cia.gov/readingroom/document/cia-rdp06t00412r000606580001-5.
17 See: Alfoneh, Ali, "Eternal Rivals? The Artesh and the IRGC," Middle East Institute, November 15, 2011. https://www.mei.edu/publications/eternal-rivals-artesh-and-irgc.
18 See: Wilson, Ben, "The Evolution of Iranian Warfighting during the Iran–Iraq War," *Foreign Military Studies Office*, July 1, 2007. https://community.apan.org/wg/tradoc-g2/fmso/m/fmso-monographs/241822.
19 See: Connell, Michael, "Iran's Military Doctrine," *Iran Primer*, October 21, 2010. https://www.Iranprimer.usip.org/resource/irans-military-doctrine.
20 Byman, Daniel, Shahram Chubin, Anoushiravan Ehteshami, and Jerrold D. Green, *Iran's Security Policy in the Post-Revolutionary Era*. RAND Corp, 2001. https://www.rand.org/content/dam/rand/pubs/monograph_reports/MR1320/RAND_MR1320.pdf.
21 See: Cordesman, Anthony H., "The Lessons of Modern War—Volume II—The Iran–Iraq War" (Chapter 2: The Conditions that Shaped the Iran–Iraq War), Center for Strategic and International Studies, May 1, 1990. https://www.csis.org/analysis/lessons-modern-war-volume-ii-iran-iraq-war-%E2%80%93-chapter-2-conditions-shaped-iran-iraq-war.
22 See: Ward, Steven R., *Immortal, Updated Edition: A Military History of Iran and its Armed Forces*. Washington, DC: Georgetown University Press, 2014.
23 See: Byman, Daniel, et al., *Iran's Security Policy in the Post-Revolutionary Era*. RAND Corp, 2001. https://www.rand.org/content/dam/rand/pubs/monograph_reports/MR1320/RAND_MR1320.pdf. Page 54.

24 Ibid.
25 See: Ward, Steven R., *Immortal, Updated Edition: A Military History of Iran and its Armed Forces*. Washington, DC: Georgetown University Press, 2014.
26 "Iran's Revolutionary Guard: Armed Pillar of the Islamic Republic," Central Intelligence Agency (CIA), January 1987. Declassified in Part—Sanitized Copy Approved for Release 2012/05/08. Page 10–11. https://www.cia.gov/readingroom/document/cia-rdp06t00412r000606580001-5.
27 See: Wilson, Ben, "The Evolution of Iranian Warfighting during the Iran–Iraq War," Foreign Military Studies Office, July 1, 2007. https://community.apan.org/wg/tradoc-g2/fmso/m/fmso-monographs/241822.
28 See: Murray, Williamson and Kevin M. Woods, *The Iran–Iraq War: A Military and Strategic History*. Cambridge: Cambridge University Press, 2014. Page 210.
29 Ibid. Page 176.
30 See: Wilson, Ben, "The Evolution of Iranian Warfighting during the Iran–Iraq War," Foreign Military Studies Office, July 1, 2007. https://community.apan.org/wg/tradoc-g2/fmso/m/fmso-monographs/241822.
31 See: Edelman, Eric S. and Whitney Morgan McNamara, "Contain, Degrade, and Defeat: A Defense Strategy for a Troubled Middle East," Center for Strategic and Budgetary Assessments, 2017.
32 See: Wilson, Ben, "The Evolution of Iranian Warfighting during the Iran–Iraq War," Foreign Military Studies Office, July 1, 2007. https://community.apan.org/wg/tradoc-g2/fmso/m/fmso-monographs/241822.
33 See: French, Spencer Lawrence, "Embracing Asymmetry: Assessing Iranian National Security Strategy, 1983–1987," *Joint Force Quarterly (JFQ)*, Issue 101, 2nd Quarter, 2021. Page 74.
34 For the most detailed view of The Tanker War, see: Zatarain, Lee Allen, *America's First Clash with Iran, 1987–1988*. Havertown, PA: Casemate Publishers, 2008.
35 See: Nadia el-Sayed El Shazly, "Iran's Silent Force and the US Navy Take Center Stage," in *The Gulf Tanker War: Iran and Iraq's Maritime Swordplay*. London: Palgrave Macmillan, 1998. Pages 260–304.
36 See: French, Spencer Lawrence, "Embracing Asymmetry: Assessing Iranian National Security Strategy, 1983–1987," in *JFQ*, Issue 101, 2nd Quarter, 2021. Page 73.
37 See: El Shazly, Nadia el-Sayed, "Iran's Silent Force and the US Navy Take Center Stage," in *The Gulf Tanker War: Iran and Iraq's Maritime Swordplay*. London: Palgrave Macmillan, 1998. Pages 260–304.

38 Connell, Michael, "Iran's Military Doctrine," *The Iran Primer,* October 11, 2010. https://iranprimer.usip.org/resource/irans-military-doctrine.

39 See: El Shazly, Nadia el-Sayed "Iran's Silent Force and the US Navy Take Center Stage," in *The Gulf Tanker War: Iran and Iraq's Maritime Swordplay.* London: Palgrave Macmillan, 1998. Pages 260–304.

40 Connell, Michael, "Iran's Military Doctrine," *The Iran Primer,* October 11, 2010. https://iranprimer.usip.org/resource/irans-military-doctrine.

41 Ibid.

42 See: Kirkpatrick, David D., Richard Pérez-Peña, and Stanley Reed, "Tankers Are Attacked in Mideast, and US Says Video Shows Iran Was Involved," *New York Times,* June 13, 2019. https://www.nytimes.com/2019/06/13/world/middleeast/oil-tanker-attack-gulf-oman.html.

43 For more on Iran's operational losses, see: Cordesman, Anthony H., "Iran's Military Forces: 1988–1993," Center for Strategic and International Studies (CSIS), September 1994. Page 30.

44 Smith, Ben, "The Quds Force of the Iranian Revolutionary Guard," International Affairs and Defence Section, October 30, 2007. https://researchbriefings.files.parliament.uk/documents/SN04494/SN04494.pdf.

45 Murray, Williamson and Kevin M. Woods, *The Iran–Iraq War: A Military and Strategic History,* Cambridge: Cambridge University Press, 2014. Page 338.

46 "Iran's Revolutionary Guard: Armed Pillar of the Islamic Republic," Central Intelligence Agency (CIA), January 1987. Declassified in Part—Sanitized Copy Approved for Release 2012/05/08. Page iii. https://www.cia.gov/readingroom/document/cia-rdp06t00412r000606580001-5.

Chapter 5

1 See: Golkar, Saeid, "The Supreme Leader and the Guard: Civil–Military Relations and Regime Survival in Iran," The Washington Institute for Near East Policy, 2019. https://www.washingtoninstitute.org/policy-analysis/supreme-leader-and-guard-civil-military-relations-and-regime-survival-iran.

2 Author interview with Ali Alfoneh, Senior Fellow at the Arab Gulf States Institute in Washington.

3 Brooks, Risa A., "Integrating the Civil–Military Relations Subfield," in *Annual Review of Political Science,* January 30, 2019. Page 391.

4 Ibid.

5 Ibid. Page 392.
6 Hashim, Ahmed S., "Civil-Military Relations in Iran: Internal and External Pressures," *Middle East Policy*, Vol. 25, No.3, Autumn 2018. Page 51.
7 See Wehrey, et al., page 78, and Hamid Ansari, "Imam Khomeini's Direct Order and Testaments to the Armed Forces," November 26, 2007.
8 Hashim. Page 49.
9 Ibid. Page 51.
10 Cordesman, Anthony H., *Iran's Military Forces in Transition: Conventional Threats and Weapons of Mass Destruction*. Westport, CT: Praeger Publishers, 1999. Page 32.
11 Vatanka, Alex, *The Battle of the Ayatollahs in Iran: The United States, Foreign Policy, and Political Rivalry Since 1979*. London: Bloomsbury Publishing, 2021. Page 88.
12 Hashim. Page 52.
13 Slavin, Barbara, *Bitter Friends, Bosom Enemies: Iran, the US, and the Twisted Path to Confrontation*. New York: St. Martin's Griffin, 2009. Page 69.
14 Golkar, Saeid, "Configuration of Political Elites in Post-Revolutionary Iran," *The Brown Journal of World Affairs*, Fall/Winter 2016, Vol. 23, Issue 1. Page 283.
15 Ibid. Page 284.
16 See Saïd Amir Arjomand, *After Khomeini*. Oxford: Oxford University Press, 2009. Page 60.
17 Ibid. Page 32.
18 Khatam al-Anbia was sanctioned by the US Department of the Treasury in 2007. Additional sanctions were implemented against several Khatam al-Anbia subsidiaries. For more information, see: Fact Sheet: Designation of Iranian Entities and Individuals for Proliferation Activities and Support for Terrorism, October 25, 2007. https://home.treasury.gov/news/press-releases/hp644.
19 See Arjomand. Page 60.
20 Hashim. Page 55.
21 Harris, Kevan, "The Rise of the Subcontractor State: Politics of Pseudo-Privatization in the Islamic Republic of Iran," *International Journal of Middle East Studies*, Vol. 45, 2013. Page 63.
22 See Arjomand. Page 57.
23 See: Vatanka, Alex, *The Battle of the Ayatollahs in Iran: The United States, Foreign Policy, and Political Rivalry since 1979*. London: Bloomsbury Publishing, 2021. Page 106.

24 Forozan, Hesam and Afshin Shahi, "The Military and the State in Iran: The Economic Rise of the Revolutionary Guards," *Middle East Journal*, Vol. 71, No. 1, Winter 2017. Page 74.
25 Ostovar, Afshon, *Vanguard of the Imam: Religion, Politics, and Iran's Revolutionary Guards*. Oxford: Oxford University Press, 2016. Pages 143–4.
26 Ibid. Page 144.
27 Ibid. Page 145.
28 Ibid. Page 146.
29 See: Arjomand. Page 59.
30 Ali Shamkhani was an early IRGC commander in 1988, and later commander of the IRGC Navy. He was also Iran's defense minister between 1997 and 2005. Shamkhani is currently Iran's Supreme National Security Council (SNSC) Secretary, a position he has held since his appointment in 2013 under former Iranian President Hasan Rouhani.
31 Hashim, Ahmed S., "Civil–Military Relations in Iran: Internal and External Pressures," *Middle East Policy*, Vol. 25, No.3, Autumn 2018. Page 58.
32 Ibid. Page 55.
33 See: Forozan and Shahi, 2017. Page 76.
34 See: Golkar, Saeid, "Configuration of Political Elites in Post-Revolutionary Iran," *The Brown Journal of World Affairs*, Fall/Winter 2016, Vol. 23, Issue 1. Page 286.
35 Ibid.
36 Ostovar. Page 154.
37 Ostovar. Page 156.
38 Vatanka. Page 139.
39 See: Geranmayeh, Ellie, "Reviving the Revolutionaries: How Trump's Maximum Pressure is Shifting Iran's Domestic Politics," European Council on Foreign Relations, June 23, 2020. https://ecfr.eu/publication/reviving_the_revolutionaries_how_trumps_maximum_pressure_is_shifting_irans/.
40 See: Wehrey, et al., "The Rise of the Pasdaran: Assessing the Domestic Roles of Iran's Islamic Revolutionary Guards Corps," RAND, 2009. https://www.rand.org/pubs/monographs/MG821.html.
41 Ibid.
42 See: Rizvi, M.A., "Evaluating the Political and Economic Role of the IRGC," *Strategic Analysis*, Vol. 36, No. 4. Page 584.
43 Eisenstadt, Michael, "Iranian Military Power: Capabilities and Intentions," The Washington Institute for Near East Studies, Policy Papers, Number 42, 1996. Page 38. https://www.washingtoninstitute.org/policy-analysis/iranian-

military-power-capabilities-and-intentions. See also: Vaziri, Haleh, "The Islamic Republic's Policy in the Persian Gulf: Who's Containing Whom, How, and Why?" *Middle East Insight,* Vol. 11, No. 5, July–August 1995.

44 Special thanks to Ambassador James Jeffrey for this point in an author interview.

Chapter 6

1 "Pasdaran" is a term in Farsi used for the IRGC.
2 Ward, Steven R., *Immortal: A Military History of Iran and its Armed Forces.* Washington, DC: Georgetown University Press, 2009. Page 308.
3 Alexander, Jonah and Milton Hoenig, *The New Iranian Leadership: Ahmadinejad, Terrorism, Nuclear Ambition, and the Middle East.* Westport, CT: Praeger Security International, 2008. Page viii.
4 See: Golkar, Saeid, "Configuration of Political Elites in Post-Revolutionary Iran," *Brown Journal of World Affairs,* Fall/Winter 2016, Vol. 23, No 1. Pages 286–8.
5 Hashim, Ahmed S., "Civil Military Relations in Iran: Internal and External Pressures," *Middle East Policy Council*, Vol. 25, No. 3, Autumn 2018. Page 59.
6 See Constitution of the Islamic Republic of Iran, http://www.moi.ir/Portal/File/ShowFile.aspx?ID=ab40c7a6-af7d-4634-af93-40f2f3a04acf (in Farsi); http://www.iranonline.com/iran/iran-info/government/constitution.html (in English).
7 "Islamic Republic of Iran's Constitution of 1979 with Amendments through 1989," https://www.constituteproject.org/constitution/Iran_1989.pdf?lang=en.
8 O'Hern, Steven, *Iran's Revolutionary Guard: The Threat that Grows While America Sleeps.* Dulles, VA: Potomac Books, 2012. Page 127.
9 Ibid.
10 Arjomand, Saïd Amir, *After Khomeini.* Oxford: Oxford University Press, 2009. Page 153.
11 Alfoneh, Ali, *Political Succession in the Islamic Republic of Iran: Demise of the Clergy and the Rise of the Islamic Revolutionary Guard Corps.* Washington, DC: Arab Gulf States Institute,2020. Page 123.
12 Ibid.
13 Ibid.
14 Khoshnood, Ardavan, "The Khatam al-Anbiya Camp and the Future of the Revolutionary Guards' Empire," The Begin-Sadat Center for Strategic Studies (BESA), No. 2, 014. May 3, 2021. https://besacenter.org/wp-content/uploads/2021/05/2014-khatam-al-anbiya-camp-and-revolutionary-guards-khoshnood-final.pdf.

15 See also: Khajehpour, Brian, "The Real Footprint of the IRGC in Iran's Economy," *Al Monitor*, August 9, 2017. https://www.al-monitor.com/originals/2017/08/iran-irgc-economy-footprint-khatam-olanbia.html.
16 See: https://www.iranwatch.org/iranian-entities/national-iranian-oil-company.
17 "Khatam al-Anbiya Construction Headquarters," *Iran Watch*, Wisconsin Project on Nuclear Arms Control, updated January 19, 2021. https://www.iranwatch.org/iranian-entities/khatam-al-anbiya-construction-headquarters-kaa.
18 See: Worldwide Ballistic Missile Inventories, https://www.armscontrol.org/factsheets/missiles and Missile Threat and Proliferation, https://missiledefenseadvocacy.org/missile-threat-and-proliferation/todays-missile-threat/iran/fateh-110/ and SS-1 "Scud," https://missilethreat.csis.org/missile/scud/.
19 Subsidiaries include Fater Institute, Garagahe Sazandegi Ghaem (GHAEM), Ghorb Karbal, Imensazan Consultant Engineers Institute (ICEI), Makin, Oriental Oil Kish (OOK), Rah Sahel, Rahab Engineering Institute, Sepanir, and Sepasad Engineering Company. See, *Iran Watch*, http://www.iranwatch.org/sites/default/files/khatam_al_anbia.jpg.
20 Ibid. Pages 44–8.
21 Arjomand, Saïd Amir, *After Khomeini*. Oxford: Oxford University Press, 2009. Page 60.
22 Wehrey, Frederic, Jerrold D. Green, Brian Nichiporuk, Alireza Nader, Lydia Hansell, Rasool Nafisi, and S.R. Bohandy, "The Rise of the Pasdaran: Assessing the Domestic Role of Iran's Islamic Revolutionary Guard Corps." RAND Corp, prepared for the Office of the Secretary of Defense, 2009. Pages 60–1.
23 Ibid.
24 See: Rubenfeld, Samuel, "Iran Business Prospects Complicated by Revolutionary Guard," *Wall Street Journal*, November 30, 2015. https://www.wsj.com/articles/BL-252B-8793.
25 Ghazvinian, John, *America and Iran: A History, 1720 to the Present*, New York: Alfred Knopf, 2021. Page 437.
26 Ibid.
27 *Iran Watch*, Khatam al-Anbia. http://www.iranwatch.org/sites/default/files/khatam_al_anbia.jpg.
28 "Khatam al-Anbiya Construction Headquarters," *Iran Watch*, Wisconsin Project on Nuclear Arms Control, updated January 19, 2021. https://www.iranwatch.org/iranian-entities/khatam-al-anbiya-construction-headquarters-kaa. See also: Wehrey, Frederic, Jerrold D. Green, Brian Nichiporuk, Alireza Nader, Lydia Hansell, Rasool Nafisi, and S.R. Bohandy, "The Rise of the Pasdaran: Assessing

the Domestic Role of Iran's Islamic Revolutionary Guard Corps," RAND Corp, prepared for the Office of the Secretary of Defense, 2009.

29   Executive Order 13382, "Blocking Property of Weapons of Mass Destruction Proliferators and Their Supporters." https://home.treasury.gov/system/files/126/wmd.pdf.

30   "Executive Order 13438: Blocking Property of Certain Persons who Threaten Stabilization Efforts in Iraq," Congressional Research Service, Updated January 24, 2014. https://crsreports.congress.gov/product/pdf/RL/RL34254/15.

31   CISADA was the first most comprehensive sanctions policy against Iran, signed into law by President Obama on July 1, 2010, which builds on United Nations Security Council Resolution (UNSCR) 1929. UNSCR 1929 targeted asset-freezing provisions to prevent financial services that could extend to Iran's nuclear ambitions. For more information on CISADA, see: "CISADA: The New US Sanctions on Iran," US Department of the Treasury, https://home.treasury.gov/system/files/126/CISADA_english.pdf.

32   For more information on EO 13574, see: "Executive Order 13574 Concerning Further Sanctions on Iran," https://obamawhitehouse.archives.gov/the-press-office/2011/05/23/executive-order-13574-concerning-further-sanctions-iran.

33   For more information on EO 13581, see: "Transnational Criminal Organizations Sanctions Regulations," Office of Foreign Assets Control, US Department of the Treasury, https://home.treasury.gov/system/files/126/fr_tco_2022-01072.pdf.

34   For more information on EO 13590, see: "Executive Order 13590—Iran Sanctions," November 21, 2011. https://obamawhitehouse.archives.gov/the-press-office/2011/11/21/executive-order-13590-iran-sanctions.

35   For more information on EO 13599, see: "Executive Order 13599 of February 5, 2012, Blocking Property of the Government of Iran and Iranian Financial Institutions," US Department of the Treasury, https://home.treasury.gov/system/files/126/iran_eo_02062012.pdf.

36   Slavin, Barbara, "Ahmadinejad's Swan Song: 'Wherever I am, Politics Will Follow,'" *Al-Monitor,* September 25, 2012. https://www.al-monitor.com/orginals/2012/al-monitor/politics-and-controversy-follow.html.

37   Ibid.

38   Author interview with Director, Iran Initiative and nonresident senior fellow at the Atlantic Council, Barbara Slavin.

39   Ibid.

40   Masters, Jonathan, "CFR Backgrounders: Hizballah." Updated January 3, 2014. Page 3. http://www.cfr.org/lebanon/Hizballah-k-hizbollah-hizbullah/p9155.

41 Ibid. Page 5.
42 See: Islamic Republic of Iran: Estimations on Smuggling of Goods, International Monetary Fund, https://www.imf.org/en/Data/Statistics/informal-economy-data/Reports/Iran-Estimations-on-Smuggling-of-Goods and Bill Samii, "Analysis: Goods Smuggling Highlights Economic Problems in Iran," Radio Free Europe/Radio Liberty, January 7, 2005. https://www.rferl.org/a/1056740.html.
43 Hoffman, Frank G., "The Hybrid Character of Modern Conflict," *Hybrid Warfare and Transnational Threats: Perspectives for an Era of Persistent Conflict*, Paul Brister, William H. Natter, III, and Robert R. Tomes (eds.). New York: Council for Emerging National Security Affairs, 2011. Page 45.
44 Author interview with Peter R. Mansoor, General Raymond E. Major Jr. Chair in Military History at Ohio State University.

Chapter 7

1 Author interview with Michael Eisenstadt, Kahn Fellow and Director of the Washington Institute for Near East Studies' Military and Security Studies Program.
2 See: Connell, Michael, "Iran's Military Doctrine," *Iran Primer,* October 21, 2010. www.Iranprimer.usip.org/resource/irans-military-doctrine.
3 Department of Justice, "Mansoor Arabsiar Sentenced in New York City Federal Court to 25 Years in Prison for Conspiring with Iranian Military Officials to Assassinate the Saudi Arabian Ambassador to the United States." May 30, 2013. http://www.justice.gov/opa/pr/manssor-arabsiar-sentenced-new-york-city-federal-court-25-years-prison-conspiring-iranian.
4 See also: Nakissa Jahanbani, "Beyond Soleimani: Implications for Iran's Proxy Network in Iraq and Syria," Combating Terrorism Center, January 10, 2020. https://ctc.usma.edu/beyond-soleimani-implications-irans-proxy-network-iraq-syria.
5 Crist, David, *The Twilight War: The Secret History of America's Thirty-Year Conflict with Iran*. New York: Penguin Press, 2012. Page 397.
6 See: DIA, "Iran Military Power: Ensuring Regime Survival and Securing Regional Dominance," 2019. https://www.dia.mil/Portals/110/Images/News/Military_Powers_Publications/Iran_Military_Power_LR.pdf. Page 23.
7 Crist, David, *The Twilight War: The Secret History of America's Thirty-Year Conflict with Iran*. New York: Penguin Press, 2012. Page 460.

8   See: Raine, John, "Iran, Its Partners, and the Balance of Effective Force," *War on the Rocks*, March 18, 2020. https://warontherocks.com/2020/03/iran-its-partners-and-the-balance-of-effective-force.

9   Eisenstadt, Michael, "Iranian Military Power: Capabilities and Intentions," The Washington Institute for Near East Studies, Policy Papers, No. 42, 1996. Page 68.

10 Ibid.

11 Author interview with Michael Eisenstadt.

12 See: DIA "Iran Military Power," 2019.

13 تدوین راهبردهای کلان جنگ ترکیبی, "Developing macro strategies for hybrid warfare," Scientific Quarterly Journal of Defense Strategy. 17 Khordad 1395 (June 6, 2016). Page 3. https://www.sid.ir%2Ffa%2Fjournal%2FViewPaper.aspx%3FID%3D2793 19&psig=AOvVaw0hP5uC6tMERvDqydK2nzu4&ust=1669687464268956.

14 Ibid. Page 6.

15 See: Connell, Michael, "The Artesh Navy: Iran's Strategic Force," *Center for Naval Analysis*, January 31, 2012. https://www.mei.edu/publications/artesh-navy-irans-strategic-force.

16 See: "United States Prevails in Actions to Seize and Forfeit Iranian Terror Group's Missiles and Petroleum," Department of Justice, December 7, 2021. https://www.justice.gov/opa/pr/united-states-prevails-actions-seize-and-forfeit-iranian-terror-group-s-missiles-and.

17 تدوین راهبردهای کلان جنگ ترکیبی, "Developing macro strategies for hybrid warfare," Scientific Quarterly Journal of Defense Strategy. 17 Khordad 1395 (June 6, 2016). Page 7. https://www.sid.ir%2Ffa%2Fjournal%2FViewPaper.aspx%3FID%3D2793 19&psig=AOvVaw0hP5uC6tMERvDqydK2nzu4&ust=1669687464268956.

18 Ibid. Page 13.

19 Author interview with Senior Historian to the Joint Chiefs of Staff, David Crist.

20 Author interview with Ambassador James Jeffrey.

21 Jenkins, Brian Michael, "New Modes of Conflict," prepared for the Defense Nuclear Agency, 1983. Page vi.

22 See: Bunker, Robert J., and Alma Keshavarz, "'Made in Yemen:' Houthi Exhibition Showcase New Drones, Missiles, and Naval Mines," *Small Wars Journal*, April 8, 2021. https://smallwarsjournal.com/jrnl/art/made-yemen-houthi-exhibition-showcase-new-drones-missiles-and-naval-mines.

23 See: Jones, Seth G., Jared Thompson, Danielle Ngo, Brian McSorley, and Joseph S. Bermudez Jr., "The Iranian and Houthi War against Saudi Arabia," CSIS, December 2021. https://www.csis.org/analysis/iranian-and-houthi-war-against-saudi-arabia.

24 A special thanks to Director, Future of Iran Initiative at the Atlantic Council Barbara Slavin on clarifying the differences between proxies and partners, which helped shape this argument. Author interview with Slavin.
25 For more information on the GCC, see: Secretariat General of the Gulf Cooperation Council, The Cooperation Council for the Arab States of the Gulf. https://www.gcc-sg.org/en-us/AboutGCC/MemberStates/pages/Home.aspx
26 Author interview with Michael Connell, Center for Naval Analysis (CNA) expert in Persian-Gulf security-related issues, the armed forces of Iran, US-GCC security cooperation, and adversary cyber policy and strategy.
27 Rice, Condoleezza, Opening Remarks before the Senate Foreign Relations Committee, October 19, 2005. https://2001-2009.state.gov/secretary/rm/2005/55303.htm.
28 Ibid.
29 Author interview with Peter R. Mansoor, General Raymond E. Major Jr. Chair in Military History at Ohio State University.
30 Rayburn, Joel D., Frank K. Sobchak (eds.), "The US Army in the Iraq War: Vol. 1, 2003–2006," US Army War College, January 2019. Pages 74–5. https://apps.dtic.mil/sti/pdfs/AD1066345.pdf.
31 Ibid. Page 187.
32 Author interview with Senior Department of Defense official.
33 Rayburn, Joel D., Frank K. Sobchak (eds.), "The US Army in the Iraq War: Vol. 2, Surge and Withdrawal," US Army War College, January 2019. https://press.armywarcollege.edu/monographs/940/.
34 Remarks by the President in Address to the Nation on the End of Combat Operations in Iraq, August 31, 2010. https://obamawhitehouse.archives.gov/the-press-office/2010/08/31/remarks-president-address-nation-end-combat-operations-iraq.
35 The US Army in the Iraq War: Vol. 1, 2003–2006. Joel D. Rayburn, Frank K. Sobchak (eds.). US Army War College, January 2019. Page 269.
36 Author interview with Senior Historian to the Joint Chiefs of Staff, David Crist.
37 Shahrudi was a senior Iranian cleric who was widely believed to be Khamenei's successor. See: Lim, Kevjn, "Iran's Next Supreme Leader is Dead," *Foreign Policy*, January 10, 2019. https://foreignpolicy.com/2019/01/10/irans-next-supreme-leader-is-dead.
38 Levy, Ido, "Shia Militias and Exclusionary Politics in Iraq," *Middle East Policy Council*, 2019. https://mepc.org/journal/shia-militias-and-exclusionary-politics-iraq.

39 Eisenstadt, Michael, Michael Knights, and Ahmed Ali, "Iran's Influence in Iraq: Countering Tehran's Whole-of-Government Approach," Washington Institute for Near East Studies, Policy Focus #111, April 2011. Page 3. https://www.washingtoninstitute.org/media/3364.
40 Mapping Militant Organizations. "Badr Organization of Reconstruction and Development." Stanford University. Last modified March 2019. https://cisac.fsi.stanford.edu/mappingmilitants/profiles/badr-organization-reconstruction-and-development. Page 2.
41 Mahdi Army is also known as Jaysh al-Mahdi (JAM), a Shi'a militia led by Muqtada al-Sadr formed in 2003. JAM was Sadr's response to the US invasion of Iraq. See: https://cisac.fsi.stanford.edu/mappingmilitants/profiles/mahdi-army#highlight_text_16994.
42 See: Katzman, Kenneth, "Iran's Influence in Iraq," Congressional Research Service (CRS), September 29, 2006. http://fpc.state.gov/documents/organization/73938.pdf.
43 Uskowi, Nader, *Temperature Rising: Iran's Revolutionary Guards and Wars in the Middle East.* Lanham, MD: Rowman & Littlefield, 2019. Page 56.
44 See: The Qayis al-Khazali Papers, American Enterprise Institute, which are declassified reports of his interrogations, detailing the Iranian network. https://www.aei.org/the-qayis-al-khazali-papers/.
45 Rayburn, Joel D. and Frank K. Sobchak (eds.), "The US Army in the Iraq War: Vol. 2, Surge and Withdrawal," US Army War College, January 2019. Page 224. https://press.armywarcollege.edu/monographs/940/.
46 Ibid. Page 225.
47 Malik, Hamdi, "Qais al-Khazali's Show of Independence," The Washington Institute for Near East Studies, 14 June 2021. https://www.washingtoninstitute.org/policy-analysis/qais-al-khazalis-show-independence.
48 Eisenstadt, Michael, Michael Knights, and Ahmed Ali, "Iran's Influence in Iraq: Countering Tehran's Whole-of-Government Approach," Washington Institute for Near East Studies, Policy Focus #111, April 2011. Page 8. https://www.washingtoninstitute.org/media/3364.
49 Ibid.
50 Mapping Militants Organizations. "Kata'ib Hizballah." Stanford University. Last modified September 2020. https://cisac.fsi.stanford.edu/mappingmilitants/profiles/kataib-Hizballah. Pages 2–3.
51 Mapping Militant Organizations. "Kata'ib Sayyid al-Shuhada." Stanford University. Last modified June 2019. mappingmilitants.cisac.fsi.stanford.edu/kataib-sayyid-al-shuhada Pages 2–3.

52 See: Chapter Four: "Iraq," in *Iran's Networks of Influence in the Middle East.* London: The International Institute for Strategic Studies (IISS), 2019. Page 124.
53 Knights, Michael, "Profile: Harakat Hizballah al-Nujaba," The Washington Institute for Near East Policy, April 27, 2021. https://www.washingtoninstitute.org/policy-analysis/profile-harakat-hezbollah-al-nujaba.
54 Ibid.
55 Ibid.
56 See: Iraq: Legislating the Status of the Popular Mobilization Forces, Library of Congress, https://www.loc.gov/item/global-legal-monitor/2016-12-07/iraq-legislating-the-status-of-the-popular-mobilization-forces/.
57 See: Alaaldin, Ranj, "Containing Shiite Militias: The Battle for Stability in Iraq," Brookings Doha Center. December 2017. https://www.brookings.edu/research/containing-shiite-militias-the-battle-for-stability-in-iraq.
58 See: Ghaddar, Hanin, "Iran's Foreign Legion: The Impact of Shia Militias on US Foreign Policy," *The Washington Institute for Near East Studies*, 2018. Page 8. https://www.washingtoninstitute.org/policy-analysis/irans-foreign-legion-impact-shia-militias-us-foreign-policy.
59 See: Mansour, Renad, "More than Militias: Iraq's Popular Mobilization Forces Are Here to Stay," *War on the Rocks*, April 4, 2018. https://warontherocks.com/2018/04/more-than-militias-iraqs-popular-mobilization-forces-are-here-to-stay/.
60 See: Chapter Two: "Lebanese Hizbullah" in *Iran's Networks of Influence in the Middle East.* London: The International Institute for Strategic Studies (IISS), 2019. Pages 39–83.
61 Rafighdoost, Mohsen, *Baraye Tareekh Megooyam (For History)*, 2015. Farsi edition.
62 Ibid. Page 43.
63 For more details on Lebanon's political process, see: Augustus R. Norton, *Hizballah: A Short History.* Princeton, NJ: Princeton University Press, 2014.
64 See: Glenn, Russell W., "Thoughts on 'Hybrid Conflict.'" *Small Wars Journal*, 2009.
65 See: Brister, Paul, "Revisiting the Gordian Knot: Strategic Considerations for Hybrid Wars," in *Hybrid Warfare and Transnational Threats: Perspectives for an Era of Persistent Conflict*, Paul Brister, William H. Natter, and Robert R. Tomes (eds.). New York: Council for Emerging National Security Affairs, 2011. Page 58.
66 Cordesman, Anthony H., "Preliminary 'Lessons' of the Israeli-Hizballah War." Center for Strategic and International Studies. September 11, 2006. Page 19.

67 See: Johnson, David E., "Hard Fighting: Israel in Lebanon and Gaza," RAND Corporation, prepared for the United States Army and the United States Air Force, 2011.
68 Seliktar, Ofira and Farhad Rezaei, *Iran, Revolution, and Proxy Wars*. London: Palgrave Macmillan, 2020. Pages 37–8.
69 Keynoush, Banafsheh. "Iran's Regional Dynamics: A Piecemeal Approach." Middle East Policy 27, No. 2, 2020. Pages 94–107.
70 Ibid.
71 See: Chapter Two: "Lebanese Hizbullah" in *Iran's Networks of Influence in the Middle East*. London: The International Institute for Strategic Studies (IISS), 2019. Page 57.
72 Keynoush, Banafsheh. "Iran's Regional Dynamics: A Piecemeal Approach." *Middle East Policy*, Vol. 27, No. 2, 2020. Pages 94–107.
73 Jones, Seth and Maxwell B. Markusen, "The Escalating Conflict with Hezbollah in Syria," CSIS, 20 June 2018. https://www.csis.org/analysis/escalating-conflict-hezbollah-syria.
74 Mehdi Taeb is Hossein Taeb's brother, another senior cleric who previously held a powerful position in Iran as the IRGC Intelligence Organization Chief.
75 Diaconu, Florin, "Iranian Grand Strategy in the Greater Middle East, the IRGC and General Qasem Soleimani," International Scientific Conference, Center for Defense and Security Strategic Studies, 2017. https://www.proquest.com/openview/3157faae6dba42807a2e494e87037538/1.pdf?pq-origsite=gscholar&cbl=2026346.
76 See: Keynoush.
77 Smyth, Phillip, "Iran's Iraqi Shiite Proxies Increase Their Deployment to Syria," The Washington Institute for Near East Studies, October 2, 2015. https://www.washingtoninstitute.org/policy-analysis/irans-iraqi-shiite-proxies-increase-their-deployment-syria/.
78 Author interview with Ambassador James Jeffrey.
79 A counter point by Groh, Tyrone L., *Proxy War: The Least Bad Option*. Stanford, CA: Stanford University Press, 2019. Page 78.
80 See: Katherine Zimmerman, "Profile: Al Houthi Movement," AEI, January 28, 2010. https://www.aei.org/articles/profile-al-houthi-movement/.
81 The Houthis eventually assassinated Saleh in December 2017, claiming it was an act of revenge for killing Hussein al Houthi. See: Nader Uskowi, *Temperature Rising: Iran's Revolutionary Guards and Wars in the Middle East*. Lanham, MD: Rowman & Littlefield, 2019. Page 117.

82 Seliktar, Ofira, "Iran's Geopolitics and Revolutionary Export: The Promises and Limits of the Proxy Empire," Foreign Policy Research Institute, November 2021. https://www.fpri.org/article/2021/01/irans-geopolitics-and-revolutionary-export-the-promises-and-limits-of-the-proxy-empire/.

83 See: Hafezi, Parisa, "UAE Security Official Pays Rare Visit to Iran to Discuss Ties, Regional Issues," *Reuters*, December 6, 2021. https://www.reuters.com/world/middle-east/uae-security-official-iran-discuss-ties-regional-issues-state-media-2021-12-06/.

84 Juneau, Thomas, "Iran's Policy towards the Houthi's in Yemen: A Limited Return on a Modest Investment," *International Affairs*, Vol. 92, No. 3, 2016. Page 647.

85 Strobel, Warren, and Mark Hosenball, "Elite Iranian Guards Training Yemen's Houthis: US Officials," *Reuters*, March 27, 2015. https://www.reuters.com/article/us-yemen-security-houthis-iran-idUSKBN0MN2MI20150327.

86 Author interview with Ambassador James Jeffrey.

87 Author interview with Barbara Slavin.

88 See: Ghaddar, Hanin, "Iran's Foreign Legion: The Impact of Shia Militias on US Foreign Policy," The Washington Institute for Near East Studies, 2018.

89 Thanks to Elliott Abrams for this thought in an author interview. Elliott Abrams is a senior fellow for Middle Eastern studies at the Council on Foreign Relations (CFR), and former deputy assistant to the president and deputy national security advisor in the administration of President George W. Bush.

90 Author interview with Gen. (ret.) Jim Mattis.

91 See: Operation Inherent Resolve, CJTF-OIR, July 1 to September 30, 2021. https://media.defense.gov/2021/Nov/04/2002886593/-1/-1/1/LEAD%20INSPECTOR%20GENERAL%20FOR%20OPERATION%20INHERENT%20RESOLVE%20QUARTERLY%20REPORT%20JULY%201,%202021%20–%20SEPTEMBER%2030,%202021 … PDF.PDF.

92 Ibid.

93 Author interview with senior Department of Defense official.

94 Ibid.

95 Kesling, Ben and Michael R. Gordon, "US to Close Consulate in Iraq, Citing Threats from Iran," *Wall Street Journal*, September 29, 2018. https://www.wsj.com/articles/u-s-to-close-consulate-in-basra-iraq-official-says-1538164084.

96 See: Gramer, Robbie, "Pompeo Seeks to Make Baghdad Embassy Pullout Permanent, Officials Say," *Foreign Policy*, July 12, 2019. https://foreignpolicy.com/2019/07/12/pompeo-seeks-to-make-baghdad-embassy-pullout-permanent-officials-say-state-department-diplomacy-middle-east-iran-tensions-embassy-drawdown-evacuation/.

97 Author interview with Daveed Gartenstein-Ross, founder and chief executive officer of Valens Global.
98 Ibid.
99 "US Civilian Contractor Killed in Iraq Base Rocket Attack: Officials," *Reuters*, December 27, 2019. https://www.reuters.com/article/us-iraq-security/u-s-civilian-contractor-killed-in-iraq-base-rocket-attack-officials-idUSKBN1YV1IX.
100 Salim, Mustafa and Liz Sly, "Militia Supporters Chanting 'Death to America' Break into US Embassy Compound in Baghdad," Washington Post, December 31, 2019. https://www.washingtonpost.com/world/iran-backed-militia-supporters-converge-on-us-embassy-in-baghdad-shouting-death-to-america/2019/12/31/93f050b2-2bb1-11ea-bffe-020c88b3f120_story.html.
101 See: Uskowi, Nader, *Temperature Rising: Iran's Revolutionary Guards and Wars in the Middle East*. Lanham, MD: Rowman & Littlefield, 2019. Page 56.
102 Schwartz, Matthew S. "Who Was the Iraqi Commander also Killed In the Baghdad Drone Strike?" *NPR*, January 5, 2020. https://www.npr.org/2020/01/04/793618490/who-was-the-iraqi-commander-also-killed-in-baghdad-drone-strike.
103 Jahanbani, Nakissa, "Beyond Soleimani: Implications for Iran's Proxy Network in Iraq and Syria," The Washington Institute for Near East Studies, January 10, 2020.
104 Rayburn, Joel D. and Frank K. Sobchak (eds.), "The US Army in the Iraq War: Vol. 2, Surge and Withdrawal," US Army War College, January 2019. Page 65. https://press.armywarcollege.edu/monographs/940/.
105 Author interview with David Crist.
106 Cullen, Patrick, "A Perspective on EU Hybrid Threat Early Warning Efforts," in *Hybrid Warfare: Security and Asymmetric Conflict in International Relations*, Mikael Weissmann, Niklas Nilsson, Björn Palmertz, and Per Thunholm (eds.). London: I.B. Tauris, 2021.
107 Author interview with Ali Alfoneh, senior fellow at the Arab Gulf States Institute in Washington.
108 Ibid.
109 Ibid.
110 Rayburn, Joel D. and Frank K. Sobchak (eds.), "The US Army in the Iraq War: Vol. 2, Surge and Withdrawal," US Army War College, January 2019. Page 639. https://press.armywarcollege.edu/monographs/940/.
111 Author interview with Peter R. Mansoor.

Chapter 8

1. Filkins, Dexter, "The Thin Red Line: Inside the White House Debate over Syria," *New Yorker,* May 6, 2013. https://www.newyorker.com/magazine/2013/05/13/the-thin-red-line-2.
2. As of June 23, 2022, Taeb was removed from his position. For more information, see: Engelbrecht, Cora, and Farnaz Fassihi, "Iran Dismisses Revolutionary Guards' Powerful Intelligence Chief," *New York Times,* June 23, 2022. https://www.nytimes.com/2022/06/23/world/middleeast/iran-revolutionary-guards-intelligence-chief-hossein-taeb.html.
3. "Iran's New Spymaster," June 20, 2010. *Iran Focus,* https://www.iranfocus.com/en/intelligence-reports/exclusive-reports/20815-irans-new-spymaster/. See also: تغییرات مهم و تجدید ساختار: سپاه آماده می شود (Important Changes and Restructuring: The IRGC is Getting Ready), BBC, October 8, 2009, https://www.bbc.com/persian/iran/2009/10/091008_op_sepah_restructuring.
4. Katzman, Kenneth, "Iran: Internal Politics and US Policy and Options," Congressional Research Service (CRS), updated May 30, 2019. https://crsreports.congress.gov/search/#/?termsToSearch=RL32048&orderBy=Relevance. Page 10.
5. Ibid.
6. The term "moderate" refers to Iran leaders who are open to economic integration while "hardliners" refers to those who strictly adhere to Islamist ideology in governance. As a point of comparison, current Iranian president Ebrahim Raisi is a hardliner.
7. See: Khalaji, Mehdi, "Great Expectations: Iran after the deal," *Washington Quarterly,* Vol. 38, No. 3, 2015. Page 66.
8. Ditto, Steven, "Who is Hassan Rouhani?" *Washington Institute for Near East Studies,* September 24, 2013. https://www.washingtoninstitute.org/policy-analysis/who-hassan-rouhani.
9. See: Alex Vatanka, "Pulling the Strings: How Khamenei will Prevent Reform in Iran," *Foreign Affairs,* November 25, 2015. https://www.foreignaffairs.com/articles/iran/2015-11-25/pulling-strings.
10. See: Keshavarz, Alma, "Iran's COVID-19 Response and US Policy," *The Caravan,* Hoover Institution, June 4, 2020. https://www.hoover.org/research/irans-covid-19-response-and-us-policy.
11. See: Forozan and Afshin Shahi, "The Military and the State in Iran: The Economic Rise of the Revolutionary Guards," *Middle East Journal,* Vol. 71, No. 1, Winter 2017. Page 82.

12. Ibid.
13. Mackey, Peg, "Iran Thaw Warms Western Oil Company Interest," *Reuters,* October 4, 2013. https://www.reuters.com/article/us-iran-oil-idINBRE9930LC20131004. See also: Forozan, Hesam and Afshin Shahi, "The Military and the State in Iran: The Economic Rise of the Revolutionary Guards," *Middle East Journal,* Vol. 71, No. 1, Winter 2017. Page 82.
14. Ibid. Page 83.
15. Vatanka, Alex, "The Iranian Industrial Complex: How the Revolutionary Guards Foil Peace," *Foreign Affairs,* October 17, 2016. https://www.foreignaffairs.com/articles/iran/2016-10-17/iranian-industrial-complex.
16. Khalaji, Mehdi, "President Rouhani and the IRGC," Washington Institute for Near East Studies, January 8, 2014. https://www.washingtoninstitute.org/policy-analysis/president-rouhani-and-irgc.
17. Saremi, Fariborz, "Iran's Islamic Revolutionary Guard Corps, the Pasdaran," *Defense & Foreign Affairs' Strategic Policy,* November/December 2007, Background Report, Page 15.
18. O'Hern, Steven, *Iran's Revolutionary Guard: The Threat that Grows While America Sleeps.* Dulles, VA: Potomac Books, 2012. Pages 72–4.
19. Bastani, Hossein, "How Powerful is Rouhani in the Islamic Republic?" Chatham House, November 2014.
20. Banerjea, Udit, "Revolutionary Intelligence: The Expanding Intelligence Role of the Iranian Revolutionary Guard Corps," *Journal of Strategic Security,* Vol. 8, No. 3, 2015. Page 94.
21. Ibid. Page 97.
22. Ibid. Page 100.
23. See: Khalaji, Mehdi, "President Rouhani and the IRGC," The Washington Institute for Near East Studies, January 8, 2014. https://www.washingtoninstitute.org/policy-analysis/president-rouhani-and-irgc.
24. "Joint Statement by IAEA and Islamic Republic of Iran," IAEA, October 29, 2013. https://www.iaea.org/newscenter/news/joint-statement-iaea-and-islamic-republic-iran.
25. Bastani, Hossein, "How powerful is Rouhani in the Islamic Republic?" Chatham House, Middle East and North Africa Program, November 2014. Page 9. https://www.chathamhouse.org/sites/default/files/field/field_document/20141124RouhaniiislamicRepublicBastani.pdf.
26. Khalaji, Mehdi, "Great Expectations: Iran after the Deal," *Washington Quarterly,* Vol. 38, No. 3, 2015. Page 72.

27 See: Erdbring, Thomas, "Iran Saps Strength of Revolutionary Guards with Arrests and Cutbacks," *New York Times,* October 21, 2017. https://www.nytimes.com/2017/10/21/world/middleeast/iran-revolutionary-guards.html.
28 Ibid.
29 Ibid.
30 DeYoung, Karen, "Trump Administration Says it's Putting Iran 'On Notice' Following Missile Test," *The Washington Post,* February 1, 2017. https://www.washingtonpost.com/world/national-security/2017/02/01/fc5ce3d2-e8b0-11e6-80c2-30e57e57e05d_story.html.
31 "*Siasat-haye kolli-ye 'eghtesad-e moghavemati'*" [The comprehensive policies of "economy of resistance"], *Islamic Students News Agency,* February 19, 2014. Available in Farsi: https://www.isna.ir/news/92113020882/سیاست-های-کلی-اقتصاد-مقاومتی-ابلاغ-شد.
32 Ibid.
33 See: Forozan, Hesam and Afshin Shahi, "The Military and the State in Iran: The Economic Rise of the Revolutionary Guards," *Middle East Journal,* Vol. 71, No. 1, Winter 2017. Pages 67–86.
34 Designated Foreign Terrorist Organizations, US Department of State, https://www.state.gov/foreign-terrorist-organizations/.
35 Ballhaus, Rebecca and Jessica Donati, "US Designates Iran's Islamic Revolutionary Guard Corps as a Terror Organization," *Wall Street Journal,* April 8, 2019. https://www.wsj.com/articles/u-s-designates-irans-islamic-revolutionary-guard-corps-a-foreign-terrorist-organization-11554733155.
36 For a chronology of US–Iran escalations, see: Kenneth Katzman, "US–Iran Tensions Escalate," *Congressional Research Service,* June 13, 2019. https://crsreports.congress.gov/product/pdf/IF/IF11212/19.
37 See: Forozan, Hesam and Afshin Shahi, "The Military and the State in Iran: The Economic Rise of the Revolutionary Guards," *Middle East Journal,* Vol. 71, No. 1, Winter 2017. Page 83.
38 Ibid.
39 See: Geranmayeh, Ellie and Sajad Jiyad, "Iraq, Iran, and the Spectre of US Sanctions," European Council on Foreign Relations, March 18, 2020. https://ecfr.eu/article/commentary_iraq_iran_and_the_spectre_of_us_sanctions/.
40 Talley, Ian, "US Adds to Sanctions against Iran," *Wall Street Journal,* March 26, 2020. https://www.wsj.com/articles/u-s-adds-to-sanctions-against-iran-11585245468.
41 "Iranian 'U-Turn' Transfers Now Prohibited," Gibson, Dunn & Crutcher LLP, International Trade Regulation and Compliance Practice Group, 2008. https://www.gibsondunn.com/iranian-u-turn-transfers-now-prohibited/.

42. Ibid. See also: Department of the Treasury, Office of Foreign Assets Control (OFAC), "Iranian Transactions Regulations," November 10, 2008. https://home.treasury.gov/system/files/126/fr73_66541.pdf.
43. Author interview with Samantha Ravich, chairman of FDD's Center on Cyber and Technology Innovation and its Transformative Cyber Innovation Lab and the principal investigator on FDD's Cyber-Enabled Economic Warfare project.
44. See: Vatanka, Alex, "Pulling the Strings: How Khamenei will Prevent Reform in Iran," *Foreign Affairs,* November 25, 2015.
45. Fassihi, Farnaz, "Iran's Foreign Minister, in Leaked Tap, Says Revolutionary Guards Set Policies," *New York Times,* April 25, 2021. https://www.nytimes.com/2021/04/25/world/middleeast/iran-suleimani-zarif.html.
46. Author interview with Henry Rome, deputy head of research and a director covering global macro politics and the Middle East at the Eurasia Group.

Chapter 9

1. Defense Intelligence Agency, "Iran Military Power: Ensuring Regime Survival and Securing Regional Dominance," 2019. https://www.dia.mil/Portals/110/Images/News/Military_Powers_Publications/Iran_Military_Power_LR.pdf. Page 35.
2. For more information, see: Rezaei, Farhad, "Iran's Military Capability: The Structure and Strength of Forces," *Insight Turkey,* No. 4, 2019. Pages 183–216.
3. Perlroth, Nicole, "In Cyberattack on Saudi Firm, US Sees Iran Firing Back," *New York Times,* October 23, 2012. https://www.nytimes.com/2012/10/24/business/global/cyberattack-on-saudi-oil-firm-disquiets-us.html?_r=0.
4. Perlroth, Nicole and Quentin Hardy, "Bank Hacking was the Work of Iranians, Officials Say," *New York Times,* January 8, 2013. https://www.nytimes.com/2013/01/09/technology/online-banking-attacks-were-work-of-iran-us-officials-say.html.
5. See: "Seven Iranians Working for Islamic Revolutionary Guard Corps-Affiliated Entities Charged for Conducting Coordinated Campaign of Cyber Attacks against US Financial Sector," Department of Justice, March 24, 2016. https://www.justice.gov/opa/pr/seven-iranians-working-islamic-revolutionary-guard-corps-affiliated-entities-charged.
6. See: Yadron, Danny, "Iranian Hackers Infiltrated New York Dam in 2013," *Wall Street Journal,* December 20, 2015. https://www.wsj.com/articles/iranian-hackers-infiltrated-new-york-dam-in-2013-1450662559.

7. Reuters Staff, "Las Vegas Sands' Network hit by Destructive Malware in Feb: Bloomberg," *Reuters,* December 11, 2014. https://www.reuters.com/article/us-lasvegassands-cybersecurity/las-vegas-sands-network-hit-by-destructive-malware-in-feb-bloomberg-idUSKBN0JQ04520141212; see also: https://www.bloomberg.com/news/articles/2014-12-11/iranian-hackers-hit-sheldon-adelsons-sands-casino-in-las-vegas.
8. Finkle, Jim, "Exclusive: Iran hackers may target US energy, defense firms, FBI warns," Reuters, December 12, 2014. https://www.reuters.com/article/us-cybersecurity-iran-fbi/exclusive-iran-hackers-may-target-u-s-energy-defense-firms-fbi-warns-idUSKBN0JQ28Z20141212.
9. Barnes, Julian E. and Siobhan Gorman, "US Says Iran Hacked Navy Computers," *Wall Street Journal,* September 27, 2012. https://www.wsj.com/articles/SB10001424052702304526204579101602356751772.
10. Sanger, David E. and Nicole Perlroth, "Iranian Hackers Attack State Dept. via Social Media Accounts," *New York Times,* November 24, 2015. https://www.nytimes.com/2015/11/25/world/middleeast/iran-hackers-cyberespionage-state-department-social-media.html.
11. Theohary, Catherine A., "Iranian Offensive Cyber Attack Capabilities," CRS, January 13, 2022. https://crsreports.congress.gov/product/details?prodcode=IF11406.
12. Lewis, James Andrew, "Iran and Cyber Power," CSIS, June 25, 2019. https://www.csis.org/analysis/iran-and-cyber-power.
13. See: Banerjea, Edit, "Revolutionary Intelligence: The Expanding Intelligence Role of the Iranian Revolutionary Guard Corps," Journal of Strategic Security, Vol. 8, No. 3, 2015.
14. "Iran's Ministry of Intelligence and Security: A Profile," Federal Research Division, Library of Congress, December 2012. http://freebeacon.com/wp-content/uploads/2013/01/LOC-MOIS.pdf.
15. See: Banerjea, Edit, "Revolutionary Intelligence: The Expanding Intelligence Role of the Iranian Revolutionary Guard Corps," *Journal of Strategic Security*, Vol. 8, No. 3, 2015. Page 103.)
16. For more information, see: DeVore, Marc R. and Sangho Lee, "APTs (Advanced Persistent Threat) and Influence: Cyber Weapons and the Changing Calculus of Conflict," *Journal of East Asian Affairs*, Spring/Summer 2017, Vol. 31, No. 1. Page 41.
17. Shample, Steph, "Iranian APTs: An Overview," *Middle East Institute.* Updated May 10, 2022. https://www.mei.edu/publications/iranian-apts-overview.

18 Threat Hunter Team, "Elfin: Relentless Espionage Groups Targets Multiple Organizations in Saudi Arabia and US," *Symantec,* March 27, 2019. https://symantec-enterprise-blogs.security.com/blogs/threat-intelligence/elfin-apt33-espionage.

19 O'Leary, Jacqueline, Josiah Kimble, Kelli Vanderlee, and Nalani Fraser, "Insights into Iranian Cyber Espionage: APT33 Targets Aerospace and Energy Sectors and has Ties to Destructive Malware," *Mandiant,* September 20, 2017. https://www.mandiant.com/resources/apt33-insights-into-iranian-cyber-espionage.

20 Newman, Lily Hay, "Iranian Hackers have been Infiltrating Critical Infrastructure Companies," *Wired,* December 7, 2017. https://www.wired.com/story/apt-34-iranian-hackers-critical-infrastructure-companies/; see also: Sardiwal, Manish, Vincent Cannon, Nalani Fraser, Yogesh Londhe, Nick Richard, Jacqueline O'Leary, "New Targeted Attack in the Middle East by APT 34, a Suspected Iranian Threat Group, Using CVE-2017-11882 Exploit," *Mandiant,* December 7, 2017. https://www.mandiant.com/resources/targeted-attack-in-middle-east-by-apt34.

21 Nakashima, Ellen, "Iranian Hackers are Targeting US Officials through Social Networks, Report Says," *Washington Post,* March 29, 2014. https://www.washingtonpost.com/world/national-security/iranian-hackers-are-targeting-us-officials-through-social-networks-report-says/2014/05/28/7cb86672-e6ad-11e3-8f90-73e071f3d637_story.html.

22 Bing, Christopher and Raphael Satter, "Exclusive: Trump Campaign Targeted by Iran-Linked Hackers—Sources," *Reuters,* October 4, 2019. https://www.reuters.com/article/us-cyber-security-iran-trump-exclusive/exclusive-trump-campaign-targeted-by-iran-linked-hackers-sources-idUSKBN1WJ2B4.

23 Cohen, Sam, "Iranian Cyber Capabilities: Assessing the Threat to Israeli Financial and Security Interests," *Cyber, Intelligence, and Security,* Vol. 3, No. 1, 2019. Page 26.

24 Author interview with John Arquilla, Emeritus Professor at the Naval Postgraduate School.

25 Author interview with John Arquilla.

26 Maresi, Costinel Nicolae, "Offensive Cyber Operations, an Essential Capability of Hybrid Threats," *Strategic Impact,* Vol. 77, No. 4, Carol I National Defence University, Centre for Defence and Security Strategic Studies, 2020. Pages 137–51.

27 Ibid.

28 McMillan, Robert, "Iranian Hackers have Hit Hundreds of Companies in Past Two Years," *Wall Street Journal,* March 6, 2019. https://www.wsj.com/articles/iranian-hackers-have-hit-hundreds-of-companies-in-past-two-years-11551906036.

29 Cohen, Sam, "Iranian Cyber Capabilities: Assessing the Threat to Israeli Financial and Security Interests," *Cyber, Intelligence, and Security,* Vol. 3, No. 1, 2019. Pages 26–7.
30 For more information, see: "Iran Government Invests $225 million Innovation Fund," *Financial Tribune,* September 6, 2019. https://financialtribune.com/articles/sci-tech/99750/iran-gov-t-invests-225m-in-innovation-fund.
31 Author interview with John Arquilla, Defense Analysis Emeritus Professor at the Naval Postgraduate School.
32 Author interview with John Arquilla, Defense Analysis Emeritus Professor at the Naval Postgraduate School.
33 Author interview with former US Treasury Department and Senate Homeland Security Committee Official John Yaros. Yaros specialized in Cybersecurity, Digital Assets, Fintech, and Illicit Finance.

Chapter 10

1 Author interview with Thomas G. Mahnken.
2 Author interview with Michael Eisenstadt.
3 Author interview with a senior Department of Defense official.
4 Author interview with a senior Department of Defense official.
5 Author interview with Peter R. Mansoor.
6 Shear, Michael D., Eric Schmitt, Michael Crowley, and Maggie Haberman, "Strikes on Iran Approved by Trump, then Abruptly Pulled Back," *New York Times,* June 20, 2019. https://www.nytimes.com/2019/06/20/world/middleeast/iran-us-drone.html.
7 Author interview with David Crist.
8 Author interview with David Crist.
9 Author interview with former US Treasury Department and Senate Homeland Security Committee Official John Yaros. Yaros specialized in Cybersecurity, Digital Assets, Fintech, and Illicit Finance.
10 Author interview with John Yaros.
11 See: McQue, Katie, "Smuggled Iranian Fuel and Secret Nighttime Transfers: Seafarers Recount How it's Done," *The Washington Post,* January 3, 2022. https://www.washingtonpost.com/world/middle_east/iran-oil-smugglng-sanctions/2022/01/02/97a6bf90-5457-11ec-83d2-d9dab0e23b7e_story.html.
12 See: Lee, Liz, "Muslim Nations Consider Gold, Barter Trade to Beat Sanctions," *Reuters,* December 21, 2019. https://www.reuters.com/article/us-malaysia-

muslimalliance/muslim-nations-consider-gold-barter-trade-to-beat-sanctions-idUSKBN1YP04C.
13. Author interview with David Crist.
14. See: Congressional Research Service, "Iran and Nuclear Weapons Production," July 25, 2022. https://crsreports.congress.gov/product/pdf/IF/IF12106.
15. Author interview with Henry Rome.
16. Author interview with Henry Rome.
17. Author interview with Ambassador James Jeffrey.
18. Author interview with David Crist.
19. Author interview with senior Department of Defense official.
20. Author interview with Jim Mattis.
21. Author interview with Michael Eisenstadt.
22. Author interview with Elliott Abrams.
23. Author interview with Barbara Slavin.
24. Author interview with a senior Department of Defense official.
25. Author interview with Michael Connell.
26. Author interview with Michael Connell.
27. Thanks to Tom G. Mahnken for his help in developing this thought in an author interview.
28. Author interview with a senior Department of Defense official.
29. Author interview with Peter R. Mansoor, General Raymond E. Major Jr., Chair in Military History at Ohio State University.

Bibliography

Alaaldin, Ranj. "Containing Shiite Militias: The Battle for Stability in Iraq." Brookings Doha Center, December 2017. https://www.brookings.edu/research/containing-shiite-militias-the-battle-for-stability-in-iraq/.

Alaei, Hossein. *Analytical History of the Iran–Iraq War*, Vol. 1, 2016. Farsi edition.

Alemzadeh, Maryam. "Revolutionaries for Life," in *Global 1979: Geographies and the Histories of the Iranian Revolution*. Cambridge: Cambridge University Press, 2021.

Alexander, Yonah and Milton Hoenig. *The New Iranian Leadership: Ahmadinejad, Terrorism, Nuclear Ambition, and the Middle East*. Westport, CT: Praeger Security International, 2008.

Alfoneh, Ali. "Eternal Rivals? The Artesh and the IRGC." Middle East Institute, November 15, 2011. https://www.mei.edu/publications/eternal-rivals-artesh-and-irgc.

Alfoneh, Ali. *Iran Unveiled: How the Revolutionary Guards is Turning Theocracy into Military Dictatorship*. Washington, DC: American Enterprise Institute Press, 2013.

Alfoneh, Ali. *Political Succession in the Islamic Republic of Iran: Demise of the Clergy and the Rise of the Islamic Revolutionary Guard Corps*. Washington, DC: Arab Gulf States Institute, 2020.

American Enterprise Institute. "The Qayis al-Khazali Papers," October 10, 2019 https://www.aei.org/the-qayis-al-khazali-papers/.

Ansari, Hamid. "Imam Khomeini's Direct Order and Testaments to the Armed Forces." November 26, 2007. As cited in Frederic Wehrey, et al., "The Rise of the Pasdaran: Assessing the Domestic Role of Iran's Islamic Revolutionary Guard Corps." RAND Corp, 2009. https://www.rand.org/pubs/monographs/MG821.html.

Arjomand, Saïd Amir. *After Khomeini*. Oxford: Oxford University Press, 2009.

Arms Control. "Worldwide Ballistic Missile Inventories." https://www.armscontrol.org/factsheets/missiles.

Arquilla, John and David F. Ronfeldt. "The Advent of Netwar." RAND Corp, 1996.

Arquilla, John, David Ronfeldt, and Michele Zanini. "Networks, Netwar, and Information-Age Terrorism," in *Countering the New Terrorism*, O. Ian Lesser, Bruce Hoffman, John Arquilla, David Ronfeldt, Michele Zanini, and Brian Michael Jenkins (eds.). Santa Monica, CA: RAND Corp, 1999. Pages 39–84.

Ballhaus, Rebecca and Jessica Donati. "US Designates Iran's Islamic Revolutionary Guard Corps as a Terror Organization." *Wall Street Journal*, April 8, 2019. https://www.wsj.com/articles/u-s-designates-irans-islamic-revolutionary-guard-corps-a-foreign-terrorist-organization-11554733155.

Bastani, Hossein. "How Powerful is Rouhani in the Islamic Republic?" Chatham House, November 2014. https://www.chathamhouse.org/sites/default/files/field/field_document/20141124RouhaniislamicRepublicBastani.pdf.

Berzins, Janis. "The New Generation of Russian Warfare." The Potomac Foundation, October 11, 2016. http://www.thepotomacfoundation.org/the-new-generation-of-russian-warfare/.

Bing, Christopher and Raphael Satter. "Exclusive: Trump Campaign Targeted by Iran-Linked Hackers—Sources." *Reuters*, October 4, 2019. https://www.reuters.com/article/us-cyber-security-iran-trump-exclusive/exclusive-trump-campaign-targeted-by-iran-linked-hackers-sources-idUSKBN1WJ2B4.

Bowers, Christopher O. "Identifying Emerging Hybrid Adversaries." *Parameters*, https://press.armywarcollege.edu/parameters/vol42/iss1/3/.

Brister, Paul, William H. Natter, III, and Robert R. Tomes (eds.). *Hybrid Warfare and Transnational Threats: Perspectives for an Era of Persistent Conflict*. New York: Council for Emerging National Security Affairs, 2011.

British Broadcasting Company (BBC). "Important Changes and Restructuring: The IRGC is Getting Ready," سپاه آماده می شود: تغییرات مهم و تجدید ساختار October 8, 2009. https://www.bbc.com/persian/iran/2009/10/091008_op_sepah_restructuring.

Brooks, Risa A. "Integrating the Civil–Military Relations Subfield," in *Annual Review of Political Science*, January 30, 2019. Pages 379–98.

Bunker, Robert J. "The Transition to Fourth Epoch War." *Marine Corps Gazette*, Vol. 78, No. 9 (1994). Pages 20–32.

Bunker, Robert J. "Battlespace Dynamics, Information Warfare to Netwar, and Bond-Relationship Targeting," in *Non-State Threats and Future War*, Robert J. Bunker (ed.). London: Frank Cass, 2003.

Bunker, Robert J. and Alma Keshavarz. "'Made in Yemen': Houthi Exhibition Showcase New Drones, Missiles, and Naval Mines." *Small Wars Journal*, April 8, 2021. https://smallwarsjournal.com/jrnl/art/made-yemen-houthi-exhibition-showcase-new-drones-missiles-and-naval-mines.

Bunker, Robert J. and Hakim Hazim. "Are We Prematurely Designating Iran's Revolutionary Guards as Criminal Soldiers?" *Small Wars Journal*, September 5, 2007. http://smallwarsjournal.com/blog/are-we-prematurely-designating-irans-revolutionary-guards-as-criminal-soldiers.

Byman, Daniel, Shahram Chubin, Anoushiravan Ehteshami, and Jerrold E. Green. *Iran's Security Policy in the Post-Revolutionary Era*. RAND Corp, 2001. https://

www.rand.org/content/dam/rand/pubs/monograph_reports/MR1320/RAND_MR1320.pdf.

Carl, Nicholas, Kitaneh Fitzpatrick, Zachary Coles, and Frederick Kagan. "Iran Crisis Update." Critical Threats Project (CTP), November 17, 2022. https://www.criticalthreats.org/analysis/iran-crisis-update-november-17.

Center for Arms Control and Non-Proliferation. "Fact Sheet: Iran and the Additional Protocol." July 14, 2015. https://armscontrolcenter.org/factsheet-iran-and-the-additional-protocol/.

Center for International Security and Cooperation (CISAC). "Badr Organization of Reconstruction and Development." Stanford University. Last modified March 2019. https://cisac.fsi.stanford.edu/mappingmilitants/profiles/badr-organization-reconstruction-and-development.

Center for International Security and Cooperation (CISAC). "Kata'ib Sayyid al-Shuhada." Stanford University. Last modified June 2019. https://cisac.fsi.stanford.edu/mappingmilitants/profiles/kataib-sayyid-al-shuhada.

Center for International Security and Cooperation (CISAC). "Mahdi Army." Stanford University. Last modified May 2019. https://cisac.fsi.stanford.edu/mappingmilitants/profiles/mahdi-army#highlight_text_16994.

Center for International Security and Cooperation (CISAC). "Kata'ib Hizballah." Stanford University. Last modified September 2020. https://cisac.fsi.stanford.edu/mappingmilitants/profiles/kataib-Hizballah.

Center for Strategic and International Studies (CSIS). "SS-1 'Scud'" https://missilethreat.csis.org/missile/scud/.

Central Intelligence Agency (CIA). "Iran's Revolutionary Guard: Armed Pillar of the Islamic Republic." January 1987. Declassified in Part—Sanitized Copy Approved for Release 2012/ 05/08. https://www.cia.gov/readingroom/document/cia-rdp06t00412r000606580001-5.

Cohen, Sam. "Iranian Cyber Capabilities: Assessing the Threat to Israeli Financial and Security Interests." *Cyber, Intelligence, and Security*, Vol. 3, No. 1 2019. Pages 71–94.

Congressionally Directed Action (CDA). "Unclassified Report on Military Power of Iran." April 2010. https://man.fas.org/eprint/dod_iran_2010.pdf.

Congressional Research Service. "Iran and Nuclear Weapons Production." July 25, 2022. https://crsreports.congress.gov/product/pdf/IF/IF12106.

Connell, Michael. "Iran's Military Doctrine." *Iran Primer*, October 21, 2010. https://www.Iranprimer.usip.org/resource/irans-military-doctrine.

Connell, Michael. "The Artesh Navy: Iran's Strategic Force." Center for Naval Analysis, January 31, 2012. https://www.mei.edu/publications/artesh-navy-irans-strategic-force.

Constitute Project. "Islamic Republic of Iran's Constitution of 1979 with Amendments through 1989." https://www.constituteproject.org/constitution/Iran_1989.pdf?lang=en.

Constitution of the Islamic Republic of Iran. http://www.moi.ir/Portal/File/ShowFile.aspx?ID=ab40c7a6-af7d-4634-af93-40f2f3a04acf (in Farsi); http://www.iranonline.com/iran/iran-info/government/constitution.html (in English).

Cooperation Council for the Arab States of the Gulf. Secretariat General of the Gulf Cooperation Council. https://www.gcc-sg.org/en-us/AboutGCC/MemberStates/pages/Home.aspx.

Cordesman, Anthony H. "The Lessons of Modern War – Volume II – The Iran–Iraq War (Chapter 2: The Conditions that Shaped the Iran–Iraq War)." Center for Strategic and International Studies, May 1, 1990. https://www.csis.org/analysis/lessons-modern-war-volume-ii-iran-iraq-war-%E2%80%93-chapter-2-conditions-shaped-iran-iraq-war.

Cordesman, Anthony H. "Iran's Military Forces: 1988–1993." Center for Strategic and International Studies (CSIS), September 1994.

Cordesman, Anthony H. *Iran's Military Forces in Transition: Conventional Threats and Weapons of Mass Destruction*. Westport, CT: Praeger Publishers, 1999.

Cordesman, Anthony H. "Preliminary 'Lessons' of the Israeli-Hizballah War." Center for Strategic and International Studies, September 11, 2006.

Cordesman, Anthony H. "Iran's Revolutionary Guards, the Al Quds Force, and Other Intelligence and Paramilitary Forces." Center for Strategic and International Studies (CSIS), August 16, 2007. https://www.csis.org/analysis/irans-revolutionary-guards-al-quds-force-and-other-intelligence-and-paramilitary-forces.

Crist, David. *The Twilight War: The Secret History of America's Thirty-Year Conflict with Iran*. New York: Penguin Press, 2012.

Cullen, Patrick. "A perspective on EU Hybrid Threat Early Warning Efforts," in *Hybrid Warfare: Security and Asymmetric Conflict in International Relations*, Mikael Weissmann, Niklas Nilsson, Björn Palmertz and Per Thunholm (eds.). London: I.B. Tauris, 2021.

Cummings, Michael and Eric Cummings. "The Costs of War with Iran: An Intelligence Preparation of the Battlefield." *Small Wars Journal*, August 31, 2012. http://smallwarsjournal.com/jrnl/art/the-costs-of-war-with-iran-an-intelligence-preparation-of-the-battlefield.

Davis, Jr., John R. "Continued Evolution of Hybrid Threats: The Russian Hybrid Threat Construct and the Need for Innovation." *The Three Swords Magazine*, 2015.

Defense Intelligence Agency (DIA). "Iran Military Power: Ensuring Regime Survival and Securing Regional Dominance." 2019. https://www.dia.mil/Portals/110/Images/News/Military_Powers_Publications/Iran_Military_Power_LR.pdf.

Department of Defense. *National Defense Strategy of the United States of America*. March 2005. https://history.defense.gov/Historical-Sources/National-Defense-Strategy/.

Department of Defense. Operation Inherent Resolve, CJTF-OIR, July 1, to September 30, 2021. https://tinyurl.com/33xxdn38.

Department of Justice. "Mansoor Arabsiar Sentenced in New York City Federal Court to 25 Years in Prison for Conspiring with Iranian Military Officials to Assassinate the Saudi Arabian Ambassador to the United States." May 30, 2013. http://www.justice.gov/opa/pr/manssor-arabsiar-sentenced-new-york-city-federal-court-25-years-prison-conspiring-iranian.

Department of Justice. "United States Prevails in Actions to Seize and Forfeit Iranian Terror Group's Missiles and Petroleum." December 7, 2021. https://www.justice.gov/opa/pr/united-states-prevails-actions-seize-and-forfeit-iranian-terror-group-s-missiles-and.

Department of State. "Designated Foreign Terrorist Organizations." https://www.state.gov/foreign-terrorist-organizations/.

Department of State. "State Sponsors of Terrorism Overview." Bureau of Counterterrorism, Country Reports on Terrorism. https://www.state.gov/j/ct/rls/crt/2014/239410.htm.

Department of the Treasury. "Iranian Transactions Regulations." Office of Foreign Assets Control (OFAC), November 10, 2008. https://home.treasury.gov/system/files/126/fr73_66541.pdf.

Department of the Treasury. "CISADA: The New US Sanctions on Iran." https://home.treasury.gov/system/files/126/CISADA_english.pdf.

Department of the Treasury. "EO 13581," "Transnational Criminal Organizations Sanctions Regulations." Office of Foreign Assets Control. https://home.treasury.gov/system/files/126/fr_tco_2022-01072.pdf.

Department of the Treasury. "Executive Order 13599 of February 5, 2012, Blocking Property of the Government of Iran and Iranian Financial Institutions." https://home.treasury.gov/system/files/126/iran_eo_02062012.pdf.

Department of the Treasury. "Fact Sheet: Designation of Iranian Entities and Individuals for Proliferation Activities and Support for Terrorism." October 25, 2007. https://www.treasury.gov/press-center/press-releases/Pages/hp644.aspx.

DeVore, Marc R. and Sangho Lee. "APTs (Advanced Persistent Threat) and Influence: Cyber Weapons and the Changing Calculus of Conflict." *The Journal of East Asian Affairs*, Vol. 31, No. 1 (Spring/Summer 2017). Pages 39–64.

DeYoung, Karen. "Trump Administration Says It's Putting Iran 'On Notice' Following Missile Test." *The Washington Post*, February 1, 2017. https://www.washingtonpost.com/world/national-security/2017/02/01/fc5ce3d2-e8b0-11e6-80c2-30e57e57e05d_story.html.

Diaconu, Florin. "Iranian Grand Strategy in the Greater Middle East, the IRGC and General Qasem Soleimani." International Scientific Conference, Center for Defense and Security Strategic Studies, 2017. https://www.proquest.com/openview/3157faae6dba42807a2e494e87037538/1.pdf?pq-origsite=gscholar&cbl=2026346.

Ditto, Steven. "Who is Hassan Rouhani?" *The Washington Institute for Near East Studies*, September 24, 2013. https://www.washingtoninstitute.org/policy-analysis/who-hassan-rouhani.

Douville, Alex. "The Iran-Contra Affair." *Case Studies Working Group Report*, Richard Weitz (ed.), Vol. 2, Chapter 2. Strategic Studies Institute, US Army War College, Carlisle Barracks, PA, 2012.

Edelman, Eric S. and Whitney Morgan McNamara. "Contain, Degrade, and Defeat: A Defense Strategy for a Troubled Middle East." Center for Strategic and Budgetary Assessments, 2017. https://csbaonline.org/research/publications/contain-degrade-and-defeat-a-defense-strategy-for-a-troubled-middle-east.

Eisenstadt, Michael. "Iranian Military Power: Capabilities and Intentions." The Washington Institute for Near East Studies, No. 42 (1996). https://www.washingtoninstitute.org/policy-analysis/iranian-military-power-capabilities-and-intentions.

Eisenstadt, Michael, Michael Knights, and Ahmed Ali. "Iran's Influence in Iraq: Countering Tehran's Whole-of-Government Approach." Washington Institute for Near East Studies, No. 111 (2011). https://www.washingtoninstitute.org/media/3364.

Erdbring, Thomas. "Iran Saps Strength of Revolutionary Guards with Arrests and Cutbacks." *New York Times*, October 21, 2017. https://www.nytimes.com/2017/10/21/world/middleeast/iran-revolutionary-guards.html.

Fassihi, Farnaz. "Iran's Foreign Minister, in Leaked Tape, Says Revolutionary Guards Set Policies." *New York Times*, April 25, 2021. https://www.nytimes.com/2021/04/25/world/middleeast/iran-suleimani-zarif.html.

Felter, Joseph and Brian Fishman. "Iranian Strategy in Iraq: Politics and Other Means." Combating Terrorism Center at US Military Academy, West Point, October 13, 2008, http://www.ctc.usma.edu/wp-content/uploads/2010/06/Iranian-Strategy-in-Iraq.pdf.

Filkins, Dexter. "The Thin Red Line: Inside the White House Debate over Syria." *New Yorker*, May 6, 2013. https://www.newyorker.com/magazine/2013/05/13/the-thin-red-line-2.

Financial Tribune. "Iran Government Invests $225 Million Innovation Fund." September 6, 2019. https://financialtribune.com/articles/sci-tech/99750/iran-gov-t-invests-225m-in-innovation-fund.

Findlater, Euan. "Islamic Republic of Iran's Strategic Culture and National Security Analysis." *Small Wars Journal*, January 19, 2020. https://www.smallwarsjournal.com/jrnl/art/islamic-republic-irans-strategic-culture-and-national-security-analysis.

Forozan, Hesam and Afshin Shahi. "The Military and the State in Iran: The Economic Rise of the Revolutionary Guards." *Middle East Journal*, Vol. 71, No. 1 (2017). Pages 67–86.

Fox, Amos C. and Andrew J. Rossow. "Assessing Russian Hybrid Warfare: A Successful Tool for Limited War." *Small Wars Journal*, August 8, 2016. https://smallwarsjournal.com/jrnl/art/assessing-russian-hybrid-warfare-a-successful-tool-for-limited-war.

Freedman, Lawrence and Efraim Karsh. "How Kuwait Was Won: Strategy in the Gulf War." *International Security*, Vol. 16, No. 2 (1991). Pages 5–41. muse.jhu.edu/article/447278.

French, Spencer Lawrence. "Embracing Asymmetry: Assessing Iranian National Security Strategy, 1983–1987." *Joint Force Quarterly (JFQ)*, No. 101 (2nd Quarter, 2021). Pages 69–77.

Friedman, Thomas. "Beyond Fourth Generation Warfare." *ROA National Security Report*, September 2007.

Galeotti, Mark. "'Hybrid War' and 'Little Green Men:' How it Works, and How It Doesn't," in *Ukraine and Russia: People, Politics, Propaganda and Perspectives*. Agnieszka Pikulicka-Wilczewska and Richard Sakwa (eds.). *E-International Relations*, March 2015. https://www.e-ir.info/pdf/55375.

Geranmayeh, Ellie. "Reviving the Revolutionaries: How Trump's Maximum Pressure is Shifting Iran's Domestic Politics." European Council on Foreign Relations, June 23, 2020. https://ecfr.eu/publication/reviving_the_revolutionaries_how_trumps_maximum_pressure_is_shifting_irans/.

Geranmayeh, Ellie and Sajad Jiyad. "Iraq, Iran, and the Spectre of US Sanctions." European Council on Foreign Relations, March 18, 2020. https://ecfr.eu/article/commentary_iraq_iran_and_the_spectre_of_us_sanctions/.

Ghaddar, Hanin. "Iran's Foreign Legion: The Impact of Shia Militias on US Foreign Policy." Washington Institute for Near East Studies, 2018. https://www.washingtoninstitute.org/policy-analysis/irans-foreign-legion-impact-shia-militias-us-foreign-policy.

Ghazvinian, John. *America and Iran: A History, 1720 to the Present*. New York: Alfred Knopf, 2021.

Gibson, Dunn & Crutcher LLP, International Trade Regulation and Compliance Practice Group. "Iranian 'U-Turn' Transfers Now Prohibited." 2008. https://www.gibsondunn.com/iranian-u-turn-transfers-now-prohibited/.

Gibson, Bryan R. "The Long Road to Tehran: The Iran Nuclear Deal in Perspective." London School of Economics, 2015.

Glenn, Russell W. "Thoughts on 'Hybrid Conflict.'" *Small Wars Journal*, 2009. https://smallwarsjournal.com/jrnl/art/thoughts-on-hybrid-conflict.

Golkar, Saeid. "Configuration of Political Elites in Post-Revolutionary Iran." *The Brown Journal of World Affairs*, Vol. 23, No. 1 (2016). Pages 281–92.

Golkar, Saeid. "The Supreme Leader and the Guard: Civil–Military Relations and Regime Survival in Iran." Washington Institute for Near East Policy, 2019. https://www.washingtoninstitute.org/policy-analysis/supreme-leader-and-guard-civil-military-relations-and-regime-survival-iran.

Government Accountability Office (GAO). "Hybrid Warfare." The GAO analysis of DoD military concept and briefing documents and academic writings. September 10, 2010. https://www.gao.gov/assets/gao-10-1036r.pdf.

Gramer, Robbie. "Pompeo Seeks to Make Baghdad Embassy Pullout Permanent, Officials Say." *Foreign Policy*, July 12, 2019. https://foreignpolicy.com/2019/07/12/pompeo-seeks-to-make-baghdad-embassy-pullout-permanent-officials-say-state-department-diplomacy-middle-east-iran-tensions-embassy-drawdown-evacuation/.

Groh, Tyrone L. *Proxy War: The Least Bad Option*. Stanford, CA: Stanford University Press, 2019.

Haaretz. "U.S. Concerned Iran Providing Weapons to Iraq Militants." July 11, 2011, http://www.haaretz.com/news/middle-east/u-s-concerned-iran-providing-weapons-to-iraq-militants-1.372670.

Hafezi, Parisa. "UAE Security Official Pays Rare Visit to Iran to Discuss Ties, Regional Issues." *Reuters*, December 6, 2021. https://www.reuters.com/world/middle-east/uae-security-official-iran-discuss-ties-regional-issues-state-media-2021-12-06/.

Haghshenass, Fariborz. "Iran's Asymmetric Naval Warfare." Washington Institute for Near East Studies, September 2008. https://www.washingtoninstitute.org/media/3446.

Hammes, Thomas X. *The Sling and the Stone: On War in the 21st Century*. St. Paul, MN: Zenith Press, 2006.

Harari, Michal. "Status Update: Shia Militias in Iraq." Institute for the Study of War, August 16, 2010. https://www.understandingwar.org/backgrounder/status-update-shia-militias-iraq.

Harris, Kevan. "The Rise of the Subcontractor State: Politics of Pseudo-Privatization in the Islamic Republic of Iran." *International Journal of Middle East Studies*, Vol. 45 (2013). Pages 45–70.

Hashim, Ahmed S. "Civil–Military Relations in Iran: Internal and External Pressures." *Middle East Policy*, Vol. 25, No. 3 (2018). Pages 47–66.

Heritage Foundation. "After the Deal: A New Iran Strategy." An interview with Mike Pompeo, May 21, 2018. https://www.heritage.org/defense/event/after-the-deal-new-iran-strategy.

Hoffman, David. "Bush Offers 'Goodwill' if Hostages are Freed." *The Washington Post*, August 10, 1989. https://www.washingtonpost.com/archive/politics/1989/08/10/bush-offers-goodwill-if-hostages-are-freed/953ab824-67de-4a3f-a69f-4a77874ab9b7/.

Hoffman, Frank G. "Conflict in the 21st Century: The Rise of Hybrid Wars." Potomac Institute for Policy Studies, 2007.

Hoffman, Frank G. "Hybrid Warfare and Challenges." *Joint Force Quarterly*, No. 52 (Ist Quarter, 2009).

Holy Defense Research and Document Center. "The Quarterly Studies of Iran–Iraq War." Vol. 3, No. 9 (2014). Research Review at Sacred Defense.

Hovsepian-Bearce, Yvette. *The Political Ideology of Ayatollah Khamenei: Out of the Mouth of the Supreme Leader of Iran*. Routledge, 2016.

Hunter, Eve and Piret Pernik. "The Challenges of Hybrid Warfare." International Center for Defence and Security, April 2015.

Illarionov, Andrei. "The Russian Leadership's Preparation for War," in *The Guns of August 2008: Russia's War in Georgia*, Svante E. Cornell and S. Frederick Starr (eds.). New York: Routledge, 2015.

International Atomic Energy Agency (IAEA). "Director General's Statement on the Announcement by the E3/EU + 3 and Iran on the Agreement of the Joint Comprehensive Plan of Action." July 14, 2015. https://www.iaea.org/newscenter/pressreleases/director-general's-statement-announcement-e3/eu-3-and-iran-agreement-joint-comprehensive-plan-action.

International Atomic Energy Agency (IAEA). "Implementation of the NPT Safeguards Agreement in the Islamic Republic of Iran and Related Board Resolutions." August 11, 2005. https://www.iaea.org/sites/default/files/gov2005-64.pdf.

International Atomic Energy Agency (IAEA). "Joint Statement on a Framework for Cooperation." November 11, 2013. https://www.iaea.org/sites/default/files/gov-inf-2013-14.pdf.

International Atomic Energy Agency (IAEA). "Statement by IAEA Director General on Geneva Agreement." November 24, 2013. https://www.iaea.org/newscenter/statements/statement-iaea-director-general-geneva-agreement.

International Atomic Energy Agency (IAEA). "Status of Iran's Nuclear Programme in Relation to the Joint Plan of Action." January 20, 2014. https://www.iaea.org/sites/default/files/govinf2014-1.pdf.

International Atomic Energy Agency (IAEA). "Status of Iran's Nuclear Programme in Relation to the Joint Plan of Action." July 20, 2015. https://www.iaea.org/sites/default/files/gov-inf-2015-15.pdf.

International Institute for Strategic Studies (IISS). "Iraq," in *Iran's Networks of Influence in the Middle East*. London: IISS, 2019.

International Institute for Strategic Studies (IISS). "Lebanese Hizbullah," in *Iran's Networks of Influence in the Middle East*. London: IISS, 2019.

International Monetary Fund. "Islamic Republic of Iran: Estimations on Smuggling of Goods." https://www.imf.org/en/Data/Statistics/informal-economy-data/Reports/Iran-Estimations-on-Smuggling-of-Goods.

Iran Focus. "Iran's New Spymaster." June 20, 2010. https://www.iranfocus.com/en/intelligence-reports/exclusive-reports/20815-irans-new-spymaster/.

Iran Watch. "Khatam al-Anbiya Construction Headquarters." Wisconsin Project on Nuclear Arms Control. Updated January 19, 2021. https://www.iranwatch.org/iranian-entities/khatam-al-anbiya-construction-headquarters-kaa.

Iran Watch. "Ministry of Defense Armed Forces and Logistics (MODAFL)." https://www.iranwatch.org/iranian-entities/ministry-defense-armed-forces-logistics-modafl.

Iran's Holy Defense Research and Document Center. Persian Archive. https://www.persianarchive.com/publisher/holy-defense-research-document-center/.

Islamic Students News Agency (ISNA). *"Siasat-haye kolli-ye 'eghtesad-e moghavemati"* [The comprehensive policies of "economy of resistance"]. February 19, 2014. Available in Persian: https://www.isna.ir/news/92113020882/سیاست‌-های‌-کلی‌-اقتصاد‌-مقاومتی‌-ابلاغ‌-شد.

Jenkins, Brian Michael. "New Modes of Conflict." RAND Corp, prepared for the Defense Nuclear Agency. 1983. https://www.rand.org/content/dam/rand/pubs/reports/2006/R3009.pdf.

Johnson, David, E. "Hard Fighting: Israel in Lebanon and Gaza." RAND Corp, prepared for the United States Army and the United States Air Force, 2011. https://www.rand.org/pubs/monographs/MG1085.html.

Jones, Seth G., Jared Thompson, Danielle Ngo, Brian McSorley, and Joseph S. Bermudez Jr. "The Iranian and Houthi War against Saudi Arabia." CSIS, December 2021. https://www.csis.org/analysis/iranian-and-houthi-war-against-saudi-arabia.

Juneau, Thomas. "Iran's Policy towards the Houthi's in Yemen: A Limited Return on a Modest Investment." *International Affairs*, Vol. 92, No. 3 (2016). Pages 647–63.

Karber, Phillip A. "Russia's 'New Generation Warfare.'" National Geospatial-Intelligence Agency, June 4, 2015. https://www.nga.mil/news/Russias_New_Generation_Warfare.html.

Katzman, Kenneth B. "Iran's Islamic Revolutionary Guard Corps: Radical Ideology Despite Institutionalization in the Islamic Republic." New York University. Dissertation. 1991.

Katzman, Kenneth. "Iran's Influence in Iraq." Congressional Research Service (CRS) Report RS73938, September 29, 2006. http://fpc.state.gov/documents/organization/73938.pdf.

Katzman, Kenneth. "Iran–Iraq Relations." Congressional Research Service (CRS) Report RS22323, August 13, 2010. http://www.fas.org/sgp/crs/mideast/RS22323.pdf.

Katzman, Kenneth. "Iran, Gulf Security, and U.S. Policy." Congressional Research Service, May 28, 2015.

Katzman, Kenneth. "Iran: Internal Politics and U.S. Policy and Options." Congressional Research Service (CRS), updated May 30, 2019. https://crsreports.congress.gov/search/#/?termsToSearch=RL32048&orderBy=Relevance.

Katzman, Kenneth. "US–Iran Tensions Escalate." Congressional Research Service (CRS), June 13, 2019. https://crsreports.congress.gov/product/pdf/IF/IF11212/19.

Keshavarz, Alma. "Iran's COVID-19 Response and US Policy." *The Caravan*, Hoover Institution, June 4, 2020. https://www.hoover.org/research/irans-covid-19-response-and-us-policy.

Keshavarz, Alma. "The United States Needs an Iran Strategy, not a Campaign." The Atlantic Council, June 23, 2020. https://www.atlanticcouncil.org/blogs/iransource/the-united-states-needs-an-iran-strategy-not-a-campaign/.

Kesling, Ben and Michael R. Gordon. "US to Close Consulate in Iraq, Citing Threats from Iran." *Wall Street Journal*, September 29, 2018. https://www.wsj.com/articles/u-s-to-close-consulate-in-basra-iraq-official-says-1538164084.

Keynoush, Banafsheh. "Iran's Regional Dynamics: A Piecemeal Approach." *Middle East Policy*, Vol. 27, No. 2 (2020). Pages 94–107.

Khajehpour, Bijan. "The Real Footprint of the IRGC in Iran's Economy." *Al Monitor*, August 9, 2017. https://www.al-monitor.com/originals/2017/08/iran-irgc-economy-footprint-khatam-olanbia.html.

Khalaji, Mehdi. "President Rouhani and the IRGC." Washington Institute for Near East Studies, January 8, 2014. https://www.washingtoninstitute.org/policy-analysis/president-rouhani-and-irgc.

Khalaji, Mehdi. "Great Expectations: Iran after the deal." *Washington Quarterly*, Vol. 38, No. 3 (2015). Pages 61–77.

Khoshnood, Ardavan. "The Khatam al-Anbiya Camp and the Future of the Revolutionary Guards' Empire." The Begin-Sadat Center for Strategic Studies (BESA), No. 2,014, May 3, 2021. https://besacenter.org/wp-content/uploads/2021/05/2014-khatam-al-anbiya-camp-and-revolutionary-guards-khoshnood-final.pdf.

Kilcullen, David. *Accidental Guerrilla*. Oxford: Oxford University Press, 2009.

Kirkpatrick, David D., Richard Pérez-Peña, and Stanley Reed. "Tankers Are Attacked in Mideast, and US Says Video Shows Iran Was Involved." *New York Times*, June

13, 2019. https://www.nytimes.com/2019/06/13/world/middleeast/oil-tanker-attack-gulf-oman.html.

Knights, Michael. "The Evolution of Iran's Special Groups in Iraq." Combating Terrorism Center (CTC) at West Point 3:11-12 (November 2010).

Knights, Michael. "Profile: Harakat Hizballah al-Nujaba." Washington Institute for Near East Policy, April 27, 2021. https://www.washingtoninstitute.org/policy-analysis/profile-harakat-hezbollah-al-nujaba.

Kofman, Michael and Matthew Rojansky. "A Closer Look at Russia's 'Hybrid War.'" Wilson Center, Kennan Institute, April 2015. https://www.wilsoncenter.org/sites/default/files/media/documents/publication/7-KENNAN%20CABLE-ROJANSKY%20KOFMAN.pdf.

Krieg, Andreas and Jean-Marc Rickli. *Surrogate Warfare: The Transformation of War in the Twenty-First Century*. Washington, DC: Georgetown University Press, 2020.

Lamothe, Dan. "Navy: 'Poorly Led and Unprepared' Sailors were Detained by Iran after Multiple Errors." *The Washington Post*, June 30, 2016. https://www.washingtonpost.com/news/checkpoint/wp/2016/06/30/navy-poorly-led-and-unprepared-sailors-were-detained-by-iran-after-multiple-errors/.

Lee, Liz. "Muslim Nations Consider Gold, Barter Trade to Beat Sanctions." *Reuters*, December 21, 2019. https://www.reuters.com/article/us-malaysia-muslimalliance/muslim-nations-consider-gold-barter-trade-to-beat-sanctions-idUSKBN1YP04C.

Levitt, Matthew. *Hezbollah: The Global Footprint of Lebanon's Party of God*. Washington, DC: Georgetown University Press, 2013.

Levy, Ido. "Shia Militias and Exclusionary Politics in Iraq." Middle East Policy Council, Vol. 3, No. 26 (2019). https://mepc.org/journal/shia-militias-and-exclusionary-politics-iraq.

Lewis, James Andrew. "Iran and Cyber Power." CSIS, June 25, 2019. https://www.csis.org/analysis/iran-and-cyber-power.

Library of Congress. "Iran's Ministry of Intelligence and Security: A Profile." December 2012. http://freebeacon.com/wp-content/uploads/2013/01/LOC-MOIS.pdf.

Library of Congress. "Iraq: Legislating the Status of the Popular Mobilization Forces." https://www.loc.gov/item/global-legal-monitor/2016-12-07/iraq-legislating-the-status-of-the-popular-mobilization-forces/.

Lim, Kevjn. "Iran's Next Supreme Leader is Dead." *Foreign Policy*, January 10, 2019. https://foreignpolicy.com/2019/01/10/irans-next-supreme-leader-is-dead/.

Lind, William S., Col. Keith Nightengale, Capt. John F. Schmitt, Col. Joseph W. Sutton, and Lt Col. Gary I. Wilson. "The Changing Face of War: Into the Fourth Generation." *Marine Corps Gazette*, October 1989.

Mackey, Peg. "Iran Thaw Warms Western Oil Company Interest." *Reuters*, October 4, 2013. https://www.reuters.com/article/us-iran-oil-idINBRE9930LC20131004.

Malik, Hamdi. "Qais al-Khazali's Show of Independence." Washington Institute for Near East Studies, June 14, 2021. https://www.washingtoninstitute.org/policy-analysis/qais-al-khazalis-show-independence.

Mansoor, Peter R. "Introduction: Hybrid Warfare in History," in *Hybrid Warfare: Fighting Complex Opponents from the Ancient World to the Present*, Williamson Murray and Peter R. Mansoor (eds.). New York: Cambridge University Press, 2012.

Mansour, Renad. "More than Militias: Iraq's Popular Mobilization Forces Are Here to Stay." *War on the Rocks*, April 4, 2018. https://warontherocks.com/2018/04/more-than-militias-iraqs-popular-mobilization-forces-are-here-to-stay/.

Mansuri, Javad. *Oral History of Establishment of the Islamic Revolutionary Guards (Tareekh-e Shafaee Tasees-e Sepah-e Pasdaran)*. Markaz-e Asnad Enqelab-e Eslami (Center for Islamic Revolutionary Documents), June 2014. Farsi edition.

Manwaring, Max G. "The New Global Security Landscape," in *Networks, Terrorism and Global Insurgency*, Robert J. Bunker (ed.). New York: Routledge, 2005.

Maresi, Costinel Nicolae. "Offensive Cyber Operations, an Essential Capability of Hybrid Threats," *Strategic Impact*, Vol. 77, No. 4 (2020). Pages 137–51.

Masters, Jonathan. "CFR Backgrounders: Hizballah." Updated January 3, 2014. http://www.cfr.org/lebanon/Hizballah-k-hizbollah-hizbullah/p9155.

Mattis, James N. and Frank Hoffman. "Future Warfare: The Rise of Hybrid Wars." *Proceedings Magazine*, United States Naval Institute, Vol. 132, November 2005. www.milnewstbay.pbworks.com/f/MattisFourBlockWarUSNINOV2005.pdf.

McCuen, John J. "Hybrid Wars." *Military Review*, March–April 2008. Pages 107–13.

McMillan, Robert. "Iranian Hackers have Hit Hundreds of Companies in Past Two Years." *Wall Street Journal*, March 6, 2019. https://www.wsj.com/articles/iranian-hackers-have-hit-hundreds-of-companies-in-past-two-years-11551906036.

McQue, Katie. "Smuggled Iranian Fuel and Secret Nighttime Transfers: Seafarers Recount How it's Done." *The Washington Post*, January 3, 2022. https://www.washingtonpost.com/world/middle_east/iran-oil-smuggling-sanctions/2022/01/02/97a6bf90-5457-11ec-83d2-d9dab0e23b7e_story.html.

Menon, Rajan and Eugene Rumer. *Conflict in Ukraine: The Unwinding of the Post-Cold War Order*. Cambridge, MA: Massachusetts Institute of Technology (MIT) Press Books, 2015.

Missile Defense Advocacy. "Missile Threat and Proliferation." https://missiledefenseadvocacy.org/missile-threat-and-proliferation/todays-missile-threat/iran/fateh-110/.

Mumford, Andrew. "Proxy Warfare and the Future of Conflict." *RUSI Journal*, Vol. 158, No. 2 (2013). Pages 40–6.

Murray, Williamson and Kevin M. Woods. *The Iran–Iraq War: A Military and Strategic History*. Cambridge: Cambridge University Press, 2014.

Nadia el-Sayed El Shazly. "Iran's Silent Force and the US Navy Take Center Stage," in *The Gulf Tanker War: Iran and Iraq's Maritime Swordplay*. London: Palgrave Macmillan, 1998.

Nadimi, Farzin. "Who is Iran's New Armed Forces Chief of Staff." Washington Institute for Near East Policy, July 5, 2016. https://www.washingtoninstitute.org/policy-analysis/who-irans-new-armed-forces-chief-staff.

Nakashima, Ellen. "Iranian Hackers are Targeting US Officials through Social Networks, Report Says." *The Washington Post*, March 29, 2014. https://www.washingtonpost.com/world/national-security/iranian-hackers-are-targeting-us-officials-through-social-networks-report-says/2014/05/28/7cb86672-e6ad-11e3-8f90-73e071f3d637_story.html.

Nemeth, William J. "Future War and Chechnya: A Case for Hybrid Warfare." Naval Postgraduate School. Master's Thesis. 2002.

Newman, Lily Hay. "Iranian Hackers Have Been Infiltrating Critical Infrastructure Companies." *Wired*, December 7, 2017. https://www.wired.com/story/apt-34-iranian-hackers-critical-infrastructure-companies/.

Norton, Augustus R. *Hizballah: A Short History*. Princeton, NJ: Princeton University Press, 2014.

Obama, Barrack. "Remarks by the President in Address to the Nation on the End of Combat Operations in Iraq." August 31, 2010. https://obamawhitehouse.archives.gov/the-press-office/2010/08/31/remarks-president-address-nation-end-combat-operations-iraq.

O'Hern, Steven. *Iran's Revolutionary Guard: The Threat that Grows while America Sleeps*. Dulles, VA: Potomac Books, 2012.

O'Keefe, Ed and Joby Warrick. "Weapons Prove Iranian Role in Iraq, US Says." *The Washington Post*, July 5, 2011. http://www.washingtonpost.com/world/war-zones/weapons-prove-iranian-role-in-iraq-us-says/2011/07/05/gHQAUnkmzH_story.html.

O'Leary, Jacqueline, Josiah Kimble, Kelli Vanderlee, and Nalani Fraser. "Insights into Iranian Cyber Espionage: APT 33 Targets Aerospace and Energy Sectors and Has Ties to Destructive Malware." *Mandiant*, September 20, 2017. https://www.mandiant.com/resources/apt33-insights-into-iranian-cyber-espionage.

Orenstein, Mitchell A. *The Lands in between: Russia vs. the West and the New Politics of Hybrid War*. Oxford: Oxford University Press, 2019.

Ostovar, Afshon. *Vanguard of the Imam: Religion, Politics, and Iran's Revolutionary Guards*. Oxford: Oxford University Press, 2016.

Perlroth, Nicole. "In Cyberattack on Saudi Firm, US Sees Iran Firing Back." *New York Times*, October 23, 2012. https://www.nytimes.com/2012/10/24/business/global/cyberattack-on-saudi-oil-firm-disquiets-us.html?_r=0.

Perlroth, Nicole and Quentin Hardy. "Bank Hacking was the Work of Iranians, Officials Say." *New York Times*, January 8, 2013. https://www.nytimes.com/2013/01/09/technology/online-banking-attacks-were-work-of-iran-us-officials-say.html.

Rafighdoost, Mohsen. *Baraye Tareekh Megooyam (For History)*. 2015. Farsi edition.

Raine, John. "Iran, Its Partners, and the Balance of Effective Force." *War on the Rocks*, March 18, 2020. https://warontherocks.com/2020/03/iran-its-partners-and-the-balance-of-effective-force/.

Rayburn, Joel D. and Frank K. Sobchak (eds.). "The US Army in the Iraq War: Vol. 1, 2003–2006." US Army War College, January 2019. https://apps.dtic.mil/sti/pdfs/AD1066345.pdf.

Rayburn, Joel D. and Frank K. Sobchak (eds.). "The US Army in the Iraq War: Vol. 2, Surge and Withdrawal." US Army War College, January 2019. https://press.armywarcollege.edu/monographs/940/.

Razoux, Pierre. *The Iran–Iraq War*. Nicholas Elliott (trans.). Cambridge, MA: The Belknap Press of Harvard University, 2015.

Reed, Donald J. "Beyond the War on Terror: Into the Fifth Generation of War and Conflict." *Studies in Conflict & Terrorism*, Vol. 31, No. 8 (2008). Pages 684–722.

Reuters. "US Civilian Contractor Killed in Iraq Base Rocket Attack: Officials." *Reuters*, December 27, 2019. https://www.reuters.com/article/us-iraq-security/u-s-civilian-contractor-killed-in-iraq-base-rocket-attack-officials-idUSKBN1YV1IX.

Rezaei, Farhad. "Iran's Military Capability: The Structure and Strength of Forces." *Insight Turkey*, No. 4, 2019. https://www.insightturkey.com/articles/irans-military-capability-the-structure-and-strength-of-forces.

Rice, Condoleezza. "Opening Remarks before the Senate Foreign Relations Committee." October 19, 2005. https://2001-2009.state.gov/secretary/rm/2005/55303.htm.

Rizvi, M.A. "Evaluating the Political and Economic Role of the IRGC." *Strategic Analysis*, Vol. 36, No. 4 (2012). Pages 584–96.

Rose, Gregory F. "The Post-Revolutionary Purge of Iran's Armed Forces: A Revisionist Assessment." *Iranian Studies*, Vol. 17, No. 2/3 (1984). Pages 153–94.

Rubenfeld, Samuel. "Iran Business Prospects Complicated by Revolutionary Guard." *Wall Street Journal*, November 30, 2015. https://www.wsj.com/articles/BL-252B-8793.

Rubin, Michael. "Iran's Basij Recruiting for Syria Fight." American Enterprise Institute (AEI), March 1, 2016. https://www.aei.org/articles/irans-basij-recruiting-for-syria-fight/.

Salim, Mustafa and Liz Sly. "Militia Supporters Chanting 'Death to America' Break into US Embassy Compound in Baghdad." *The Washington Post*, December 31, 2019. https://www.washingtonpost.com/world/iran-backed-militia-supporters-converge-on-us-embassy-in-baghdad-shouting-death-to-america/2019/12/31/93f050b2-2bb1-11ea-bffe-020c88b3f120_story.html.

Samii, Bill. "Analysis: Goods Smuggling Highlights Economic Problems in Iran." *Radio Free Europe/Radio Liberty*, January 7, 2005. https://www.rferl.org/a/1056740.html.

Sanger, David E. and Nicole Perlroth. "Iranian Hackers Attack State Dept. via Social Media Accounts." *New York Times*, November 24, 2015. https://www.nytimes.com/2015/11/25/world/middleeast/iran-hackers-cyberespionage-state-department-social-media.html.

Sardiwal, Manish, Vincent Cannon, Nalani Fraser, Yogesh Londhe, Nick Richard, and Jacqueline O'Leary. "New Targeted Attack in the Middle East by APT 34, a Suspected Iranian Threat Group, Using CVE-2017-11882 Exploit." *Mandiant*, December 7, 2017. https://www.mandiant.com/resources/targeted-attack-in-middle-east-by-apt34.

Saremi, Fariborz. "Iran's Islamic Revolutionary Guard Corps, the Pasdaran." *Defense & Foreign Affairs' Strategic Policy*, November/December 2007.

Schwartz, Matthew S. "Who Was The Iraqi Commander also Killed in the Baghdad Drone Strike?" *NPR*, January 5, 2020. https://www.npr.org/2020/01/04/793618490/who-was-the-iraqi-commander-also-killed-in-baghdad-drone-strike.

Scientific Quarterly Journal of Defense Strategy. "Developing Macro Strategies for Hybrid Warfare." 17 Khordad 1395 (June 6, 2016). https://www.sid.ir%2Ffa%2Fjournal%2FViewPaper.aspx%3FID%3D279319&psig=AOvVaw0hP5uC6tMERvDqydK2nzu4&ust=1669687464268956.

Seliktar, Ofira. "Iran's Geopolitics and Revolutionary Export: The Promises and Limits of the Proxy Empire." Foreign Policy Research Institute, November 2021. https://www.fpri.org/article/2021/01/irans-geopolitics-and-revolutionary-export-the-promises-and-limits-of-the-proxy-empire/.

Seliktar, Ofira and Farhad Rezaei. *Iran, Revolution, and Proxy Wars*. London: Palgrave Macmillan, 2020.

Shear, Michael D., Eric Schmitt, Michael Crowley, and Maggie Haberman. "Strikes on Iran Approved by Trump, then Abruptly Pulled Back." *New York Times*, June 20, 2019. https://www.nytimes.com/2019/06/20/world/middleeast/iran-us-drone.html.

Sinkaya, Bayram. *Revolutionary Guards in Iranian Politics: Elites and Shifting Relations*. London: Routledge, 2016.

Slavin, Barbara. *Bitter Friends, Bosom Enemies: Iran, the US, and the Twisted Path to Confrontation*. New York: St. Martin's Griffin, 2009.

Slavin, Barbara. "Ahmadinejad's Swan Song: 'Wherever I am, Politics will Follow.'" *Al-Monitor*, September 25, 2012. https://www.al-monitor.com/orginals/2012/al-monitor/politics-and-controversy-follow.html.

Smith, Ben. "The Quds Force of the Iranian Revolutionary Guard." International Affairs and Defence Section, October 30, 2007. https://researchbriefings.files.parliament.uk/documents/SN04494/SN04494.pdf.

Smyth, Phillip. "From Karbala to Sayyida Zaynab: Iraqi Fighters in Syria's Shia Militias." Combating Terrorism Center (CTC) at West Point, Vol. 6, No. 8 (2013).

Smyth, Phillip. "Iran's Iraqi Shiite Proxies Increase Their Deployment to Syria." Washington Institute for Near East Studies, October 2, 2015. https://www.washingtoninstitute.org/policy-analysis/irans-iraqi-shiite-proxies-increase-their-deployment-syria/.

Sofaer, Abraham D. *Taking on Iran: Strength, Diplomacy, and the Iranian Threat*. Stanford, CA: Hoover Institution Press, 2013.

Strobel, Warren and Mark Hosenball. "Elite Iranian Guards Training Yemen's Houthis: US Officials." *Reuters*, March 27, 2015. https://www.reuters.com/article/us-yemen-security-houthis-iran-idUSKBN0MN2MI20150327.

Talley, Ian. "US Adds to Sanctions against Iran." *Wall Street Journal*, March 26, 2020. https://www.wsj.com/articles/u-s-adds-to-sanctions-against-iran-11585245468.

The Holy Defense Research & Document Center. *Quarterly Studies of the Iran–Iraq War*, Vol. 3, No. 9 (Spring 2014). Research and Review at Sacred Defense. Farsi edition.

The Jerusalem Quarterly. "An Open Letter: The Hizballah Program." Fall 1988. https://web.archive.org/web/20060821215729/http://www.ict.org/il/Articles/Hiz_letter.htm.

The White House. "Executive Order 13574 Concerning Further Sanctions on Iran." https://obamawhitehouse.archives.gov/the-press-office/2011/05/23/executive-order-13574-concerning-further-sanctions-iran.

The White House. "Executive Order 13590—Iran Sanctions." November 21, 2011. https://obamawhitehouse.archives.gov/the-press-office/2011/11/21/executive-order-13590-iran-sanctions.

Theohary, Catherine A. "Iranian Offensive Cyber Attack Capabilities." Congressional Research Service, January 13, 2022. https://crsreports.congress.gov/product/details?prodcode=IF11406.

Threat Hunter Team. "Elfin: Relentless Espionage Groups Targets Multiple Organizations in Saudi Arabia and U.S." *Symantec*, March 27, 2019. https://symantec-enterprise-blogs.security.com/blogs/threat-intelligence/elfin-apt33-espionage.

Tower, John, Edmund Muskie, and Brent Scowcroft. *The Tower Commission Report*, joint publication of Bantam Books, Inc., and Time Books, Inc., New York,

February 1987. https://archive.org/details/towercommission00unit/page/n5/mode/2up?ref=ol&view=theater.

United Nations Security Council (UNSC). "Security Council Imposed Sanctions on Iran for Failure to Halt Uranium Enrichment, Unanimously Adopting Resolution 1737 (2006)." Press Release December 23, 2006. https://www.un.org/press/en/2006/sc8928.doc.htm.

United Nations Security Council (UNSC). "Security Council Toughens Sanctions against Iran, Adds Arms Embargo, with Unanimous Adoption of Resolution 1747 (2007)." Press Release March 24, 2007. https://www.un.org/press/en/2007/sc8980.doc.htm.

United Nations Security Council (UNSC). "Security Council Authorizes More Sanctions against Iran over Nuclear Issue." March 3, 2008. https://news.un.org/en/story/2008/03/251122-security-council-authorizes-more-sanctions-against-iran-over-nuclear-issue.

United States District Court for the District of Columbia. *Welch v Islamic Republic of Iran*. 2008. https://www.gpo.gov/fdsys/pkg/USCOURTS-dcd-1_01-cv-00863/pdf/USCOURTS-dcd-1_01-cv-00863-1.pdf.

United States District Court for the District of Columbia. *Brewer v Islamic Republic of Iran*. 2009. http://docs.justia.com/cases/federal/district-courts/district-of-columbia/dcdce/1:2008cv00534/130417/20/0.pdf.

Uskowi, Nader. *Temperature Rising: Iran's Revolutionary Guards and Wars in the Middle East*. Lanham, MD: Rowman & Littlefield, 2019.

van Creveld, Martin. *The Transformation of War*. New York: Free Press, 1991.

Vatanka, Alex. "Pulling the Strings: How Khamenei will Prevent Reform in Iran." *Foreign Affairs*, November 25, 2015. https://www.foreignaffairs.com/articles/iran/2015-11-25/pulling-strings.

Vatanka, Alex. "The Iranian Industrial Complex: How the Revolutionary Guards Foil Peace." *Foreign Affairs*, October 17, 2016. https://www.foreignaffairs.com/articles/iran/2016-10-17/iranian-industrial-complex.

Vatanka, Alex. *The Battle of the Ayatollahs in Iran: The United States, Foreign Policy, and Political Rivalry Since 1979*. London: Bloomsbury Publishing, 2021.

Vaziri, Haleh, "The Islamic Republic's Policy in the Persian Gulf: Who's Containing Whom, How, and Why?" *Middle East Insight*, Vol. 11, No. 5 (July–August (1995).

von Clausewitz, Carl. *On War*. Michael Howard and Peter Paret (ed. and trans.). Princeton, NJ: Princeton University Press, 1976.

Ward, Steven M. *Immortal: A Military History of Iran and its Armed Forces*. Washington, DC: Georgetown University Press, 2009.

Wehrey, Frederic, Jerrold D. Green, Brian Nichiporuk, Alireza Nader, Lydia Hansell, Rasool Nafisi, and S.R. Bohandy. "The Rise of the Pasdaran: Assessing the Domestic Role of Iran's Islamic Revolutionary Guard Corps." RAND Corp, prepared for the Office of the Secretary of Defense, 2009. https://www.rand.org/pubs/monographs/MG821.html.

Wilson, Ben. "The Evolution of Iranian Warfighting during the Iran–Iraq War." Foreign Military Studies Office, July 1, 2007. https://community.apan.org/wg/tradoc-g2/fmso/m/fmso-monographs/241822.

Wolfowitz, Paul. "What Was and What Might Have Been—the Threats and Wars in Afghanistan and Iraq." *Strategika*, Issue 76, Hoover Institution. https://www.hoover.org/research/what-was-and-what-might-have-been-threats-and-wars-afghanistan-and-iraq.

Zabih, Sepehr. *The Iranian Military in Revolution*. Oxford: Routledge, 1988.

Zatarain, Lee Allen. *America's First Clash with Iran, 1987–1988*. Havertown, PA: Casemate Publishers. 2008.

Zimmerman, Katherine. "Profile: Al Houthi Movement." *AEI*, January 28, 2010. https://www.aei.org/articles/profile-al-houthi-movement/.

Index

4GW *see* Fourth Generation Warfare
5GW *see* Fifth Generation Warfare

AAH *see* Asa'ib Ahl al-Haq
Ababil (Operation) 122–3
Abraham Accords 140–1
Abrams, Elliott 140
Accidental Guerrilla (Kilcullen) 23
Adelson, Sheldon 122–3
advanced persistent threats (APTs) 124–5, 128
"The Advent of Netwar" (Arquilla & Ronfeldt) 21–2
Afghanistan 9–10, 25, 34, 102–3, 141
   see also Taliban
AFGS *see* Armed Forces General Staff
After Khomeini (Arjomand) 30–1
Ahmadinejad, Mahmoud 1–2, 30–1, 73–7, 79–81, 91–2
Air Force (Iran) 29–30, 55
Air Force (US) 14
air strikes 23, 55, 98, 104, 105
Alaei, Hossein 40, 52
Alfoneh, Ali 42–3, 48, 62, 105
Amano, Yukiya 114
AMIA Jewish Community Center attack, Buenos Aires, 1994 44
Amir-Abdollahian, Hossein 111
al-Amiri, Hadi 93
The Analytical History of the Iran–Iraq War (Alaei) 40
Ansarallah *see* Houthis
Ansari, Hamid 70
anti-Sandinista policy 7–8
Anti-Tank Guided Missiles (ATGMs) 15, 81
APTs (advanced persistent threats) 124–5, 128
Arab Spring 6, 45, 111
Arafat, Yasser 52
Araghchi, Abbas 114–15

Aramco 122
Arjomand, Saïd Amir 30–1
Armed Forces General Staff (AFGS) 41–2
arms embargoes 52–3
Army (US) 14
   see also Iraq War
Arquilla, John 21–2, 121, 125, 129–30
Artesh *see* Shah Imperial Army
Article 44 of the Constitution 74–5
Article 150 of the Constitution 39
Asa'ib Ahl al-Haq (AAH) 89, 94, 105, 118–19
al-Assad, Bashar 45–6, 88–9, 98–9
asymmetric warfare 54–6, 57, 59
ATGMs (Anti-Tank Guided Missiles) 15, 81
Axis of Evil 9–10
   see also Iraq War
axis points of 5GW (Reed) 27

Badr al Din al Houthi, Hussein 100
Badr Corps (Badr organization) 45–6, 84, 88–9, 91, 93, 105
Baghdad Embassy (US) 103, 104
banking sector 122–3, 135
   see also economics
Basij paramilitary force 45–6, 55
Basra, US Consulate 103
Beirut Bombings, 1983 7–8, 44
"Beyond Fourth Generation Warfare" (Friedman) 26–7
"Beyond the War on Terror: Into the Fifth Generation of War and Conflict" (Reed) 27
Biden, Joe and Administration 17, 136
Bitter Friends, Bosom Enemies: Iran, the US, and the Twisted Path to Confrontation (Slavin) 30, 79–80
Bolshevik Revolution, 1917 32

bombings 7–8, 44
    see also air strikes
Bowers, Christopher O. 24, 49
Bowman Dam in Rye, New York 122–3
Brewer vs Islamic Republic of Iran 44
Brooks, Risa 63
Bunker, Robert J. 25–6
Bush, George H.W. 9–10
Bush, George W. 90–3
    see also Iraq War

capability (hybrid threats) 24
Carter, Jimmy 7
Central Bank of Iran 135
Central Command (CENTCOM) 102, 117
Central Intelligence Agency (CIA) 8, 53, 59
Chamran, Mostafa 31, 38
"The Changing Face of War: Into the Fourth Generation" (Lind *et al.*) 24–5
Charming Kitten (cyber warfare) 125, 128
Chechnya 22
China 29–30, 32, 52, 54–5, 128, 141
    Liberation Army 29–30
    Mao Zedong 20
    Revolution, 1949 32
civil war 1, 4, 23, 44, 46, 97
civil–military relations 61–71, 107–8
Classical warfare 26
Clinton, Bill 9
cognitive domains of conflict (5GW) 26
Cold War 34
common vulnerability and exploit (CVE) – APTs 124
competitive control for influence 138–9
complex terrain (hybrid threats) 24
Comprehensive Iran Sanctions, Accountability, and Divestment Act of 2010 (CISADA) 78
Connell, Michael 89–90, 141
Constitution of the Islamic Republic 39–40, 74–5
conventional warfare 20, 54–6
Cordesman, Anthony H. 30
counterterrorism 103
    see also terrorism
Covid-19 pandemic 119–20

Crimea, annexation 2014 27
Crist, David 31, 84, 87, 92–3, 101, 104
    "Maximum Pressure Campaign" 134, 136
    policy concepts and strategic thought 138–9
"cult of martyrdom" *see* martyrdom
cyber warfare 21–2, 121–30
    capabilities and networks 123–5
    hybrid warfare 125–30
    Iranian way of war 86–7
    Stuxnet 122–3
    as tool for hybrid warfare 127–30
    "U-Turn" transfers and the FDD 119
Cyber-Enabled Economic Warfare Project (FDD) 119

Da'wa party 45–6
Defense Intelligence Agency (DIA) 102
Dehghan, Hossein 97, 110
Democratic Republic of North Korea (DPRK) 52, 121
Department of Defense (DoD) 7–8, 14
Department of State (DoS) 7–8
Department of the Treasury (DoT) 46, 119
distributed denial of service (DDoS) attacks 122–3
"Doha Talks" 140
drones 86–7, 134
Dubai 140
Dynastic warfare 26

Eastern Europe 54–5
economics 73–81
    Khatam al-Anbia 76–7
    Mahmoud Ahmadinejad 79–81
    reimagined 74–5
    "resistance economy" and FTO 116–17
    see also sanctions
Eisenstadt, Michael 37–8, 47–8, 85, 139–40
electronic warfare 86–7
    see also cyber warfare
elite military 15, 28, 38–40, 50–3, 55
    see also Quds Force
embargoes 52–3, 62
    see also sanctions

Embassies 7, 40–1, 103, 104
espionage 125
European union (EU) 12
Executive Orders 46, 78–9
explosively formed penetrators (EFP) 45

Facebook 123
factionalism 104, 105
Faqih (Jurist) 50
　see also *velayat-e faqih* ideology
Fatah coalition/Fatah Alliance 93
Fellow, Kahn 37–8
Feudal warfare 26
Fifth Generation Warfare (5GW) 26–8
financial sanctions 78–9
　see also sanctions
FireEye 124–5
Flynn, Michael 115–16
foreign policy
　future of 140–2
　and hybrid warfare 1–18, 131–42
　Iranian way of war 83
　modern, and hybrid warfare 131–42
　Rouhani and Shadow Government 107–8
　and strategic thought 137–40
Foreign Terrorist Organization (FTO) 116–17, 119
Foundation for the Defence of Democracies (FDD) 119
Fourth Generation Warfare (4GW) 24–7
French Revolution (1789) 32
French revolutionary army 29–30
Fridman, Ofer 28
Friedman, George 26
Friedman, Milton 6
Friedman, Thomas 6
Fukuyama, Francis 6
"The Future War and Chechnya: A Case for Hybrid Warfare" (Nemeth) 22

Gaddafi, Muammar 52
Gartenstein-Ross, Daveed 103
gas resources 76–7, 122, 140
GCC see Gulf Cooperation Council
Ghabban, Mohammed 93
Ghalibaf, Mohammad Bagher 77, 110
Ghani, Esmail 84, 94
Ghasemi, Rostam 77
Ghorb Nooh 77

Glenn, Russell, W. 23
global trade 135–6
Great Britain 52–3
green berets 42–3
Groh, Tyrone L. 33
"Guardians of the Islamic Revolution: Ideology, Politics, and the Development of Military Power in Iran (1979–2009)" (Ostovar) 31–2
guerilla warfare 20, 23, 47, 55, 56, 88
　see also Hizballah
Gulf Cooperation Council (GCC) 89–90
Gulf of Oman 114–15
Gulf region 30, 57
Gulf War 9, 30

hackers 122–3
　see also cyber warfare
Hamas 9, 46, 112
Hammes, Thomas X. 25, 26
Hara (company) 76, 77
Harakat Hizballah al-Nujaba (HaN) 96
Hatami, Amir 110
Hizballah 3, 15, 23, 46, 112, 135
　economics 80–1
　Iranian way of war 87–8, 97–9
　JCPOA 114–15
　state sponsorship 44, 45
　way of war 89–90
Hoffman, Frank G. 22–3
Holy Defense Research and Document Center 50
"holy warriors" see Quds Force
hostage situations 7–8, 9
Houthis 33–4, 89, 100–1, 114–15, 139–40
human rights abuse sanctions 78
Huntington, Samuel P. 29
Hussein, Saddam 90–3
　see also Iraq War
The Hybrid Age: International Security in the Era of Hybrid Warfare (Najžer) 28
Hybrid Conflicts and Information Warfare: New Labels, Old Politics 28
Hybrid Warfare: Fighting Complex Opponents from the Ancient World to the Present (Mansoor) 4–5

Hybrid Warfare: Security and Asymmetric Conflict in International Relations 28
hybridity/hybrid warfare
 applying the concept 3–6, 19
 civil–military relations 61–4, 70–1
 cyber warfare 125–30
 foreign policy 1–18, 131–42
 Iranian way of war 83, 86–90, 98
 models of coercion 107–8
 "resistance economy" and FTO 116–17
 Rouhani and Shadow Government 107–8, 112–13
 scope of 13–15
 Tanker War 57
 unanswered questions 20–8

"Identifying Emerging Hybrid Adversaries" (Bowers) 24
ideology of IRGC 37–42, 50, 98
IDF (Israeli Defense Forces) 15, 98
Imam Khomeini International Airport 76
Immortal: A Military History of Iran and its Armed Forces (Ward) 31
Imperial Army (the Artesh) 28, 38–40, 50–2, 53, 55
improvised explosive devices (IEDs) 45, 94
Indian proxy war in Sri Lanka 33–4
Indyk, Martin 9
information domains of conflict (5GW) 27
information technology (IT) 21–2, 28, 78
 see also cyber warfare
Inherent Resolve (Operation) 102
intelligence bodies
 CIA 8, 53, 59
 DIA 102
 MOIS 41–2, 44, 78, 107–8, 112–13
 SIGINT 15, 81, 86–7, 127
International Atomic Energy Association (IAEA) 10, 11, 114
Iran, Revolution, and Proxy Wars (Seliktar & Rezaei) 33
Iran Sanctions Act (ISA) 78–9
Iran-Contra Affair 8, 13
Iran–Iraq War 6, 15, 29–30, 41–2, 49–51
 Analytical History of the Iran–Iraq War (Alaei) 40
 civil–military relations 61, 65–6

conventional to asymmetric warfare 55–6
Hossein Alaei 40
hybrid warfare/civil–military relations 64
Iranian way of war 83–5, 87, 88, 97
legacy 59 60
lessons learned 58–60
A Military and Strategic History (Murray & Woods) 29
Tanker War 57–8
Iran's Revolutionary Guard, The Threat that Grows While America Sleeps (O'Hern) 31
Iraq 43, 55–6, 139–40
 air strikes on Iran 55
 Baghdad Embassy (US) 103, 104
 Fourth Generation Warfare 25
 invasion of Kuwait 9, 30
 ISCI 45–6
 killing of Soleimani and Muhandis 104, 105
 SCIRI 56
Iraq War 10, 30–3
 Islamic Republic Revolution 44
 modern foreign policy/hybrid warfare 131–2
 way of war 84, 90–3, 101–2, 105
IRGCN (Islamic Revolutionary Guard Corps Navy) 29–30, 42, 57–8
ISA *see* Iran Sanctions Act
ISCI (Islamic Supreme Council of Iraq) 45–6
ISIL (Islamic State in the Levant and Syria) 3, 84, 98, 102, 103, 107
Islam
 Jahan-e Islam (the way of Islam in the Koran) 41
 Jihad 46
 Shia Islam 39–40
 Sunni Islam 9, 46, 100, 112
 velayat-e faqih ideology 39–40, 50, 98
Islamic Republic 9, 49, 59
 Asa'ib Ahl al-Haq 94
 Brewer vs Islamic Republic of Iran 44
 Constitution 39–40, 74–5
 intelligence units and leadership 112
 Iranian way of war 85, 89, 94
 offspring 37–48
 structure and ideology 37–42

Welch vs Islamic Republic of Iran 44
Islamic Revolution 1–2, 7, 37, 52–3, 55–6, 88, 97
  civil–military relations 65
  exporting of by IRGC 41
  Iranian way of war 84–5
  state sponsorship 44
  US foreign policy 7
  velayat-e faqih ideology 39–40, 50, 98
Islamic Revolutionary Guard Corps Navy (IRGCN) 29–30, 42, 57–8
Islamic State in the Levant and Syria (ISIL) 3, 84, 98, 102, 103, 107
Islamic Supreme Council of Iraq (ISCI) 45–6
Israel
  invasion of Lebanon, 1982 47–8
  Iranian hybrid war strategy 88
  Israel–Hizballah War, 2006 15
  and Palestine 40–1
  US–Israel relationships 9
Israeli Defense Forces (IDF) 15, 98

Jahan-e Islam (the way of Islam in the Koran) 41
Jaysh al-Mahdi (Mahdi Army) 45–6, 94
Jeffrey, James 88, 99–100
Jeffrey, Jim 138
Jenkins, Brian Michael 20, 88
Jerusalem Force *see* Quds Force
Jewish communities 44
Jihad 46
Joint Comprehensive Plan of Action (JCPOA) 6, 10, 12, 19, 110, 111
  "Doha Talks" 140
  modern foreign policy and hybrid warfare 133, 137
  Rouhani and Shadow Government 107, 108, 109, 113–16
  US withdrawal 115–16, 133
Joint Plan of Action (JPoA) 6, 10
"Joint Statement on a Framework for Cooperation" 11

Kabernik, Vitaly 28
Kata'ib Hizballah (KH) 45–6, 94–5, 104, 105, 118–19
Kata'ib Sayyid al-Shuhada (KSS) 95
Katzman, Kenneth 29–30

Khalaji, Mehdi 111
Khamenei, Ali 38–9, 48, 50, 61–2, 64–8
Khamenei, Mojtaba
  economics 74–5
  future of foreign policy 140–1
  intelligence units and leadership 112–13
  policy concepts and strategic thought 137
  "resistance economy" and FTO 116
  Rouhani and Shadow Government 107–8, 111, 112–13, 116, 118
  strategic thought and foreign policy 137
Khatam al-Anbia 66, 76–7, 115, 117, 118
Khatami, Seyyed Mohammad 61, 63, 64, 68–9, 73
al-Khazali, Laith 94
al-Khazali, Qais 89, 94
  see also Asa'ib Ahl al-Haq
Khedery, Ali 95
Khobar Towers bombing, 1996 44
Khomeini, Ruhollah 5, 40, 41, 44, 48, 49, 59
  civil–military relations 61, 62, 64
  Hamid Ansari (biographer) 70
  the purge 51
  structure and ideology of IRGC 37–8, 40, 41
Khomeinism 50
  velayat-e faqih ideology 39–40, 50, 98
Khuzestan 55
Kilcullen, David 23
Krieg, Andreas 34
KSS (Kata'ib Sayyid al-Shuhada) 95
Kuwait 9, 30

Laos proxy war 33–4
  see also Houthis
Lebanon
  Beirut Bombings, 1983 7–8, 44
  Israeli invasion, 1982 47–8
  US foreign policy 8
  way of war 97–100
  see also Hizballah
"legacies of modernity" 22
Levant, the 3, 84, 98, 102, 103, 107
Libya 52, 54–5
Lind, William S. 25–6

"Look to the East" policy 76–7
low-intensity conflict (LIC) 20, 21

McCuen, John 23–4
McFarlane, Robert "Bud" 8
Mahan Airlines 45–6
Mahdi Army 45–6, 94
Mahdi al-Muhandis, Abu 94–5, 104, 105
Mahnken, Thomas G. 5, 131
Malik, Hamdi 94
malware 122, 124–5
man-portable air defense systems (MANPADS) 23
Mansoor, Peter R. 4–5, 81, 91, 133, 142
Manwaring, Max G. 26
Mao Zedong 20
Marine barracks bombings in Beirut *see* Beirut Bombings, 1983
Marine Corps (US) 14
martyrdom 50–1, 55
Mattis, James 4, 15, 102–3, 139
maturity (hybrid threats) 24
"Maximum Pressure Campaign" 132–7
Medieval warfare 26
Meta (Facebook) 123
Microsoft 128
Middle East scholarship and integration of the IRGC 34–5
mines 57–8
Ministry of Defense and Armed Forces Logistics (MODAFL) 41–2, 67
Ministry of Intelligence and Security (MOIS) 41–2, 44, 78, 107–8, 112–13
Ministry of Oil, Transportation, and Energy 76–7
models of coercion 107–8
Modern warfare 26
Mosul 96–7
Muhammad, Saeed 77
Mujahedin-al Khalk (MeK) 37
Mumford, Andrew 34
Muqtada al Sadr 45–6
Murray, Williamson 4, 29
Muskie, Edmund 8

Najžer, Brin 28
Nasrallah, Hassan 98
Natanz nuclear facilities 122–3

National Defense Strategy (NDS) 22–3
National Oil Company of Iran 76–7
National Security Council (NSC) 7–8
natural gas 140
  see also gas resources
naval forces 14, 29–30, 42, 57–8, 123, 127
Nemeth, William J. 22
netwar 21–2
"New Modes of Conflict" 20
Newscaster (cyber warfare) 125, 128
Nicaraguan Contras 7–8, 13
Nilsson, Niklas 28
Non-Proliferation Treaty (NPT) 10
North Korea 52, 54–5, 121
North, Oliver 8
nuclear deals, negotiations and programs 10, 11, 109, 114, 115–16
  cyber warfare 122–3
  economics 77–9, 80
  "Maximum Pressure Campaign" 133–4, 136
nuclear facilities, Natanz 122–3
nuclear warfare 122–3

Obama, Barack & Administration 10, 77, 78–9, 92
offensive cyber operations (OCO) 126
Office of the Secretary of Defense (OSD) 30–1
O'Hern, Steven 31, 47
oil 76–7
Oman (Sultanate of Oman) 140
  see also Gulf of Oman
Omran Sahel 77
Operation
  Ababil 122–3
  Inherent Resolve 102
  Praying Mantis 57–8
  Ramadan 55–6
Oriental Kish Company 76–7
Ostovar, Afshon 31–2, 67, 69

Pahlavi, Reza Shah 7, 37
Palestine
  Hamas 9, 46, 112
  Islamic Jihad 46
  Palestine–Israeli conflict 40–1
Palmertz, Björn 28
partners and proxies 139–40

Pearce, James D. 28
Petraeus, David 94
phishing 124–5
Phosphorus (cyber warfare) 125, 128
Picco, Giandomenico 9
policy concepts
　anti-Sandinista policy 7–8
　and strategic investments 101–5
　and strategic thought 137–40
　see also foreign policy
Pompeo, Michael 103
Popular Front for the Liberation of Palestine (PFLP-GC) 46
Popular Mobilization Forces (PMF) 84, 96–7, 104, 105
Powell, Colin 6
Praying Mantis (Operation) 57–8
propaganda 86–7
proxy wars 33–4, 139–40
purge (Artesh) 51–2

al-Qaeda (AQ) 3, 131–2
Qatar 140
　RasGas malware attacks 122
Quds Force (QF) 6, 9–10, 29–31, 33, 42–4, 59
　economics 80–1
　policy concepts and strategic thought 139–40
　Rouhani and Shadow Government 110, 112, 119
　sanctions 78
　state sponsorship 44, 45, 46
　US foreign policy 9–10
　way of war 83–93, 96–7, 101–5

Rafighdoost, Mohsen 44, 52, 97
Rafsanjani, Ali Akbar Hashemi 38, 52, 61, 63–70, 73
Raider warfare 26
Raisi, Ebrahim 137
RasGas malware attacks 122
Ravich, Samantha 119, 128
Reagan, Ronald 7–8
Red Army (Soviet) 29–30, 32
Reed, Donald J. 27
religion 99–100
　see also Islam
"resistance economy" and FTO 116–17
Revolution see Islamic Revolution

Revolutionary Council 40–1
Revolutionary Guards in Iranian Politics: Elites and Shifting Relations (Sinkaya) 32
Rezaei, Farhad 33
Rezaei, Mohsen 30, 50, 52, 67, 68–9
Rice, Condoleezza 90
Rickli, Jean-Marc 34
Rocket Kitten (cyber warfare) 125, 128
Rome, Henry 120, 137
Ronfeldt, David 21–2, 121
Ross, Dennis 9
Rouhani, Hasan 107–20
　cyber warfare 127–8
　"diplomatic Sheikh" 108–9
　intelligence units and leadership 112–13
　IRGC 110–11
　JCPOA 107, 108, 109, 113–16
　"resistance economy" and FTO 116–17
Russia
　annexation of Crimea 2014 27
　Bolshevik Revolution, 1917 32
　future of foreign policy 141, 142
　invasion of Ukraine, 2022 27, 136
　Russo–Georgian War, 2008 27
　Soviet Red Army 29–30
　see also Soviet Union

Saffron Rose (cyber warfare) 125, 128
Sahel Consultant Engineers 77
Salami, Hossein 123
sanctions 9, 62, 77–9
　countermeasures 141–2
　ISA 78–9
　JCPOA 114
　modern foreign policy/hybrid warfare 132–3
　"resistance economy" and FTO 116–17
　Rouhani and Shadow Government 118–19
Sands Casino, Las Vegas 122–3
SAR (synthetic-aperture radars) 86–7
Saudi Arabia 44, 100, 122
SCADA (supervisory control and data acquisition) 122–3
Schahgaldian, Nikola B. 28–9
scholarship and integration of the IRGC 34–5

SCIRI (Supreme Council for the Islamic Revolution in Iraq) 56
Scowcroft, Brent 8
Seliktar, Ofira 33
Sepasad (company) 76
September 11th terrorist attacks 9–10
Shadow Government/Networks 90–3, 107–20
Shah Imperial Army (the Artesh) 28, 38–40, 50–2, 53, 55
Shahrudi, Hashemi (Ayatollah) 93
Shamkhani, Ali 31, 84, 109
Shamoon malware 122, 128
Shia Islam 39–40
Shia militia groups (SMGs) 44–6, 56, 99–100, 103–4, 139–40
   Iranian way of war 87–8, 92–3
   JCPOA 114–15
   state sponsorship 45–6
   way of war 89–90, 105
Shia populations 85
shipping and global trade 135–6
Signals Intelligence (SIGINT) 15, 81, 86–7, 127
Sinkaya, Bayram 32
Slavin, Barbara 30, 38, 79–80, 89, 101, 139–40, 141
The Sling and the Stone: On War in the 21st Century (Hammes) 25
SLO (Supreme Leaders' Office) 64
SNSC (Supreme National Security Council) 41–2, 108–9
SOC (Special Operations Command) 14
social domains of conflict (5GW) 26–7
social media propaganda 86–7
SOFA (Status of Forces Agreement) 92
Sofaer, Abraham D. 31
soft power 59
"soldiers of the Last Days" *see* Quds Force
Soleimani, Qasem 6, 32, 43, 88
   future of foreign policy 140
   Kata'ib Hizballah 94–5
   policy concepts and strategic thought 139–40
   Rouhani and Shadow Government 110
   state sponsorship 45–6
   strategic investments and US policy 104, 105
South African proxy war in Angola 33–4
South Pars Gas Development (SPGD) 76–7

Soviet Union 54–5
   Bolshevik Revolution, 1917 32
   Cold War 34
   Red Army 29–30, 32
   Tanker War 57–8
spear phishing 124–5
Special Operations Command (SOC) 14
state sponsorship 44–6, 98–9
state-on-state violence 21
   see also von Clausewitz
Status of Forces Agreement (SOFA) 92
strategy
   calculus and civil–military relations 69–71
   investments and US policy 101–5
   Iranian hybrid warfare 86–90
   "strategic crime" 125
   "strategic deterrence" 84
   thought and foreign policy 137–40
   see also individual warfare strategies …
structure and ideology of IRGC 37–41
Stuxnet (cyber warfare) 122–3
suicide bombings 44
Sunni Islam 100
   Hamas 9, 46, 112
supervisory control and data acquisition (SCADA) 122–3
Supreme Council for the Islamic Revolution in Iraq (SCIRI) 56
Supreme Leaders' Office (SLO) 64
Supreme National Security Council (SNSC) 41–2, 108–9
"Surge", 2007 91–2
"surrogate warfare" 34
Surrogate Warfare: The Transformation of War in the Twenty-First Century (Krieg & Rickli) 34
synthetic-aperture radars (SAR) 86–7
Syria 43, 78, 97–100
   Bashar al-Assad 45–6, 88–9, 98–9
   ISIL 3, 84, 98, 102, 103, 107
   state sponsorship 45–6

tactics, techniques, and procedures (TTPs) 2, 4, 121–2
   see also hybridity/hybrid warfare
Taeb, Hossein 107–8
Taeb, Mehdi 99
Taking on Iran (O'Hern) 31
Taliban 46, 102–3, 112, 140

Tanker War 57–8, 127
Tehran Embassy (US) 7, 40–1
Telecommunications Company of Iran 123–4
Temperature Rising: Iran's Revolutionary Guards and Wars in the Middle East (Uskowi) 32
terrorism 3, 20, 44, 46, 77
  Axis of Evil 9–10
  bombings 7–8, 44
  hostage situations 7–8, 9
  Iraq War 90–1
  "resistance economy" and FTO 117
  strategic investments and US policy 102–3
  see also individual terrorist groups ...
Thunholm, Per 28
tools for hybrid warfare 127–30
Tower Commission 8
Tower, John 8
The Transformation of war (van Creveld) 21
"The Transition to Fourth Epoch War" (Bunker) 25–6
Trump, Donald J. and Administration 12, 77, 103, 104, 105, 139–40
  modern foreign policy and hybrid warfare 132–7
  "resistance economy" and FTO 117
  US withdrawal from JCPOA 115–16
TTP (tactics, techniques, and procedures) 2, 4, 121–2
The Twilight War: The Secret History of America's Thirty-Year Conflict with Iran (Crist) 31

UAVs (Unmanned Aerial Vehicles) 15, 24, 81
Ukraine 27, 136
United Arab Emirates (UAE) 101, 140
United Nations Security Council (UNSC) 10–11
United Nations (UN) 9
United States
  arms embargoes 52–3
  banking systems and cyberwarfare 122–3
  Basra Consulate 103
  Beirut Bombings, 1983 7–8, 44
  blending modes of conflict 22–3

Central Command, CENTCOM 102, 117
civil–military relations 63
competitive control for influence 138–9
cyber warfare 122–5, 128, 129
"Doha Talks" 140
Embassies 7, 40–1, 103, 104
Executive Orders 46, 78–9
foreign policy
  future of 140–1
  hybrid warfare 1, 2–3, 6–13, 19
  Iranian way of war 83, 84, 85–6
  modern and hybrid warfare 131–42
  and strategic thought 137–40
green berets 42–3
hybrid warfare 1, 2–3, 6–13, 19, 63
Iranian proxy involvement 34
Iranian way of war 83, 84, 85–6, 94
Iran's strategic investments 101–5
killing of Soleimani and Muhandis 104, 105
National Defense Strategy 22–3
nuclear programs and sanctions 77–9
proxy war in Laos 33–4
"resistance economy" and FTO 116–17
Rouhani and Shadow Government 116–17, 119
state sponsorship 45–6
support of the Taliban 46
Tanker War 57–8
US-Israel relationships 9
withdrawal from Afghanistan 102–3
withdrawal from JCPOA 115–16, 133
see also individual US presidents ...; Iraq War
United States, Cold War 34
Unmanned Aerial Vehicles (UAVs) 15, 24, 81
UNSC (United Nations Security Council) 10–11
uranium stockpiles 117
  see also nuclear deals, negotiations and programs
Uskowi, Nader 32
"U-Turn" transfers 118–19

Vahidi, Ahmad 43
van Creveld, Martin 21

Vanguard of the Imam: Religion, Politics, and Iran's Revolutionary Guards (Ostovar) 32
velayat-e faqih ideology 39–40, 50, 98
von Clausewitz, Carl 1, 15, 21

Ward, Steven M. 47
Ward, Steven R. 30
The Warriors of Islam: Iran's Revolutionary Guard (Katzman) 29–30
"watering hole" attacks 125
way of war 83–105
    Asa'ib Ahl al-Haq 94
    Badr Corps 84, 88, 89, 91, 93, 105
    Harakat Hizballah al-Nujaba 96
    invasion by the US 90–3
    Iranian hybrid strategy 86–90
    Kata'ib Hizballah 94–5, 104, 105
    Kata'ib Sayyid al-Shuhada 95
    Lebanon and Syria 97–100
    Popular Mobilization Forces 84, 96–7, 104, 105
    shadow networks 90–3
    strategic investments and US policy 101–5
    Yemen 100–1
weapons of mass destruction (WMD) 77, 78, 122–3
    see also nuclear deals, negotiations and programs
Wehrey, Frederic 30–1
Weissmann, Mikael 28
Welch vs Islamic Republic of Iran 44
WinRAR 124
Woods, Kevin M. 29

Yaros, John 129–30, 135
Yemen 89, 100–1
    see also Houthis

Zabih, Sepehr 29
Zangeneh, Bijan Namdar 110
Zarif, Mohammad Javad 109, 111, 119
Zaydi Shia *see* Houthis